THE TALMUD OF BABYLONIA

Number 87
THE TALMUD OF BABYLONIA
An American Translation
XXIIIC: Tractate Sanhedrin
Chapters 9-11

translated by
Jacob Neusner

THE TALMUD OF BABYLONIA
An American Translation
XXIIIC: Tractate Sanhedrin
Chapters 9–11

translated by
Jacob Neusner

Scholars Press
Chico, California

THE TALMUD OF BABYLONIA
An American Translation
XXIIIC: Tractate Sanhedrin
Chapters 9–11

translated by
Jacob Neusner

Library of Congress Cataloging in Publication Data

Talmud. Sanhedrin IX–XI. English.
  Tractate Sanhedrin, chapters 9–11.

  (The Talmud of Babylonia ; 23C) (Brown Judaic studies ;
no. 87)
  Includes index.
  1. Neusner, Jacob, 1932–   . II. Title. III. Series: Talmud.
English. 1984 ; 23C. IV. Series: Brown Judaic studies ; no. 87.
BM499.5.E4 1984   vol. 23C 296.1'2505 s   85–2032
[BM506.S2E5]   [296.1'2505]
ISBN 0–89130–803–2 (alk. paper)
ISBN 0–89130–804–0 (pbk. : alk. paper)

Printed in the United States of America
on acid-free paper

For

my dear colleagues and friends

Calvin Goldscheider
and
Frances E. Kobrin Goldscheider

A token of celebration
of the first year of their marriage

and of the beginning
of their association with the
Program in Judaic Studies at Brown University

and of the appearance of
The Transformation of the Jews
by Calvin Goldscheider and Alan S. Zuckerman

All of us rejoice at the
advent of these splendid colleagues
and take pleasure in joining their lives to ours.

CONTENTS

INTRODUCTION

To place into proper context the chapters covered in the present volume of the translation of tractate Sanhedrin, we review the tractate as a whole.

This tractate deals with two subjects, first, the organization of the Israelite government and court-system, second, punishments administered to those convicted by the courts of having committed various crimes. The two topics are treated in sections of approximately equal length. The tractate has attracted interest out of all proportion to its intellectual merits. The reason is that it is supposed to tell us whether or not the diverse accounts of the trial of Jesus conform to the laws of "the Jews." Since the only available statement purporting to give those rules is in Mishnah-tractate Sanhedrin, it is natural for people to pay close attention to what they find here. But, self-evidently, we may be certain only that the tractate, for its part, records the state of opinion as it was at the time of its own redaction, which, it is generally supposed, is at A.D. 200. Whether its picture is accurate for the procedures of the Temple nearly two hundred years earlier remains to be demonstrated and surely cannot be taken for granted.

If, however, the tractate has to stand on its own, it is hardly so compelling. It provides a sizable repertoire of extremely well-organized facts, enlivened by narratives illustrating the workings of the courts and rules for conducting trials. But, unlike the three Babas, the tractate asks no important questions about its facts, hardly attempts to show their complex potentialities, and undertakes no strikingly fresh intellectual initiatives. The framers of the tractate are satisfied to paint a picture and tell a story. They may claim significant success only in the excellent way in which the tractate is organized, since it is still more cogent and follows an even more disciplined pattern than the three tractates which precede.

Part of the reason for the tractate's logical and orderly treatment of its topic is that the framers choose to ignore the way Scripture handles the same set of themes. The make ample use of the facts they find in the Mosiac law codes. But these they lay out and organize entirely in their own way. When "Moses" does not provide information which their scheme or order and substance requires, they do not hesitate to make things up for themselves. Once more we shall see that fact most clearly by comparing the substance and sequence of Scriptures, laid out in accord with Mishnah's plan (Albeck, pp. 159-161), with the topical unfolding of the Mishnah tractate itself. These are the relevant verses, in the order in which the tractate calls upon them or upon information contained in them.

Deut. 16:18-20:

> You shall appoint judges and officers in all your towns which the Lord your God gives you, according to your tribes; and they shall judge the people with righteous judgment. You shall not pervert justice; you shall not show partiality; and you shall not take a bribe, for a bribe blinds the eyes of the

wise and subverts the cause of the righteous. Justice, and only justice, you shall follow, that you may live and inherit the land which the Lord you God gives you.

Deut. 17:8-13:

If any case arises requiring decision between one kind of homicide and another, one kind of legal right and another, or one kind of assault and another, any case within your towns which is too difficult for you, then you shall arise and go up to he place which the Lord your God will choose, and coming to the Levitical priests, and to the judge who is in office in those days, you shall consult them, and they shall declare to you the decision. Then you shall do according to what they declare to you from that place which the Lord will choose; and you shall be careful to do according to all that they direct you, according to the instructions which they give you, and according to the decision which they pronounce to you, you shall do; you shall not turn aside from the verdict which they declare to you, either to the right hand or to the left. The man who acts presumptuously, by not obeying the priest who stands to minister there before the Lord your God, or the judge, that man shall die; so you shall purge the evil from Israel. And all the people shall hear, and fear, and not act presumptuously again.

Exodus 23:21:

Give heed to him and hearken to his voice, do not rebel against him, for he will not pardon your transgression; for my name is in him.

Numbers 35:30:

If any one kills a person, the murderer shall be put to death on the evidence of witnesses; but no person shall be put to death on the testimony of one witness.

Deut. 17:6-7:

On the evidence of two witnesses or of three witnesses he that is to die shall be put to death; a person shall not be put to death on the evidence of one witness. The hand of the witnesses shall be first against him to put him to death, and afterward the hand of all the people. So you shall purge the evil from the midst of you.

Lev. 21:10-12:

The priest who is chief among his brethren, upon whose head the anointing oil is poured, and who has been consecrated to wear the garments, shall not let the hair of his head hand loose, nor rend his clothes; he shall not go in to any dead body, nor defile himself, even for his father or for his mother; neither shall he go out of the sanctuary, nor profane the sanctuary of his god; for the consecration of the anointing oil of his God is upon him: I am the Lord.

Deut. 17:14-20:

     When you come to the land which the Lord your God gives you, and you possess it and dwell in it, and then say, 'I will set a king over me, like all the nations that are round about me'; you may indeed set as king over you him whom the Lord your God will choose. One from among your brethren you shall set as king over you; you may not put a foreigner over you; who is not your brother. Only he must not multiply horses for himself, or cause the people to return to Egypt in order to multiply horses, since the Lord has said to you, 'You shall never return that way again.' And he shall not multiply wives for himself, lest his heart turn away; nor shall he greatly multiply for himself silver and gold.

     And when he sits on the throne of his kingdom, he shall write for himself in a book a copy of this law, from that which is in charge of the Levitical priests; and it shall be with him, and he shall read in it all the days of his life, that he may learn to fear the Lord his God, by keeping all the words of this law and these statutes, and doing them; that his heart may not be lifted up above his brethren, and that he may not turn aside from the commandment, either to the right hand or to the left; so that he may continue long in his kingdom, he and his children, in Israel.

Deut. 21:22-23:

     And if a man has committed a crime punishable by death and he is put to death, and you hang him on a tree, his body shall not remain all night upon the tree, but you shall bury him the same day, for a hanged man is accursed by God; you shall not defile your land which the Lord your God gives you for an inheritance.

Deut. 21:18-21:

     If a man has a stubborn and rebellious son, who will not obey the voice of his father or the voice of his mother, and, though they chastise him, will not give heed to them, then his father and his mother shall take hold of him and bring him out to the elders of his city at the gate of the place where he lives, and they shall say to the elders of his city, 'This our son is stubborn and rebellious, he will not obey our voice; he is a glutton and a drunkard.' Then all the men of the city shall stone him to death with stones; so you shall purge the evil from your midst; and all Israel shall hear, and fear.

Deut. 13:12-18:

     If you hear in one of your cities, which the Lord you God gives you to dwell there, that certain base fellows have gone out among you and have drawn away the inhabitants of the city, saying, 'Let us go and serve other gods,' which you have not known, then you shall inquire and make search and ask diligently; and behold, if it be true and certain that such an abominable thing has been done among you, you shall surely put the inhabitants of that city to the sword, destroying it utterly, all who are in it and its cattle, with the edge of the sword. You shall gather all its spoil into the midst of its open square, and burn the city and all its spoil with fire, as a whole burnt offering to the Lord your God; it shall be a heap forever, it shall not be built again. None of the devoted things shall cleave to your hand; that the Lord may turn from the fierceness of his anger, and show you mercy, and have compassion on you, and multiply you, as he swore to your fathers, if you obey the voice of the Lord your God, keeping all his commandments which I command you this day, and doing what is right in the sight of the Lord your God.

The outline of the entire tractate is as follows:

I.   The Court-System. 1:1-5:5

A.   Various kinds of courts and their jurisdiction. 1:1-6

1:1   Property cases are decided by three judges.
1:2   Various other sorts of cases which are decided by a court of three judges.
1:3   Continuation of the foregoing.
1:4   Cases involving the death-penalty are judged by twenty-three judges.
1:5   Political crimes are judged by seventy-one judges, e.g., a tribe, a false prophet, a high priest.
1:6   The large court had seventy-one members, and the small one, twenty-three.

B.   The heads of the Israelite nations and the court-system. 2:1-5

2:1   The high priest judges and others judge him.
2:2   The king does not judge, and others do not judge him.
2:3   Continuation of the foregoing.
2:4-5 The prerogatives of the king.

C.   The procedures of the court-system: Property cases. 3:1-8

3:1-2 Choosing the judges for a property-case.
3:3   These are not valid to serve as judges or as witnesses.
3:4   These relatives are prohibited from serving as one's witnesses or judges.
3:5   Others who may not serve as judges or witnesses.
3:6   How do they examine the testimony of witnesses. Procedures for reaching a decision.
3:7   Procedures for reaching a decision, continued.
3:8   Avenues of appeal.

D.   The procedures of the court-system: Capital-cases. 4:1-5:5

4:1-2   The difference of capital cases and their procedures from property cases.

4:3-4   The layout of the sanhedrin, the places of the judges.

4:5   How they admonish witnesses in capital cases.

5:1   The points of interrogation of witnesses (in capital cases).

5:2   The more they interrogate witnesses, the more is one to be praised.

5:3   Contradictory testimony.

5:4   The foregoing continued. The discussion of the case. The possibility of appeal.

5:5   Reaching a decision. Voting procedures in capital cases.

II.   The death-penalty. 6:1-11:6

A.   Stoning. 6:1-6

6:1-4   When the trial is over, they take the convicted felon out and stone him. Description of the penalty.

6:5   Appended homily.

6:6   Disposition of the corpse of the felon.

B.   Four modes of execution lie in the power of the court and how they are administered. 7:1-3

7:1   Four modes of execution: stoning, burning, decapitation, and strangulation.

7:2   How burning is carried out.

7:3   How decapitation and strangulation are carried out.

C.   Those who are put to death by stoning. 7:4-8:7

7:4   These are the ones who are put to death by stoning.

7:5   Continuation of the foregoing list and its exegesis.

7:6   Continuation of the foregoing list and its exegesis.

7:7   Continuation of the foregoing list and its exegesis.

7:8   Continuation of the foregoing list and its exegesis.

7:9   Continuation of the foregoing list and its exegesis.

7:10   Continuation of the foregoing list and its exegesis.

7:11   Continuation of the foregoing list and its exegesis.

8:1-4   Continuation of the foregoing list and its exegesis.

8:5-7   Appended homiletical materials.

D.   Those put to death through burning or decapitation. 9:1-6

9:1   And these are the ones who are put to death through burning, decapitation.
9:2   Murderers.
9:3   Continuation of the foregoing.
9:4   He who is liable to be put to death through two different modes of execution
         is judged to be executed by the more severe.
9:5-6   Extra-judicial modes of punishment, e.g., of recidivists.

E.   Those put to death through strangulation. 10:1-6

10:1   These are the ones who are to be strangled.
10:2   Continuation of the foregoing list and its exegesis.
10:3   Continuation of the foregoing list and its exegesis.
10:4   Continuation of the foregoing list and its exegesis.
10:5   Continuation of the foregoing list and its exegesis.
10:6   Continuation of the foregoing list and its exegesis.

F.   Appendix. 11:1-6

11:1-3   Homiletical expansion of M. 9:5-6: extra-judicial punishment, at the hands
         of Heaven. All Israelites share in the world to come except....
11:4-5   Exegesis of M. 9:1's list for decapitation.
11:6   Homiletical continuation of the foregoing.

Both units of the tractate are very carefully organized. There is, moreover, a careful and obvious effort to link the two, since M. 6:1ff. carry forward the narrative begun at M. 5:5, and it is only in the unfolding of the new materials that we realize a decisive shift in the topic has taken place. The tractate unpacks the opening topic, the court system, by describing, first, the several types of courts, I.A. (I.B. is important and can go nowhere else), then the procedures followed for the two distinct kinds of cases with which they deal, property litigation, I.C., and capital-cases, I.D. This latter has to have its present position, for it serves as a prologue to the second unit.

The important pericope in unit II is M. 7:1, which lays the foundations for all which follows. First, the four modes of execution are described. Then, still more important, those who are subjected to each of the four modes of execution are specified. The spelling out is at II.C, D, and E. As is clear, except for some inserted or appended homiletical materials, the entire construction systematically expounds the facts important for a full understanding of M. 7:1. I cannot imagine a more cogent or logically and formally coherent tractate than this one. As I said, the facts so elegantly put together are considerably less interesting than the way in which they are organized and given linguistic and syntactic form.

In addition to using my already-available translations of the Mishnah and the Tosefta, I made reference throughout to Sanhedrin. Translated into English with notes, glossary, and indices. Chapters I-VI by Jacob Shachter. Chapters VII-XI by H. Freedman (London, 1948: Soncino). Where I have followed translations proposed by Shachter and Freedman, I have so indicated. From time to time I interpolate their footnotes verbatim (these commonly provide a precis of what Rashi says), and here too I have, of course, indicated that fact.

My students, Paul Flesher (Chapters Nine and Ten) and Howard Eilberg-Schwartz (Chapter Eleven) took time out from their busy graduate studies to proof-read this book and to check my translation against the original text. The contributed numerous valuable corrections, and I thank them both.

9:1 A-C

A. And these are those who are put to death through burning:

B. he who has sexual relations with both a woman and her daughter [Lev. 18:17, 20:14], and a priest's daughter who committed adultery [Lev. 21:9].

C. In the same category as a woman and her daughter are [the following]: his daughter, his daughter's daughter, his son's daughter, his wife's daughter, the daughter of her daughter, the daughter of her son, his mother-in-law, the mother of his mother-in-law, and the mother of his father-in-law.

I.

A. The framer of the passage does not say, "He who has sexual relations with a woman whose daughter he has married," but rather, He who has sexual relations with both a woman and her daughter [M. 9:1B].

B. What follows is that both of them are prohibited.

C. And who are they? They are his mother-in-law and the mother of his mother-in-law.

D. Then it further goes on, In the same category as a woman and her daughter..., which leads to the inference that the two that are specified are stated explicitly in Scripture, with the others derived by exegesis [from them].

E. That poses no problem to the view of Abayye, who has said, "[Aqiba and Ishmael, cited below, XI], differ on the basis on which the rule at hand is derived."

F. In accord with whose view is the Mishnah-passage at hand?

G. It is R. Aqiba [who maintains that the prohibition of marriage to the mother-in-law's mother is explicitly prohibited by Scripture (Freedman, p. 507, n. 4)].

H. But in the view of Raba, who has said, "At issue [between Aqiba and Ishmael] is the status of his mother-in-law after his wife's death [at which point the woman is no longer his mother-in-law]," in accord with authority is the Mishnah-passage at hand?

I. Raba will tell you, "Repeat it as follows: 'He who has sexual relations with a woman whose daughter one has married' [so obviating the question with which we began, A]."

J. In the same category as a woman and her daughter are...his mother-in-law, the mother of his mother-in-law, and the mother of his father-in-law [M. 9:1C].

K. In Abayye's view [Freedman, p. 508, n. 2: that burning for the first two is explicitly decreed, so that they cannot be included in 'a woman, etc.,' but are identical therewith], since the framer of the passage wished to make reference to the mother of his father-in-law, he stated also, "His mother-in-law and the mother of his mother-in-law." [that only the mother-in-law is forbidden on pain of death by fire, but not her mother (Freedman, p. 508, n. 3)].

L.   In Raba's view since the framer of the passage wanted to make reference to the mother of his father-in-law and the mother of his mother-in-law, he made reference also to his mother-in-law.

II.

A.   What is the source of the rule at hand?

B.   It is in accord with what our rabbis have taught on Tannaite authority:

C.   "And if a man takes a woman and her mother [it is wickedness, they shall be burned with fire, both he and they]" (Lev. 20:14).

D.   I know only that the law applies to marriage with both a woman and her mother. How do I know that the same law applies to [marriage with] the daughter of the woman, the daughter of her daughter, or the daughter of her son?

E.   In the present passage, the word "wickedness" appears, and elsewhere the same word appears [namely, at Lev. 18:17: "You shall not uncover the nakedness of a woman and her daughter, neither shall you take her son's daughter or her daughter's daughter to uncover her nakedness, for they are her near kinswomen; it is wickedness"].

F.   Just as, when the word "wickness" occurs elsewhere, it encompasses her daughter and the daughter of her daughter as well as the daughter of her son, so here it encompasses her daughter, the daughter of her daughter, and the daughter of her son.

G.   How do we know that one should treat the males as equivalent to the females [explained at unit III]?

H.   Here the word "wickedness" occurs, and elsewhere, that same word occurs.

I.   Just as there [at Lev. 18:17] males are treated as equivalent to females [so the son's daughter is forbidden as much as the daughter's daughter], so here the males are treated as equivalent to females.

J.   How do we know that those below are treated as equivalent to those above [a question to be explained at unit IV]?

K.   Here the word "wickedness" occurs, and elsewhere the word wickedness occurs. Just as elsewhere those below are treated as equivalent to those above, so here those below are to be treated as equivalent to those above. And just as here, those above are treated as equivalent to those below, so elsewhere, those above are treated as equivalent to those below.

III.

A.   A master has said, "How do we know that one should treat the males as equivalent to the females?"

B.   What is the sense of "the males as equivalent to the females"?

C.   If we should say that one should treat the daughter of her son as equivalent to the daughter of her daughter, these derive together [from the same proof-text, based on "wickedness"].

D.   Rather, it means to treat his father-in-law's mother as equivalent to his mother-in-law's mother [in both cases, incest is punished by execution through burning].

E.   But if at this point we have not proved that fact in the case of the mother of his mother-in-law, can we proceed to take up the case of the mother of his father-in-law?

F.   [75B] Said Abayye, "This is the sense of the passage: 'How do we know that we should treat his issue as equivalent to hers? Here the word 'wickedness' is used, and elsewhere, the word 'wickedness' is used,' and so on. [Freedman, p. 509, n.5: So we prove that his daughter, his son's daughter, or his daughter's daughter by a mistress are forbidden to him on pain of burning, just as are the wife's daughter, her son's daughter, and her daughter's daughter. For Lev. 18:17 refers to the offspring of marriage, not of seduction or outrage. On this interpretation 'male' refers to his issue, 'female' to his wife's.]"

G.   But lo, with reference to his issue, the word "wickedness" in point of fact is not used at all. [Freedman, p. 509, n. 6: For that his issue is at all forbidden is derived not from Lev. 18:17 but from Lev. 18:10]

H.   Said Raba, "R. Isaac bar Abodimi said to me, 'We derive the application of the law to both cases from the facts, first, that 'they'appears in two related passages and the fact that 'wickedness' occurs in two. [Freedman, p. 509, n. 7: In Lev. 18:10 it is stated, "The nakedness of thy son's daughter, or of thy daughter's daughter, even their nakedness thou shalt not uncover: for they (hennah) are thine own nakedness." Further, it is written (ibid. 18:17): "Thou shalt not uncover the nakedness of a woman and her daughter, neither shall thou take her son's daughter, or her daughter's daughter, to uncover her nakedness; for they (hennah) are her near kinswomen; it is wickedness (zimmah)." Since hennah occurs in these two passages, they are identified with each other, and zimmah in the second passage, referring to her issue, is understood to be implicit in the first too, which refers to his issue. Then the first passage is further identified with Lev. 20:14. "And if a man take a wife and her mother, it is wickedness (zimmah): They shalt be burnt with fire:" thus we derive burning for incest with his issue.]

IV.

A.   The master said, "How do we know that those below are treated as equivalent to those above?"

B.   What is the meaning of the phrase, "those below as those above"?

C.   If one should wish to propose that the sense [of "those below"] is that the daughter of her son and the daughter of her daughter are equivalent to her daughter ["those above"], these derive all together from the same proof-texts.

D.   Rather, it refers to the mother of his father-in-law and the mother of his mother-in-law, treating them as equivalent to his mother-in-law.

E.   But if so, then instead of saying, "Those below are equivalent to those above," what is required is "Those above are equivalent to those below". [The older generation are "those above."]

F.   Repeat the passage in just this way: "Those above are equivalent to those below" [exactly as you propose].

G.   If so, then the statement, "Here, 'wickedness' is stated, and there 'wickedness' is
      stated" [makes no sense]. For, at this point, the prohibition they themselves have
      not yet been established through proof-texts, so the use of the word "wickedness" in
      their connection also can prove nothing. [Freedman, p. 509. n. 4: At this stage,
      nothing has been adduced to show that incest with his mother-in-law's mother us
      thus punished, for 'a woman' has been translated literally. Consequently, only his
      mother-in-law is forbidden in this verse.]

H.   Said Abayye, "This is the sense of the passage:

I.   "How do we know that we should treat the third generation above as equivalent to
      the third generation below [that is, the daughter's daughter and the son's daughter
      are forbidden, so too the father-in-law's mother and the mother-in-law's mother]?

J.   "With respect to the generations below, the word 'wickedness' is used, and with
      reference to the generations above, the word 'wickedness' is used.

K.   "Just as for the generations below, the prohibition extends for three generations, so
      for the generations above, the prohibitions extend for three generations.

L.   "And just as with respect to the penalty, the law has treated the generations below
      as equivalent to the generations above, so with regard to the admonition the same is
      the case, the law having treated the generations above as equivalent to the
      generations below." [Freedman, p. 510, n. 10: For in Lev. 18:10, where the third
      lower generation is forbidden, nothing is said about punishment, which is derived
      from Lev. 20:14, as stated above. On the other hand, in Lev. 20:14, which is made
      to include the third generation above, though only explicitly stating the second, no
      formal prohibition is given. This in turn is derived from Lev. 18:10. (Both are
      derived through the medium of Lev. 18:17, the connecting link between the other
      two.) One Abayye's interpretation it is necessary to emend the Baraitha from 'and
      the lower is as the upper', to 'that the upper is as the lower etc.']

M.   R. Ashi said, "Indeed, matters are just as stated [and require no revision, contrary to
      Abayye's view]. And what is the sense of "those below"? It is "those below" in the
      seriousness of the prohibition. [Freedman, pp. 510-511, n. 12: 'the upper' or higher
      prohibition is that of his mother-in-law, his more immediate relation, whilst the
      prohibition of her mother, as also of his father-in-law's mother, is regarded as
      'lower', i.e. weaker, as they are a generation further removed. Hence this is its
      meaning: Whence do we know that his mother-in-law's mother and his
      father-in-law's mother, whose relationships are lower (i.e., further removed, and
      consequently weaker) than his mother-in-law's, are treated as his mother-in-law? It
      is derived from his wife's daughter: just as in the latter case, the 'lower' relation is
      as the 'upper' (stronger), i.e., his wife's daughter's daughter is as his wife's
      daughter, though more distant; so here too, his mother-in-law's mother is as she
      herself. This deduction is in respect of equal punishment. The second clause is
      explained by R. Ashi as Abayye, as referring to the prohibition.]"

V.

A.   [Referring back to III A, how do we know that the male's relations are regarded as the female's relations], if so, then just as the mother of her mother is forbidden, so the mother of his mother is forbidden.

B. Said Abayye, "Scripture says, 'The nakedness of your father or the nakedness of your mother you shall not uncover; she is your mother' (Lev. 18:7) -- On account of [incest with] one's mother you impose a penalty, on account of the mother of his mother you do not impose a penalty."

C. Said Raba, "Whether matters accord with him who has said, [Freedman:] 'Judge from it in its entirety,' or 'Judge from it and place it on its own basis,' this could not be deduced. [Freedman, p. 511, n. 5: A verse is unnecessary, because his maternal grandmother could not be deduced from the gezerah shawah based on zimmah, whatever view be held on the scope of a gezerah shawah. There are two views on this. One is that the identity of law taught by a gezerah shawah must hold good in all respects, so that the case deduced is equal to the premise in all points; this is called 'judge from it and from (all) of it.' An opposing view is that the analogy holds good only in respect of the main question at issue, but that thereafter, the case deduced may diverge from its premise. This is called, 'judge from it, but place it on its own basis', i.e., confine the analogy to the main question, not to the subsidiary points.]

D. "[Freedman, p. 11:] For on the view, 'judge from it in its entirety', [the deduction would proceed thus:] Just as her [his wife's] maternal grandmother is forbidden [to him], so is his maternal grandmother forbidden. [Then carrying the analogy] to its uttermost, just as in her case [i.e., incest with the former] is punished by fire so in his case [i.e., incest with the latter] is punished by fire.

E. "In the view of him who says that the execution through burning is the more severe penalty, there is the possibility of raising the following question: What is the particular trait affecting his wife's maternal grandfather [that she should be forbidden and the penalty of burning applies]?

F. "It is that his wife's mother is subject to the same penalty. [Freedman, p. 512, n. 2: Hence, since the prohibition of his wife's mother is so severe, it is natural that it should extend to her maternal grandmother too.]

G. "But will you make such a statement in his case, for [should he have incest with] his wife, the penalty is stoning?

H. "Furthermore, the penalty for incest with his mother is through stoning. Will the penalty for incest with his mother's mother be burning?

I. "And furthermore, just as there is no distinction made in her case between her mother and her mother's mother, so in his case, there should be no distinction between the penalty inflicted in the case of incest with his mother and with the mother of his mother.

J. "And in the position of him who maintains that stoning is the more severe, on account of this problem, there is in any event no analogy.

K. "[Freedman, p. 512:] Whilst on the view, 'judge from it and place it on its own basis', [the deduction would proceed thus:] Just as her [his wife's] maternal grandmother is forbidden [to him], so is his maternal grandmother forbidden. But 'place it on its own basis', thus: in the former case the punishment is burning; but in the latter, stoning, the penalty which we find prescribed for incest with his mother. Now, in the view that burning is severer, this can be refuted, [76A] [Thus]: Why is her case [i.e., his wife's maternal grandmother forbidden]? Because her mother is [forbidden] on pain of death by fire. But can you say the same in his case, seeing that his mother is forbidden on pain of stoning [only]? Further, his maternal grandmother is like her's: just as in the latter case no distinction is drawn between his wife's maternal grandmother and her [his wife's] daughter, so in the former, no distinction should be allowed between his own maternal grandmother and his daughter. Whilst on the view that stoning is severer, the analogy cannot be made on account of this last difficulty."'

L.   If [we compare his relatives to hers], then just as his daughter-in-law is forbidden, so her daughter-in-law should be forbidden [to him, that is Freedman, p. 513, n. 5: the wife of her son by a previous husband. But she is not forbidden to him.]

M.   Said Abayye, "Scripture has said, 'You shall not uncover the nakedness of your daughter-in-law, she is your son's wife' (Lev. 18:15), meaning, on account of the wife of your son you impose liability, but you do not impose liability on account of the wife of her son."

N.   Raba said, "[Freedman, p. 513:] Whether it be maintained, 'judge from it in its entirety,' or 'judge from it and place it on its own basis', this could not be deduced. For on the first view, [the deduction would proceed thus:] just as his daughter-in-law is forbidden him, so is her's forbidden him. [Then carrying through the analogy] 'in its entirety,' just as in his case [the penalty] is stoning, so in her case is the penalty stoning. But if we regard stoning severer, this analogy can be refuted. [Thus]: Why is his [daughter-in-law forbidden]? Because his mother is forbidden him on pain of stoning: Can you then say the same of her daughter-in-law, seeing that incest with her mother incurs only death by fire? Moreover, her daughter is forbidden on pain of burning: shall her daughter-in-law be forbidden on pain of stoning? [No.]"

O.   [In reply to Raba:] Let his own circumstance prove to the contrary, for his daughter [should he have incest with her] produces the penalty of burning, while his daughter-in-law produces that of stoning.

P.   Rather: Just as in his case you do not draw a distinction between his own case and that of his mother and his daughter-in-law, so in her case you should draw no distinction between her mother and her daughter-in-law. [Freedman, p. 514, n .1: Hence, incest with the latter should be punished by burning. But as has already been proved, stoning is the proper punishment; therefore the entire analogy is impossible.]

Q.   [Freedman, p. 514:] And on the view that burning is considered more severe, the analogy cannot be made because of this last difficulty. Whilst on the view, 'judge from it and place it on its own basis,' [the deduction would proceed thus:] just as his daughter-in-law is forbidden him, so is her daughter-in-law forbidden; and place it on its own basis, thus: in the former case, [his daughter-in-law] the punishment is stoning; but in the latter, burning, the punishment we find for incest with her mother. But if stoning is severer, this can be refuted. [Thus]: Why is his daughter-in-law forbidden? Because his mother is forbidden him on pain of stoning. But can you say the same of her daughter-in-law, seeing that her mother is forbidden only on pain of burning! Moreover, just as in his case, you draw a distinction between his daughter [punished by burning] and his daughter-in-law [by stoning], so in her case, you should draw a distinction between her daughter and her daughter-in-law. [Freedman, p. 514, n. 3: i.e., just as the punishment for his daughter-in-law is severer than for his daughter, viz., stoning instead of burning, so her daughter-in-law should be more stringently interdicted than her daughter, viz., by stoning, instead of burning. But if we compare her daughter-in-law to her mother, the punishment is burning. Hence the entire deduction is impossible.]

VI.

A.   How do we know that one's [own] daughter born of a woman one has raped [is forbidden]?

B.   Has not Abayye said, "It is an argument _a fortiori._ If one is punished on account of incest with the daughter of his daughter, will he not all the more so be punished on account of his daughter?"

C.   But do [courts] inflict punishment because of a logical argument?

D.   It serves to clarify the matter in general [but Lev. 18:10 in fact prohibits relationships with any sort of daughter].

E.   Raba said, "R. Isaac bar Abohdimi said to me, "The matter derives from the use of the word 'they' in the two passages and the word 'wickedness' in two [as above]."

VII.

A.   The father of R. Abin taught on Tannaite authority, "It is because have we have not derived from Scripture that **a man's incest with his daughter produced by a rape is punishable that it was necessary for Scripture to state, 'And the daughter of a man and a priest,** [if she profane herself through her father, she profanes him, she shall be burned with fire]' (Lev. 21:9) [cf. T. San. 12:1H]. [Freedman, p. 515, n. 4: Lev. 21:9, 'A man' is superfluous, and therefore teaches that even if she is only his daughter, not his wife's, this law holds good. By translating the rest of the verse as in the text, we deduce that an illegitimate daughter is burnt for incest with her father; and by regarding 'a man' as distinct from 'priest' (the latter being attached to the former with the copula 'and'), the deduction is made to refer to any illegitimate daughter, not only a priest's]'

B.   [Might one then reason as follows:] Just as the daughter of a priest is punished by execution through burning, but her lover is not punished by execution through burning, so incest with one's daughter produced by a rape produces the penalty of death through burning for her but not for her lover [her father]?

C.   Said Abayye, "Scripture has said, 'She profanes her father' (Lev. 21:9). The law applies to one who profanes her father, thus excluding the case at hand, in which her father has profaned her. [So her lover, that is, her father, shares the same punishment.]"

D. Raba said, "In the case [of the lover of a priest's daughter, guilty with her of adultery] you have removed such a one from the penalty inflicted on the daughter of a priest and imposed upon him the penalty that applies to the daughter of an Israelite [stoning, not burning].

E. "But in the present case, in accord with the death penalty of what classification of woman will you have him put to death? Will it be to that of an unmarried woman? [Freedman, p. 516, n. 2: For if an incestuous paramour be excluded from the punishment of an adulterous woman, whether the daughter of a priest or an Israelite (since the relationship is independent of these), his law can only be assimilated to that of an unmarried woman, whose unchastity is not punished at all. But surely it cannot be maintained that an illegitimate daughter is burnt for incest with her father, though her offense is a passive one, and less than the man's, whilst he goes scot free! Hence the limitation of 'she' cannot apply to this.]

VIII.

A. Whence do we derive the admonition that a man not commit incest with his daughter produced by his act of rape?

B. Now with respect to Abayye and Raba, from the very same source from which they derive the mode of execution, they also derive the admonition [since the verses they cite contain both elements].

C. But what is the equivalent for the Tannaite teaching transmitted by the father of R. Abin?

D. Said R. Ilaa, "Scripture has said, 'Do not profane your daughter to cause her to be a whore' (Lev. 19:29) [including incest, and 'daughter' involves an illegitimate one too (Freedman, p. 516, n. 5)]."

E. R. Jacob, brother of R. Aha bar Jacob, objected to this statement, "Does the cited verse, 'Do not profane your daughter to cause her to be a whore' (Lev. 19:29) serve the stated purpose?

F. "To the contrary, it is required for a quite different purpose, namely, for that in the following teaching, taught on Tannaite authority:

G. "'Do not profane your daughter to cause her to be a whore' (Lev. 19:29)"

H. "'Is it possible to maintain that Scripture speaks of a priest who may marry his daughter to a Levite or an Israelite [indicating that, since the daughter is thereby profaned, because she may no longer eat priestly rations, he is not to marry her off to a Levite or an Israelite]?

I. "'Scripture says, "To cause her to be a whore" (Lev. 19:29), meaning to refer to that sort of profanation that takes place through whoredom [and not in the context of profanation resulting in her disqualification from eating priestly rations].

J. "'So at issue is one who hands over his daughter [for a sexual liaison] not involving marriage.'"

K. [Ilaa replies], "If so, Scripture should have said, 'Do not treat profanity' [spelling the verb with one L, rather than two Ls]. Why does Scripture say, 'Do not profane [spelling the verb with two Ls]? It is to teach both lessons."

L. And how do Abayye and Raba interpret this same verse, "Do not profane your daughter to cause her to be a whore" (Lev. 19:29)?

M. Said R. Mani, "This refers to one who marries his young daughter off to an old man."

N. It accords with that which has been taught on Tannaite authority:

O. "Do not profane your daughter to cause her to be a whore" (Lev. 19:29):

P. R. Eliezer says, "This is one who marries off his young daughter to an old man."

Q. R. Aqiba says, "This refers to one who postpones marrying off his daughter once she has reached puberty."

IX.

A. Said R. Kahana in the name of R. Aqiba, "You have none who is poor in Israel except because of one who is clever in acting wickedly and one who delays marrying off his daughter once she has passed puberty."

B. But is not the one who delays marrying off his daughter once she has passed puberty also in the category of a person who is clever in acting wickedly?

C. Said Abayye, "[76B] This is the sense of the statement at hand: 'Who is one who is clever in acting wickedly? It is he who delays marrying off his daughter once she has passed puberty.'"

D. And R. Kahana said in the name of R. Aqiba, "Be careful about someone who gives you advice in accord with his own interest."

E. Said R. Judah said Rab, "He who marries off his daughter to an old man, and he who takes a wife for his minor son, and he who returns a lost object to a Samaritan -- in respect to all of these, Scripture says, '[That he bless himself in his heart, saying, I shall have peace, though I walk in the imagination of my heart] to add drunkenness to thirst. The Lord will not spare him' (Deut. 29:18-20)."

F. An objection was raised: "He who loves his first wife as he loves himself, he who honors her more than he honors himself, he who raises up his sons and daughters in the right path, and he who marries them off close to the time of their puberty -- of such a one, Scripture says, 'And you shall know that your tabernacle shall be in peace and you shall visit your habitation and you shall not sin' (Job 5:24). [So it is good to marry off a minor.]"

G. If the marriage is arranged just prior to puberty, the case is different [and meritorious].

X.

A. Our rabbis have taught on Tannaite authority:

B. He who loves his neighbors, he who draws his relatives near, he who marries his sister's daughter, and he who lends a sela to a poor person when he needs it --

C. concerning such a person Scripture says, "Then you will call, and the Lord will answer" (Is. 58:9).

XI.

A. Our rabbis have taught on Tannaite authority:

B. "[And if a man take a wife and her mother, it is wickedness; they shall be burned with fire,] both he and they" (Lev. 20:14).

C.   "He and one of them," the words of R. Ishmael.

D.   R. Aqiba says, "He and both of them."

E.   What is at issue between them?

F.   Said Abayye, "At issue is interpreting the implication of the passage at hand.

G.   "R. Ishmael takes the view that the meaning of 'he and they' is that they are to burn him and one of them, for in the Greek language, the word for 'one' is hena [in the biblical text at hand, 'THN]. And the penalty against incest with one's mother-in-law's mother derives from exegesis [of Scripture].

H.   "R. Aqiba maintains that 'he and they' means 'he and both of them,' in which case the penalty against incest with one's mother-in-law derives from what is explicitly written in the passage at hand directly [and not through exegesis]."

I.   Raba said, "At issue between them is the case of having sexual relations with his mother-in-law after his wife's death.

J.   "R. Ishmael takes the position that if one has sexual relations with his mother-in-law after his wife's death, he is put to death through burning.

K.   "R. Aqiba takes the view that he merely violates a general prohibition [but not penalized]. [Freedman, p. 518, n. 6: R. Ishmael interprets the verse, 'he and one of them' i.e., even if only one of them is alive (viz., his mother-in-law), the penalty for incest is burning, whilst R. Aqiba maintains, 'he and both of them' i.e., only during the lifetime of both is incest with his mother-in-law punished by fire. Otherwise, there is no penalty, though it is forbidden.'"

The fact that the composition was planned at the outset and follows a clear program is shown by the fact that unit I is incomprehensible without the information provided, in an appendix, only at unit XI. What we want to know is the basis for prohibiting incest with certain female relations: on the one side, the man's mother-in-law after the wife's death, on the other, the man's daughter produced through a rape. The latter of the two categories come under discussion at unit II, and the exegesis of the materials of unit II occupies units III, IV, V. Unit VI then reverts to the proof-texts for the prohibition against incest with a daughter produced by a rape, and units VII, VIII, pursue the same topic. Units IX, X, are attached prior to inclusion of the whole in the present composition and do not belong, and then, as I said, unit XI presents the locus classicus for the dispute to which unit I has made reference. If then we turn back to the Mishnah-paragraph and ask whether the exegesis of the statements we find there has generated the composition at hand, we look in vain for a reference to the daughter of a man produced by his act of rape. So the issue is essentially a theoretical one, resting on how we can prove, on the basis of Scripture or reason, that such a relationship is incestuous. Then the entire composition is attached to the Mishnah-paragraph at hand, on the pretext supplied by unit I's reading of the exegetical foundations of what turns out to be an oblique and secondary issue -- the mother-in-law. In fact, we begin with reference to the mother-in-law, but we mean the daughter produced in a rape. In all, it would be difficult to find a more subtle exercise in the theory of the exegesis of Scripture in relationship to the exegesis of the law. I in no way claim to have done justice to the presentation of the passage at hand, relying upon Freedman, as indicated.

9:1 D-M

D. And these are those who are put to death through decapitation:

E. the murderer, and the townsfolk of an apostate town.

F. A murderer who hit his neighbor with a stone or a piece of iron [Ex. 21:18],

G. or who pushed him under water or into fire, and [the other party] cannot get out of there and so perished,

H. he is liable.

I. [If] he pushed him into the water or into the fire, and he can get out of there but [nonetheless] he died, he is exempt.

J. [If] he sicked a dog on him, or sicked a snake on him, he is exempt.

K. [If] he made a snake bite him,

L. R. Judah declares him liable.

M. And sages declare him exempt.

I.

A. Said Samuel, "Why [at Num. 35:16-18, where we take up murder with iron, stone, or wooden weapons] the word 'hand' is not stated when we speak of an iron weapon [indicating that the weapon must be sufficiently large to be held in the hand only when it is a weapon of stone or wood, but not of iron]?

B. "It is because an iron weapon may inflict death no matter its size."

C. It has been taught on Tannaite authority to the same effect:

D. Rabbi says, "It is obvious to Him who spoke and brought the world into being that iron inflicts death no matter what its size.

E. "Therefore the Torah did not assign a minimum measure to it."

F. That rule pertains, however, only in the case of piercing someone with iron [but if one hit him with iron, it must be of requisite size actually to inflict death].

II.

A. Or pushed him under water [and he cannot get out...he is liable. If he pushed him into water...and he can get out...he is exempt] [M. 9:1G, I]:

B. The first of the two statements [M. 9:1G] makes its own point, and the second of the two statements [M. 9:1I] makes its own point, too.

C. The former of the two statements makes its own point, namely, even though he is not the one who pushed the other into the water, since the other cannot get up from there and so dies, he is liable.

D. The latter of the two statements makes its own point, namely, even though he is the one who pushed the other into the water, since the other can climb up out of the water and nonetheless dies, he is exempt from penalty.

III.

A.   How do we know that one keeps the other under [is liable]?

B.   Said Samuel, "It is because Scripture has stated, 'Or if with enmity he smote him with his hand' (Num. 35:21).

C.   "This serves to encompass who one holds his neighbor [under the water]."

IV.

A.   A man confined the beast of his fellow in the sun, and it perished.

B.   Rabina declared him liable [to pay the value of the beast].

C.   R. Aha, son of Rab, declared him exempt.

D.   Rabina declared him liable on the basis of an argument a fortiori:

E.   "Now if in the case of murder, in which the law does not treat inadvertent action as equivalent to deliberate action, or action done under constraint as equivalent to action done willfully, the law has imposed liability in the case of one who confines his neighbor [and so causes his death],

F.   "[77A] in the case of property damage, in which the law did not distinguish but treated as equivalent an act done inadvertently and one done deliberately, and an act done under constraint as equivalent to an act done willfully, is it not a matter of reason that one should impose liability on one who causes damage by confining [a beast]?"

G.   R. Aha, son of Rab, declares such a one exempt [from penalty].

H.   Said R. Mesharshia, "What is the scriptural basis on which the father of my father declares such a one exempt?

I.   "Scripture has said, 'He who smote him shall surely be put to death, for he is a murderer' (Num. 35:21). It is in the case of a murderer that the law has made such a one liable in the consequence of an act of confinement, but in a case of causing civil damages, the law has not made such a one liable in the consequence of an act of confinement."

VI.

A.   Said Raba, "If one tied up [another person] and the latter dies of starvation, he is exempt."

B.   And Raba said, "If one tied up a beast in the heat and it died, or if he did so in the cold and it died, he is liable.

C.   "If he did so when the sun was going to come [but had not yet risen], or that the cold had not yet taken effect, he is exempt. [In this case he is merely an indirect cause (Freedman, p. 520, n. 4)]."

D.   And Raba said, "If he tied him up before a lion, he is exempt. If he tied him up before mosquitoes, he is liable."

E.   R. Ashi said, "Even if he did so before mosquitoes, he also is exempt, because the ones who are there [when he tied the man up] go along, and others come and take their place."

VI.

A.   It has been stated on Amoraic authority:

B.   If one turned a vat over upon someone [who died of suffocation] or broke open a ceiling above him [and he caught cold and died],

C.   Raba and R. Zira:

D.   One said, "He is liable," and the other said, "He is exempt."'

E.   You may conclude that it is Raba who said that he is exempt, for Raba said, "If he tied him up and he died on account of starvation, he is exempt."

F.   To the contrary, you may draw the conclusion that R. Zira is the one who has said that he is exempt, for R. Zira said, "He who brought his fellow into a marble chamber and lit a lamp there so that the latter dies [because of the fumes], he is liable."

G.   What is the reason?

H.   It is that he lit a lamp.

I.   Lo, had he not lit a lamp, he would not have been liable [even though the other had died because of lack of air]. [So Zira, too, does not impose a penalty for indirectly causing death.]

J.   One might say that if there had been no lamp, the heat would not have begun [to affect the man] [77B] at the moment [at which he put him in the room].

K.   But in the present case [that of the overturned vat,] the heat begins to produce its effects immediately.

VII.

A.   Said Raba, "If one pushed someone into a pit, and there was a ladder in the pit, and someone else came along and took it away, or even if he himself removed the ladder, he still is exempt.

B.   "For at the point at which he threw the man into the pit,. [the victim] could climb out of it."

C.   And Raba said, "If one shot an arrow, and there was a shield in the hand [of the person at whom he shot the arrow], and someone else came long and took the shield away, or even if he came along and took it away, he is exempt.

D.   "For at the moment at which he shot the arrow at him, the force of the arrow would have been broken [on the shield]."

E.   And Raba said, "If one shot an arrow at someone, and the latter had ointment in his hand [which would heal the wound of the arrow], and someone else came along and scattered the ointment, or even if he came along and scattered it, he is exempt.

F.   "For at the moment at which he shot the arrow, the man could have healed himself."

G.   Said R. Ashi, "Therefore, even in the case of ointment in the market-place [the same rule applies, since someone could have gotten the ointment when it was needed]."

H.   Said R. Aha, son of Raba, to R. Ashi, "If [when the man was hit, he did not have ointment, but] ointment came to hand, what is the law?"

I.   He said to him, "Lo, this one goes forth from court a free man."

J.   And Raba said, "If one threw a stone against the wall and it bounced back and killed someone, he is liable."

K.   And a Tannaite authority repeats: "It would be exemplified in a case of people playing with a ball, who deliberately committed murder. They are put to death.

L.   "If this happened inadvertently, they go into exile."

M.   The point that, if it was inadvertent, they go into exile, is self-evident. It was included only because the framer of the passage wished to make the point concerning those who do so deliberately, stressing that they are put to death.

N.   What might you have said? It is a case in which it was an admonition that was subject to doubt. Nor who may say for sure that the ball will bounce back.

O.   So we are taught to the contrary.

VIII.

A.   R. Tahalipa of the West repeated on Tannaite authority before R. Abbahu, "In a case of people playing ball, if the one who was killed was within four cubits [of the wall], the player is exempt. If he was outside of four cubits, he is liable."

B.   Said Rabina to R. Ashi, "What would such a case involve? If it suited [the player that the ball rebound], then even if the man was nearer than four cubits [and the ball rebounded], he should be liable, and if he did not want [the ball to rebound], then even if the man were at a greater distance, he should be exempt from liability."

C.   He said to him, "Ordinary ball-players want the ball to rebound more. [Freedman, p. 522, n. 9: Therefore it may be presumed that he intended it to rebound at least four cubits, hence if less, he is not liable.]"

D.   May we then conclude that in a case such as this, [the murder is deemed to happen] by the man's direct action? An objection was raised on the basis of the following:

E.   He who mixes ash and water in a trough and the ash fell on his hand or on the side of the trough and afterward it fell into the trough -- the act of mixing is unfit, [since the mixing must be done by human action] [M. Par. 6:1A-E]. [Here, therefore, in a parallel case, human action does not encompass what happens on a rebound].

F.   With what sort of a case do we deal? With a case in which [ash] was dripping down [into the trough]. [But had the ash fallen with force, the fall would be regarded as part of the man's action in dropping them onto the utensil (Freedman, p. 523, n. 2)].

G.   Come and take note: A needle which is fixed in an earthenware utensil, and one sprinkled on it -- one is in doubt whether he sprinkled on the needle, or whether from the clay utensil water merely dripped on the needle -- the sprinkling is unfit [M. Par. 12:2F-H]. [The sprinkling has not been done by human action].

H.   Said R. Hinena b. R. Judah in the name of Rab, "The word should be read, 'It was found' [so the water was found on the needle, and we do not know how it got there.' That explains the unfitness.]"

IX.

A.   Said R. Papa, "If someone tied up his fellow and inundated him with a column of water, it is as if it was done by his arrows and he is liable.

B.   "That is the case if the death was due to the first flow of the water [directly], but if it was through the second flow of the water, he is merely a secondary cause of death. [Freedman, p. 523, n. 5: If the victim was lying immediately in front of the burst, where the strength of the water's flow is still due to the man's action, the drowning is by his direct agency. But if he was lying at some distance, he is held to be an indirect or secondary cause]."

C.   And R. Papa said, "If one threw a stone upward and it went to the side and killed someone, he is liable."

D.   Said Mar, son of R. Ashi, to R. Pappa, "What is the reason for that ruling? It is because of the man's direct action. But then, if it is because of what the man as done, the stone should continue to go upward.

E.   [78A] "And if it is not because of his direct action, then it should come straight down."

F.   "Rather, it is because of his direct action, but it was weakened [Freedman, p. 524, n.3: Most of the force with which he threw it was already expended but sufficient was left to impel it in the direction in which it fell]."

X.

A.   Our rabbis have taught on Tannaite authority:

B.   If ten men hit someone with ten sticks and the victim died, whether they did so simultaneously or sequentially, they are exempt.

C.   R. Judah b. Betera says, "If they did so sequentially, the last one is liable, because he brought the death nearer."

D.   Said R. Yohanan, "And both authorities [B, C] interpret the same verse: 'And he who kills an entire life of a man shall surely be put to death' (Lev. 24:17).

E.   "Rabbis understand by 'an entire life' to mean that one is liable only if the whole of the life of the man is intact [when he inflicts the death blow].

F.   "R. Judah b. Betera takes the position that an aspect of the entire life is at issue [Freedman, p. 524, n. 8: however little life the man has, even if he is nearly dead, the man who actually kills him is liable]."

G.   Said Raba, "Both parties concur in the case of one who kills one afflicted with a fatal disease that he is exempt.

H.   "If he killed someone dying because of heavenly action [that is, of natural causes] he is liable.

I.   "The dispute concerns only one who is dying on account of the act of man.

J.   "One party compares the case to that of one who is dying because of an incurable diseases [and so exempts the killer].

K.   "The other party compares the case to that of one who is dying because of heavenly action [of natural causes, so imposes liability on the murderer].

L.   "As to the one who compares the case to that of one who is dying because of an incurable disease, what is the reason that he does not compare the case to that of one who is dying because of heavenly action?

M.   "To one who is dying at the hand of heaven, no concrete injury has been done, while to the other, a concrete injury has been inflicted.

N.   "As to the one who compares the case to that of one who is dying because of heavenly action, what is the reason that he does not compare the case to that of one who is dying because of an incurable disease?

O. "In the case of one who is dying because of an incurable disease, [Freedman:] the vital organs are affected, while in the case of the other, the vital organs are not affected."

XI.

A. A Tannaite authority repeated before R. Sheshet:

B. "'And he that kills all of the life of man' (Lev. 24:17):

C. "This serves to encompass the case of one who hits his fellow, and in his blow there is not sufficient force to inflict death, and then another party comes along and actually delivers the death blow, indicating that the latter is liable."

D. Since the blow that the former gave him was not sufficient to inflict death, it is self-evident [that the former is not liable].

E. Rather, it should be that the blow that the former gave <u>was</u> sufficiently strong to inflict death, but another party came and actually inflicted the death blow, and that second party is liable.

F. The unattributed teaching belongs to R. Judah b. Betera [at X C].

XII.

A. Said Raba, "He who kills someone afflicted with an incurable disease is exempt.

B. "And someone inflicted with an incurable disease who committed murder in the presence of a court is liable.

C. "If it was not in the presence of a court, he is exempt.

D. "If it was in the presence of a court, he is liable, for it is written, 'So shall you put away evil from the midst of you' (Deut. 13:6). [The court acts on what it sees on its own.]

E. If it was not in the presence of the court, he is exempt, for you have in hand an act of testimony that is not subject to the test of conspiratorial perjury [since in this case, the perjurers are beyond penalty. Who so? One has to do to them what they conspired to do to their victim. He is regarded as legally dead. They therefore cannot have conspired to kill him.] So their testimony is not subject to the usual test and thus is null.

F. And said Raba, "One who commits pederasty with someone afflicted with an incurable disease is liable.

G. "If one inflicted with an incurable disease committed pederasty, if it was before a court, he is liable.

H. "If it was not before a court, he is exempt.

I. "If it was before a court, he is liable, for it is written, 'So shall you put away evil from the midst of you. (Deut. 13:6).

J. "If it was not before the court, he is exempt, for you have in hand an act of testimony that is not subject to the test of conspiratorial perjury."

K. What need to I have for this further case [having made the same point with reference to the former]? The latter case is identical to the former!

M. The matter is at issue because of the clause about having sexual relations with a person dying of an incurable disease.

N. So we are informed that, because of the pleasure assumed to have been gained, [a penalty is imposed], and in this case we do invoke the principle that pleasure may be presumed to have been gained through the act [and so penalize the pederast].

O. And said Raba, "Witnesses who gave testimony against someone dying of an incurable disease and who were then proved to be a conspiracy for perjury are not put to death.

P. "Witnesses who were suffering an incurable disease who were proved to be a conspiracy for perjury are put to death."

Q. R. Ashi said, "Even in the case of witnesses suffering from an incurable disease who were proved to be a conspiracy for perjury are not put to death.,

R. "For the testimony against them [proving that they constituted a conspiracy for perjury] itself is not subject to the same test [since those who testify against them cannot be put to death. Why not? The men were dying anyhow, as Raba originally said]."

S. And said Raba, "An ox, dying of an incurable disease, that killed someone is liable, and an ox belonging to a man suffering from an incurable disease that killed someone is exempt.

T. "What is the scriptural basis for this rule?

U. "Scripture has said, 'The ox shall be stoned and its owner shall also be put to death' (Ex. 21:29).

V. "Wherever we can invoke the rule, 'And also its owner shall be put to death,' we also do not invoke the rule, 'The ox will be stoned.'"

W. "And wherever we cannot invoke the rule, 'And also its owner shall be put to death,' we also do not invoke the rule, 'The ox will be stoned.'"

X. R. Ashi said, "Even an ox that is suffering from an incurable disease that killed a man would be exempt [under the stated circumstance].

Y. "What is the reason for this ruling? Since, were it the owner, it would have been exempt [dying from an incurable disease, the owner would not be liable in this case, as Raba has said], the ox also is exempt [in a parallel case]."

XIII.

A. If he sicked a dog on him, etc. [M. 9:1J]:

B. Said R. Aha bar Jacob, "When you look into the matter [A at M. 9:1K-M], you will find that, in R. Judah's opinion [who holds one liable who makes a snake bite a man], the poison of a snake is between its teeth. Therefore the one one makes the snake bite a man is put to death through decapitation, while the snake itself is exempt.

C. "In the opinion of sages, the poison of the snake its vomited up out of its midst [on its own], and therefore the snake is put to death through stoning, and the one who made the snake bite the man is exempt. [Freedman, p. 526, n. 8: On Judah's view the fangs themselves are poisonous. Consequently the snake does nothing, the murder being committed by the person. But the sages maintain that even when its fangs are embedded in the flesh, they are not poisonous, unless it voluntarily emits poison. Consequently the murder is committed by the snake, not the man.]"

Unit I turns immediately to the proof-text on the basis of which the Mishnah's rule is framed. Unit II then deals with the exegesis of the Mishnah-paragraph. Unit III provides a proof-text for the same. Unit IV then expands upon the matter. Unit V introduces the first of a long series of Raba's excellent clarifications of the principle of the law. These run on through unit VI, VII, (the theme of which is continued at units VIII, IX), and units XI-XIII. Unit XIII then reverts to a later passage of the Mishnah-paragraph. So the entire composition involving Raba is inserted whole, in the appropriate position at which a compositor aiming at Mishnah-commentary chose for it.

9:1 N-T

N.   He who hits his fellow, whether with a stone or with his fist,

O.   and they diagnosed him as likely to die,

P.   but he got better than he was,

Q.   and afterward he got worse and he died

R.   he is liable.

S.   R. Nehemiah says, "He is exempt,

T.   "for there is a basis to the matter [of thinking that he did not die from the original injury]."

I.

A.   Our rabbis have taught on Tannaite authority:

B.   [In T.'s version:] **And this is yet another exegesis which R. Nehemiah stated, "[When men quarrel, and one strikes the other with a stone or with his fist, and the man does not die but keeps his bed], then if the man rises again and walks abroad [78B] with his staff, he that struck him shall be clear; only he shall pay for the loss of his time, and shall have him thoroughly healed (Ex. 21:18-19)**

C.   **"Now would it enter one's mind that this one should walk around in the market, while the other should be put to death on his account?**

D.   **"But the meaning is that, if he should recover somewhat, then get worse, and finally even if he should die [on account of the original blow], the other is exempt," [T. B.Q. 9:7A-C].**

E.   And how do rabbis deal with the proof-text [important to Nehemiah], "And then shall he who smote him be quit" (Ex. 21:19)?

F.   It teaches that the court imprisons the man [until we see whether the victim dies of the original blow].

G.   And how does R. Nehemiah prove that one imprisons the man?

H.   He derives it from the case of the wood-gatherer (Num. 15:32-36) [who was held in prison until the case was settled on high].

I.   And why should the rabbis also not derive their principle from the case of the woodgatherer?

J.   The woodgatherer was subject to the death penalty, and what Moses did not know was simply how he was to be put to death. But that would exclude the present case, in which we do not know whether the one who hit the other is subject to the death penalty or not subject to the death penalty.

K.   And R. Nehemiah points to a parallel in the case from that of the blasphemer, [at Lev. 24:10-14], in which, not knowing whether he was subject to the death penalty or not, the court imprisoned the man [until the decision would come from on high.]

L.   And rabbis? The case of the blasphemer involved decisions on an ad hoc basis. [Such a decision cannot be taken as precedent for normal procedure.]

M.   This foregoing report accords with the following teaching on Tannaite authority:

N.   Moses, our rabbi, knew that the woodgatherer was subject to the death penalty.

O.   For it is said, "Those who defile [the Sabbath] shall surely be put to death" (Ex. 31:14).

P.   But he did not know by what means he was to be put to death, for it is written, "And they put him in ward, because it was not declared what should be done to him" (Num. 15:34).

Q.   But as to the blasphemer, it is stated only, "And they put him in ward, that the mind of the Lord might be showed to them" (Lev. 24:12).

R.   This teaches that Moses did not know whether or not he was subject to the death penalty at all.

S.   Now with respect to the view of R. Nehemiah, that is why the Scripture twice makes reference to assessing the man's condition [Ex. 21:18-19: And if men strive together and one smite another with a stone...and he die not but keeps his bed, if he rises again and walk abroad upon his staff, then he that hit him shall be quit."] [Freedman, p. 528, n. 4: Two phrases are superfluous, that is, "And he die not," and "If he rise again and walk abroad upon his staff," for it is self-evident that the assailant cannot be executed under such circumstances; hence they must refer to two judicial calculations that he would not die, which was, however, subsequently falsified].

T.   One reference to an assessment concerns a case in which the court assessed the victim, holding that he would die, and he turned out to live.

U.   The other deals with a case in which the court assessed that he would die, then be recovered somewhat.

V.   The one refers to a case in which the court assessed the man's condition and held that he would die and he lived, and the other treats a case in which the court assessed the man's condition and held that he would live, but he died.

W.   And in R. Nehemiah's view?

X.   The case of the court's assessing the man and holding that he would live, and in which he then dies, does not require a verse of Scripture, since in such a case, the accused has already left the court a free man.

II.

A.   Our rabbis have taught on Tannaite authority:

B.   He who hits his fellow, and the court made an assessment that the man would die
      but he lived -- they free the accused.

C.   If they assessed that he would die and he got somewhat better, they make a second
      assessment as to the monetary compensation that he is to pay.

D.   If after a while the ailment grew worse and the man died, one is guided by the
      second assessment [and the accused pays for the monetary claim, as originally
      assessed, but is not liable to death], "the words of R. Nehemiah.

E.   And sages say, "There is no assessment after [the original one].

F.   There is a further teaching on Tannaite authority:

G.   [T:] He who hit his fellow.

H.   [if] they formed a prognosis that he would die, they again assess that he would live.

I.   [If they formed a prognosis] that he would live, they do not again assess that he
      would die.

J.   [T. adds: If they assessed that he would die, then the defendant is liable to the
      death penalty but exempt from having to pay monetary compensation. If they made
      an estimate as to the monetary compensation, the defendant is liable to pay
      monetary compensation and exempt from the death penalty.]

K.   If they assessed that he would die, and he got better, they make an estimate of the
      monetary compensation to be paid a second time.

L.   [If] they assessed that he would live and he died, [the defendant] pays compensation
      for injury, pain, medical costs, loss of income, and indignity, to the estate of the
      deceased.

M.   From what point does he pay him off?

N.   From the point at which he hit him.   [T. B.Q.9:5A-H, 9:6A]

O.   This unattributed teaching represents the view of R. Nehemiah [that one pays
      financial compensation and the accused is not put to death].

Both units of the Talmud take up and analyze the Tosefta's complement to the
Mishnah-paragraph at hand.

                              9:2

      A.   [If] he intended to kill a beast and killed a man,

      B.   a gentile and killed an Israelite,

      C.   an untimely birth and killed an offspring that was viable,

      D.   he is exempt.

      E.   [If] he intended to hit him on his loins with a blow that was not sufficient
            to kill him when it struck his loins, but it went and hit his heart, and
            there was sufficient force in that blow to kill him when it struck his
            heart, and he died,

      F.   he is exempt.

G. [If] he intended to hit him on his heart, [79A] and there was in that blow sufficient force to kill when it struck his heart, and it went and hit him on his loins, and there was not sufficient force in that blow to kill him when it struck his loins, but he died,

H. he is exempt.

I. [If] he intended to hit a large person, and there was not sufficient force in that blow to kill a large person, but it went and hit a small person, and there was sufficient force in that blow to kill a small person, and he died,

J. he is exempt.

K. [If] he intended to hit a small person, and there was in that blow sufficient force to kill a small person, and it went and struck the large person, and there was not sufficient force in that blow to kill the large person, but he died,

L. he is exempt.

M. But: [if] he intended to hit him on his loins, and there was sufficient force in the blow to kill him when it struck his loins, and it went and hit him on his heart and he died,

N. he is liable.

O. [If] he intended to hit a large person, and there was in that blow sufficient force to kill the large person, and it went and hit a small person and he died,

P. he is liable.

Q. R. Simeon says, "Even if he intended to kill this party, and he actually killed some other party, he is exempt."

I.

A. To what passage does R. Simeon make reference [at Q]?

B. Should we say that it is to the final clause [M-P]? Then what is required is, "R. Simeon declares exempt," [Freedman, p. 530, n. 2: Why repeat, "Even if he intended..."? Since it bears upon the clause immediately preceding, the circumstances having been stated, it is sufficient just to give Simeon's ruling].

C. Rather, he refers to the opening clause: If he intended to kill a beast and killed a man, a gentile and killed an Israelite, an untimely birth and killed an offspring that was viable, he is exempt [M. 9:2A-D].

D. Thus the contrary intent is: "If one intended to kill this party but killed another party, he is liable."

E. [Then the sense of Simeon follows:] R. Simeon says, "Even if he intended to kill this party, and he actually killed some other party, he is exempt" [M. 9:2Q].

F. Now the point is self-evident that if Reuben and Simeon were standing [together], and [the killer] said, "I intended Reuben, I did not intend Simeon," here we have the dispute [of R. Simeon and the anonymous authority].

G. But if he had said, "I had in mind one of them," or if he had said, "I was thinking it was Reuben but it was Simeon," what is the law?

H.   Come and take note of the following: R. Simeon says, "He is liable only if he states, 'I intended to kill So-and-so.'"

II.

A.   What is the Scriptural basis for the position of R. Simeon?

B.   Scripture has said, "[But if any man hates his neighbor] and lies in wait for him and rises up against him" (Deut. 19:11) meaning that [one is liable only if the killer] has hostile intentions against him in particular.

C.   And rabbis [view of the language, "for him" and "against him"?]

D.   Members of the house of R. Yannai say, "[The language, 'for him' or 'against him' serves] to exclude one who throws a stone into the midst [of Israelites and gentiles]."

E.   Now what sort of case is at hand? Should we say that there were nine Samaritans and only one Israelite among them? Then you should conclude that the majority of those [among whom he threw the stone] were Samaritans.

F.   Or again, if half were of one group and half of the other group, you have a case of doubt, and in a case of doubt as to capital crimes, one must impose the more lenient ruling.

G.   The matter is made pressing by the case in which there were one Samaritan and nine Israelites, in which case the Samaritan is a settled fact [as one of those present], and where there is a settled fact, it counts as one half of the facts at hand [where there is a case of doubt]. [The verse at hand applies to this case and tells us that in such a case, one is not liable; in the other possible cases, it is self-evident that he is not liable, and no proof-text is required].

III.

A.   Now from the viewpoint of rabbis, there is no problem, for they maintain that if one intended to kill one party and killed another, he is liable, for it is written, "If men strive and hurt a woman with child: (Ex. 21:22). In this connection, said R. Eleazar, "Scripture addresses the case of a fight involving intent to kill, for it is written, 'And if any accident follow, then you shall give life for life' (Ex. 21:23).

B.   But how does R. Simeon deal with the clause, "You shall give life for life" (Ex. 21:23) [Freedman, p. 53, n. 8: Since the murder of the woman was unintentional, according to Simeon there is no death penalty]?

C.   It means that there has to be a payment of monetary compensation for the death, in accord with the view of Rabbi.

D.   For it has been taught on Tannaite authority:

E.   Rabbi says, "'You shall give life for life' (Ex. 21:23).

F.   That means that monetary compensation is paid.

G.   "You maintain that monetary compensation is paid. But perhaps it means that a life must actually be taken?

H.   "The word 'giving' is stated here [at Ex. 21:23] and the same word is stated [79B] elsewhere ["If no accident follow, he shall give what the judges determine"].

I.   "Just as in that passage what is at hand is a monetary payment, so here what is expected is a monetary payment."

IV.

A.   Said Raba, "The following Tannaite authority of the house of Hezekiah differs from both Rabbi and rabbis."

B.   For a Tannaite authority of the house of Hezekiah taught, "'And he who kills a beast [shall pay for it] and he who kills a man [shall be put to death]' (Lev. 24:21). [Freedman, p. 532, n. 4: This verse, by coupling the two, likens them to each other; it also implies that where monetary compensation has to be made for an animal, it is not so for a man, since 'shall pay for it' is only prescribed for the former.]

C.   "Just as in the instance of one who hits a beast, you make no distinction between doing so inadvertently and deliberately, doing so intentionally and unintentionally, doing so with a downward blow or an upward blow, in no instance declaring one exempt from having to make monetary compensation but imposing liability in all cases to monetary compensation,

D.   "so in the case of one who hits [and kills] a man, you should make no distinction between doing so inadvertently and deliberately, doing so intentionally and unintentionally, doing so with a downward blow or an upward blow, in no instance declaring one liable to make monetary compensation but in all cases declaring one exempt from monetary compensation [since the death penalty may be involved]."

E.   [Reverting to Raba's observation,] "Now what is the sense of 'unintentionally'?

F.   "Should we say that one is totally unintentional in what he has done? Then we deal with nothing other than a case of inadvertence.

G.   "Rather, it is self-evident, it is a case that one does not intend to kill this one but rather that one.

H.   "And it has been taught, '...not imposing a monetary compensation but declaring him free of monetary compensation'?

I.   "Now if the person at hand is subject to the death penalty, why is it necessary to indicate that he is exempt from monetary compensation?

J.   "[Rather, does it not emerge from the passage at hand that such a one is neither subject to the death penalty nor subject to the requirement to pay monetary compensation. [Rabbi, by contrast, imposes the requirement of monetary compensation, and rabbis hold that he is subject to the death penalty]."

M.9:2 A-C introduce the whole, stating the basic principle which the triplet will proceed to unpack. The matter of intention is at issue. Simeon will reject the entire construction of M.9:2 E-P, because, so far as he is concerned, so long as one's intention has not been carried out, he remains exempt, without regard to the distinctions of the antecedent triplet. Their point is clear in the contrast between E-H+I-L, and M-P. If the death is caused in such a way that the person's original intent in no way leaves him culpable, he is exempt. But if what he did would have caused death to the person to whom he intended to do it, then he is liable on account of the death of the other person, to whom he actually did it. Units I-IV of the Talmud provide a careful exegesis of the meaning of the Mishnah's statements, with special reference to Simeon's position and the scriptural basis for it. Unit II then carries forward discussion of an item introduced by unit III, so the whole, at the end, is a unitary composition.

9:3

A. A murderer who was confused with others -- all of them are exempt.

B. R. Judah says, "They put them [all] in prison."

C. All those who are liable to death who were confused with one another are judged [to be punished] by the more lenient mode of execution.

D. [If] those to be stoned were confused with those to be burned -

E. R. Simeon says, "They are to be judged [to be executed] by stoning, for burning is the more severe of the two modes of execution."

F. And sages say, "They are adjudged [to be executed] by burning, for stoning is the more severe mode of execution of the two."

G. Said to them R. Simeon, "If burning were not the more severe, it would not have been assigned to the daughter of a priest who committed adultery."

H. They said to him, "If stoning were not the more severe of the two, it would not have been assigned to the blasphemer and to the one who performs an act of service for idolatry."

I. Those who are to be decapitated who were confused with those who are to be strangled -

J. R. Simeon says, "They are killed with the sword."

K. And sages say, "They are killed by strangling."

I.

A. Who are the others [mentioned at M. 9:3A]?

B. If we should maintain that these others are upright people, then the rule [at M. 9:3A] is self-evident.

C. Furthermore, in such a case would R. Judah say, "They put them into prison"? [Surely not!]

D. Said R. Abbahu said Samuel, "Here we deal with a case in which a murderer whose trial was not complete got mixed up with other murderers, whose trials had come to an end.

E. "Rabbis maintain that the court concludes the trial of a person only in that person's presence. Therefore all of them are treated as exempt [and released].

F. "And R. Judah holds that one cannot free them entirely, since they are, after all, murderers.

G. "Therefore, they put them into prison."

H. R. Simeon b. Laqish said, "If it is a case involving human beings all parties concur that they free [all of those who are confused with one another].

I. "But here we deal with a dispute involving the case of an ox, the trial of which had not been completed, and which was confused with other oxen, the trial of which had been completed.

J. "Rabbis hold that the capital trial of the master defines the rules governing the capital trial of the ox, and so the court may conclude the trial of an ox only in that ox's presence. Therefore all of them are treated as exempt [and released].

K. "R. Judah maintains that they put them into prison."

L. Said Raba, [80A] If so, then we must take up what R. Yose observed on this passage, namely, 'Even if my father, Halapta, [a pious man] were among them, [would Judah take the view that he does]?'"

M. Rather, said Raba, "The sense [of Yose's statement] is as follows: If two people were standing, and an arrow came forth from their midst and killed someone, both of them are exempt [since we do not know who shot the arrow].

N. "And said R. yose, 'Even if my father, Halapta, were among them [The rule would be the same, and the thought of Halapta's committing murder is unthinkable. Still, the other party cannot be convicted.]

O. "But if an ox that had been tried and convicted was confused with other oxen of a perfectly good [character, not gorers], [the court nonetheless has] them stoned.

P. "R. Judah says, 'They are put into prison.'"

Q. And so it has been taught on Tannaite authority:

R. In the case of a cow which killed someone and then gave birth, if before the trial was complete it gave birth, the offspring is permitted.

S. If after the trial was completed it gave birth, the offspring is forbidden [as part of the mother at the point at which the cow was condemned to stoning. Hence the calf may not be utilized].

T. If the cow was confused with others, and others with others, they put them all into prison.

U. R. Eleazar b. R. Simeon says, "They bring them all to court and they stone them."

II.

A. A master said: "If before the trial was complete, it gave birth, the offspring is permitted."

B. And is that the case, even though, when it gored, it was pregnant?

C. And has Raba not said, "The offspring of a cow that gored is forbidden [for use in the cult], both the cow and the offspring are deemed to have gored.

D. "If the offspring was used for bestiality, both the cow and the offspring are deemed to have been used for bestiality. [If the cow was pregnant, therefore, when it gored, the calf is regarded as identical with its mother (Freedman, p. 534, n. 9)]."

E. Then read the passage in this way: If before the trial was completed, it became pregnant and produced an offspring, the offspring is permitted. If after the trial was complete, the cow became pregnant, and it produced the offspring, the offspring is forbidden.

F. That version of matters poses no problem to him who has said, "[If] both this and that constitute the causes [here: if both an ox and a cow have produced the offspring] [and one of the causes, that is, the cow, is forbidden, then] the offspring is likewise forbidden."

G.   [80B] But in the view of him who maintains that in such a case, it is permitted, what is there to be said?

H.   Rather, said Rabina, "This is how the rule is to be stated: If before the trial was completed the cow became pregnant and produced the offspring, the offspring is permitted.

I.   "And if before the trial was completed, the cow became pregnant, but it was only after the trial was completed that the cow gave birth, the offspring is forbidden.

J.   "The reason is that the embryo is deemed an integral part of the mother. [Freedman, p. 535, n. 3: In this case, it is forbidden, not because it is the product of its mother, but because before birth it is part of its mother, and the prohibition applicable to the latter applies to the embryo too.]"

III.

A.   All those who are liable to death [who were confused with one another are judged to be punished by the more lenient mode of execution] [M. 9:3C]:

B.   That indicates that admonition [not to commit a crime] which serves for a more severe infringement of the law applies as an admonition for a less severe infringement of the law. [The criminals had been admonished with a statement on the mode of execution that applies to the crime they had been about to commit. The admonition referred to a more severe mode of execution. The stated law then indicates that admonition served for a less severe mode of execution.]

C.   Said R. Jeremiah, "[Not so,] for with what sort of a case do we deal here? It is with one in which an admonition was given without specification [as to the mode of execution].

D.   "And the rule at hand accords with the Tannaite authority who stands behind this following on Tannaite teaching:

E.   "'And as to all others liable to the death penalty imposed by a court, they convict them only on the testimony of witnesses, after warning, and after they inform him that what he is going to do subjects him to liability to the death penalty in court.

F.   "'R. Judah says, "Only if they will inform him specifically as to the sort of death penalty to which he will be subjected"' [T. San. 11:1A-C].

G.   "The former of the two authorities derives the rule from the case of the wood-gatherer, R. Judah takes the view that the wood-gatherer represented an ad hoc case."

IV.

A.   If those to be stoned were confused with those to be burned [M. 9:3D]:

B.   R. Ezekiel repeated the passage at hand for Rami, his son, as follows: 'If those to be burned were confused with those to be stoned, R. Simeon says, "They are judged to be executed by stoning, for burning is the more severe of the two modes of execution" [M. 9:3E].'"

C.   Said R. Judah to him, "Father, do not repeat it in this way. Why give as the reason, 'Because burning is more stringent'?

D.   "Rather, derive the fact that the larger number of those who are put to death are put to death through stoning. [Freedman, p. 536, n. 3: For 'if criminals condemned to burning became mixed up with others condemned to stoning' implies that the latter were in the majority, as the smaller number is lost in the larger].

E.   "Instead, this is how it should be repeated:

F.   "'If those to be stoned were confused with those to be burned,

G.   "R. Simeon says, "They are judged to be executed by stoning, for burning is the more severe of the two modes of execution"' [M. 9:3D-E]."

H.   Then take up the concluding clause:

I.   But sages say, "They are adjudged to be executed by burning, for stoning is the more severe mode of execution of the two" [M. 9:3F].

J.   But derive that point from the simple fact that the greater number of those who are put to death are put to death through burning?

K.   In that case, it is rabbis who frame matters so as to state to R. Simeon, "In accord with your view, for you maintain that burning is more severe, but to the contrary, stoning is the more severe. [Freedman, p. 536, n. 4: But their ruling could be deduced from the fact that the majority are to be executed through burning]."

L.   Said Samuel to R. Judah, "Sharp one! [81A] Do not say things in this way to your father!

M.   "This is what has been taught on Tannaite authority:

N.   "Lo, if one's father was violating the teachings of the Torah, he should not say to him, 'Father, you have violated the teachings of the Torah.'

O.   "Rather, one should say to him, 'Father, this is what is written in the Torah.'"

P.   Still, this [O] is the same as that [N]!

Q.   Rather, he says to him, "Father, there is a verse of Scripture that is written in the Torah, and this is what it says. [He does not state the law directly but lets the father draw his own inference (Freedman, p. 536, n. 8)]."

Unit I provides an important clarification for the rule of the Mishnah. Unit II continues unit I. Unit III takes up the implications for an extraneous issue of the rule at M. 9:3C, and unit IV clarifies the wording of M. 9:3D.

9:4

A.   He who is declared liable to be put to death through two different modes of execution at the hands of a court is judged [to be executed] by the more severe.

B.   [if] he committed a transgression which is subject to the death penalty on two separate counts, he is judged on accont of the more severe.

C.   R. Yose says, "He is judged by the penalty which first applies to what he has done."

I.

A.   It is self-evident [that he is subject to the more severe mode of execution]. [For, after all], should he profit [from committing the further crime]?

B.   Said Raba, "With what sort of case do we deal here? It is one in which the man committed a lesser transgression and was convicted for the lesser transgression. Then he went and committed a greater transgression.

C.   "Now it might have entered your mind to rule that, since he was tried and convicted for the lesser transgression, this man is as if dead [for he is going to be put to death no matter what else he does].

D.   "So we are informed [to the contrary, that we do try him for the offense that produces the more severe mode of execution]."

II.

A.   The brother of R. Joseph bar Hama asked Rabbah bar Nathan, "What is the source of this view of rabbis: He who is declared liable to be put to death through two different modes of execution at the hands of a court is judged to be executed by the more severe [M. 9:4A]?"

B.   [The reply:] "As it is written, 'If [the righteous man] beget a son who is a robber, a shedder of blood...who has eaten upon the mountains and defiled his neighbor's wife' (Ez. 18:10-11).

C.   "'If he beget a son who is a robber, a shedder of blood' -- such a one is subject to the death penalty of decapitation.

D.   "'And defiled his neighbor's wife' -- this is adultery, punished through [the more severe penalty] strangulation.

E.   "'And has lifted up his eyes to idols' (Ez. 18:12) -- this is idolatry, punished through stoning.

F.   "And it is written, 'He shall surely die, his blood shall be upon him' (Ex. 18:13) -- this refers to stoning. [Freedman, p. 537, n. 6: Thus we see that the severest penalty is imposed, and it must be under the circumstances posited by Raba, for otherwise the verse is unnecessary.]'

G.   To this proof R. Nahman b. Isaac raised an objection, "May I propose that all of the clauses refer to crimes punished by stoning?

H.   "'If he beget a son, a robber, a shedder of blood' -- this refers to a wayward and incorrigible son, who is put to death through stoning.

I.   "'And defiled his neighbor's wife' -- this refers to a betrothed girl, on account of intercourse with whom one is put to death through stoning.

J.   "'And has lifted up his eyes to the idols' -- this refers to idolatry, penalized by the death-penalty of stoning."

K.   "If that is the case, then what is it that Ezekiel tells us?"

L.   "Perhaps he was simply reviewing the teachings of the Torah."

M.   "If so, he should have reviewed it in the way in which Moses, our master, reviewed it."

III.

A.   R. Aha, son of R. Hanina, interpreted Scripture, "What is the meaning of the verse, '[But if a man be just and do what is lawful and right...], and has not eaten upon the mountains' (Ez. 18:16)?

B. "It means that he did not eat only on account of the merit of his ancestors [but on his own merit].

C. "'And did not lift up his eyes to the idols of the house of Israel' - that he did not walk about in a proud way [but in a humble way].

D. "'Nor did he defile his neighbor's wife' -- that he did not compete with his fellow in trade.

E. "'And did not have sexual relations with a menstruating woman' -- that he did not derive benefit from the charity-fund.

F. "And it is written, 'He is just, he shall surely live' (Ez. 18:9)."

G. When Rabban Gamaliel reached this verse of Scripture, he would weep, saying, "If someone did all of these [virtuous deeds], then he will live, but not merely on account of one of them."

H. Said R. Aqiba to him, "But take account of the following: 'Do not defile yourselves in all of these things' (Lev. 18:24). Here too does it mean that one is liable only for doing all of the [vile deeds that are catalogued], but not if he did only one of them?

I. "Rather, the meaning is in 'only one of these things' [one violates the law], and so here to, if one does only one of all of these things, [he shall live]."

IV.

A. If he committed a transgression... [M. 9:4B-C]:

B. It has been taught on Tannaite authority:

C. Said R.Yose, "He is judged by the penalty which first applies to what he has done [M. 9:4C]:

D. "If he had sexual relations with her when she was his mother-in-law, and then she got married and so was a married woman, he is judged on the count of her being his mother-in-law.

E. "If she was a married woman and then became his mother-in-law, he is judged on the count of her being a married woman" [T. San. 12:5D-I].

F. Said Ada bar Ahbah to Raba, "If she was his mother-in-law and then became a married woman, should he be judged only on account of having sexual relations with his mother-in-law? Let him be judged also on account of the prohibition applying to having sexual relations with a married woman!

G. "For lo, R. Abbahu said, 'R. Yose concurs in the case of a prohibition that adds [to the prohibition already in place].'"

H. [81B] He said to him, "Ada, my son, are you going to kill him twice?"

The point of concurrence at M. 9:3C is repeated. The important point is not at M. 9:4A, but at M. 9:4B. Once more, we find ourselves engaged in the exposition of the materials of Chapter Seven, now M. 7:4K-R, the sages' view that there may be two counts of culpability on the basis of a single transgression. A's point is that if one has intercourse with a married woman and is liable for strangulation, and afterward he has sexual relations with his mother-in-law and is liable for burning, he is judged on the count of burning. If his mother-in-law had been married, we should have the problem of B. He then would be tried on the count of the mother-in-law, which produces the execution by burning, rather than on the count of the married woman, which produces the penalty of strangulation.

Yose's clarification requires that the woman have passed through several relationships to the lover. First she was a widow, whose daughter he had married, and so she was his mother-in-law. Afterward she was married. He had sexual relations with her. He is tried for having had sexual relations with his mother-in-law, thus for burning, since that was the first aspect in which the woman was prohibited to him. If the story were reversed, he would be tried under the count of strangulation for his sexual relations with a married woman.

Unit I of the Talmud clarifies the allegation of M. 9:A, and unit II provides a proof-text for that proposition. Unit III then adds a further exegesis of the same proof-text. Unit IV proceeds to the clarification of M. 9:4B-C.

9:5 A-B

A.   He who was flogged [and did the same deed] and was flogged again --

B.   [if he did it yet a third time] the court puts him in prison and feeds him barley until his belly explodes.

I.

A.   Merely because he was flogged and flogged again does the court put him in prison?

B.   Said R. Jeremiah said R. Simeon b. Laqish, "here we deal with flogging administered in a case in which the real penalty is extirpation [but in which the felon was warned only of the penalty of flogging], so that the felon in point of fact is subject to the death penalty.

C.   "Now as yet, death has not drawn near this man, and, since he has allowed himself [to violate the law again], we bring him near to death."

D.   Said R. Jacob to R. Jeremiah b. Tahalifa, "Come and I shall explain this matter to you.

E.   "The passage at hand refers to flogging administered on account of a single sort of sin that involves the penalty of extirpation.

F.   "But in the case of one who commits two or three different sorts of sins that are penalized by extirpation, this man is just trying out [different sorts of sins] and has not abandoned himself to sink to such an extent [that we hasten his death]."

II.

A.   He who was flogged and flogged again [M. 9:5A]:

B.   He did it twice and not a third time. Then may we say that the Mishnah-passage at hand does not accord with the view of R. Simeon b. Gamaliel?

C.   For in the view of Rabban Simeon b. Gamaliel, lo, he has said, "Only in the case of three occurrences [of a given phenomenon] do we recognize a presumption [that such a thing is regularly going to happen]."

D.   Said Rabina, "You may maintain even that it is in accord with Rabban Simeon b. Gamaliel.

E.   "He takes the view that in the case of the commission of transgressions, even less than three actions establish a presumption as to the character of the man."

F.   An objection was raised [on the basis of the following passage:]

G.   Those who are liable for flogging who were flogged [and did the same deed] and were flogged again [M, 9:5A] --

H.   and this happened once, twice, and yet a third time --

I.   they put him into prison.

J.   Abba Saul says, "Also on the third occasion they flog him.

K.   "But if he repeats it a fourth time,

L.   they put him into prison and feed him barley until his belly explodes" [M. 9:5B]. [T. San. 12:8B-G].

M.   May we not say that all parties concur that the fact that one has been flogged establishes a presumption [about his character], and at issue is the dispute between Rabbi and Rabban Simeon b. Gamaliel. [Freedman, p. 540, n. 4: The first Tannaite authority agrees with Rabbi that twice affords presumption, Abba Saul with R. Simeon b. Gamaliel. But since the first authority is identical with that of our Mishnah, it follows that it cannot agree with R. Simeon b. Gamaliel. This refutes Rabina.]

N.   No, all parties concur with the view of Rabban Simeon b. Gamaliel. And in the present case, the point at issue is this: One authority takes the view that the commission of transgressions establishes a presumption [as to one's character] and the other party takes the view that inflicting a flogging establishes the presumption [as to one's character].

O.   But has it not been taught on Tannaite authority:

P.   [If] they warn him and he remains silent,

Q.   warn him and he nods his head,

R.   warn him once, twice, and a third time [and he repeated the same transgression],

S.   they put him into prison [cf. M. 9:5A-B].

T.   Abba Saul says, "Also on the third occasion they warn him.

U.   "but if he repeats it a fourth time,

V.   "they put him into prison and feed him the bread of adversity and the water of affliction (Is. 30:20)" [M. 9:5C] [T. San. 12:7A-G].

W.   Now in this case there is no issue of flogging! [Here, therefore, there is no flagellation to afford a basis for presumption (Freedman, p. 540, n. 8)].

X.   So what is at issue?

Y.   Said Rabina, "What is at issue is whether there is necessity to give an advance admonition concerning the punishment of imprisonment in a cell."

III.

A.   And what is a cell?

B.   Said R. Judah, "It was the height of the prisoner."

C.   And where in Scripture do we find an allusion to such a thing?

D.   Said R. Simeon b. Laqish, "'Evil shall slay the wicked' (Ps. 34:2)."

E.   And said R. Simeon b. Laqish, "What is the meaning of that which is written, 'For man also knows not his time, as the fishes that are taken in an evil trap' (Qoh. 9:12)?

F.   "What is an evil trap?"

G.   Said R. Simeon b. Laqish, "It is a hook."

Unit I clarifies the reasoning behind M. 9:5A. Unit II then investigates its own problem, using the materials of M. 9:5A for that purpose. But the problem is integral to the Mishnah-paragraph, as Tosefta's contribution shows. Unit III then deals with the definition of the prison of M. 9:5B.

9:5C

A.   He who kills a someone not before witnesses they put him in prison and feed him the bread of adversity and the water of affliction (Is. 30:20).

I.

A.   How do we know [that this man has killed someone]?

B.   Said Rab, "We deal with a case in which the testimony is disjoined [since the two witnesses saw the act individually, but were not on a line of sight with one another]."

C.   And Samuel said, "It was an act committed without prior admonition [as to the consequences]."

D.   And R. Hisda said Abimi said, "We deal with a case in which the testimony as contradicted in some minor detail as to circumstance but was not disproved as to major details of what had actually been done.

E.   "This is as we have learned in the Mishnah: There was the case in which Ben Zakkai examined a witness as to the character of the stems of figs under which the incident took place [M. 5:2B]."

II.

A.   And feed him the bread of adversity and th water of affliction [M. 9:5C]:

B.   Why does the passage at hand frame matters as, And they feed him the bread of adversity and the water of affliction [M. 9:5C], while the other passage states, The court puts him in prison and feeds him barley until his belly explodes [M. 9:5B]?

C.   Said R. Sheshet, "Both, in point of fact, mean that they feed him the bread of adversity and the water of affliction. This is until his innards shrink. Then they give him barley-bread until his belly explodes."

The Talmud at Unit I asks the obvious question and in unit II explains divergent formulations of the law at hand.

9:6

A.   He who stole a sacred vessel [of the cult (Num. 4:7)], and he who curses using the name of an idol, and he who has sexual relations with an Aramaean woman --

B.   zealots beat him up [on the spot (Num. 25:8, 11)].

C.   A priest who performed the rite in a state of uncleanness --

D.   his brothers, the priests, do not bring him to court.

E.   But the young priests take him outside the courtyard and break his head with clubs.

F.   A non-priest who served in the Temple --

G.   R. Aqiba says, "[He is put to death] by strangling [Num. 18:7]."

H.   And sages say, "[He is put to death] at the hands of Heaven."

I.

A.   What is a sacred vessel [M. 9:6A]?

B.   Said R. Judah, "It is a utensil used in the ministry. And so it says, 'And the vessels of libation' (Num. 4:7).

C.   "And where in Scripture do we find an allusion to the matter?

D.   "'That they come not to see how the holy things are stolen, lest they [who stole them] die' (Num. 4:20)."

II.

A.   He who curses using the name of an idol. [M. 9:6A]:

B.   R. Joseph taught on Tannaite authority, "May the idol smite its enchanter."

C.   Rabbis, and others say, Rabbah b. Mari, say, "'May the idol slay him, his master, and the one who gives him ownership.'"

III.

A.   He who has sexual relations with an Aramaean woman [M. 9:6A]:

B.   R. Kahana asked Rab, [82A] "What is the law if the zealots do not beat him up [M. 9:6B]?"

C.   Rab had forgotten his learning on the subject, and in a dream, R. Kahana received the following verse of Scripture, "As Judah has dealt treacherously, and an abomination is committed in Israel and in Jerusalem, for Judah has profaned the holiness of the Lord which he loved and has been intimate with the daughter of a strange god" (Mal. 2:11).

D.   He came to Rab and said to him, "This is what I was made to recite in my dream."

E.   Rab then remembered what he had learned: "Judah has dealt treacherously -- this refers to idolatry, and so it is written, 'Surely as a wife departs treacherously from her husband, so have you dealt treacherously with me, O house of Israel, says the Lord' (Jer. 3:20).

F.   "'And an abomination is committed in Israel and in Jerusalem' -- this refers to pederasty. And so it is written, 'You shall not lie with mankind as with womankind; it is an abomination' (Lev. 18:22).

G.   "'For Judah has profaned the holiness of the Lord' -- this refers to prostitution, and so it is written, 'There shall be no consecrated harlot of the daughters of Israel' (Deut. 3:18).

H.   "'And has been intimate with the daughter of a strange god' -- this refers to one who has sexual relations with a Samaritan woman.

I.   "And thereafter it is written, 'The Lord will cut off the men who do this, the master and scholar, out of the tabernacles of Jacob, and him who offers an offering to the Lord of hosts' (Mal. 2:12).

J.   "If he is a disciple of a sage, he will have no witness among sages or response among disciples.

K.   "If he is a priest, he will have no son to make a meal offering to the Lord of hosts."

IV.

A.   Said R. Hiyya bar Abbuyah, "Whoever has sexual relations with a Samaritan woman is as if he marries an idol.

B.   "For it is written, 'And has had sexual relations with the daughter of a strange god' (Mal. 2:11).

C.   "And does a strange god have a daughter?

D.   "Rather, this refers to someone who has sexual relations with a Samaritan woman."

E.   And said R. Hiyya bar Abbuyah, "On the skull of Jehoiakim is written 'This and yet another.'"

F.   The grandfather of R. Perida found a skull which was tossed near the gates of Jerusalem, and written on it were the words, "This and yet another."

G.   He buried it and it came up again. He buried it and it came up again.

H.   He said, "This must be the skull of Jehoiakim, concerning whom it is written, 'He shall be buried with the burial of an ass, drawn and cast forth beyond the gates of Jerusalem'" (Jer. 22:19).

I.   He said, "Still, he was a king, and it is not proper to treat him with disrespect."

J.   He took the skull and wrapped it in silk and put in in a chest.

K.   His wife came along and saw it. She took it out and showed it to the neighboring women, who said to her, "It must be his [that is, your husband's] first wife, for he cannot forget her."

L.   "She lit the oven and burned it.

M.   When he came home he said, "This is in line with what is written on [the skull], 'This and yet another.'"

V.

A.   When R. Dimi came, he said, "The court of the Hasmoneans made a decree that one who has sexual relations with a Samaritan woman is liable on her account on the counts of having sexual relations with a menstruating woman, a gentile maid servant, a gentile woman, and a married woman."

B.   When Rabin came, he said, "He is liable on the counts of having sexual relations with a menstruating woman, a gentile maidservant, a gentile woman, and a prostitute, but not on the count of having relations with a married woman, since valid marital relations do not apply to them."

C.   And the other [Dimi]?

D.   They most assuredly do not allow their women to have sexual relations freely [with any man other than the husband].

VI.

A.   Said R. Hisda, "[If a zealot] comes to take counsel [as to punishing a law violator, such as is listed at M. 9:6A], they do not give him instructions to do so."

B.   It has been stated along these same lines on Amoraic authority:

C.   Said Rabbah bar bar Hannah said R. Yohanan, "[If a zealot] comes to take counsel, they do not give him instructions to do so.

D.   "And not only so, but if Zimri had separated from [his girl-friend] and had Phineas then killed him, Phineas would have been put to death on his account.

E.   "[Under these same conditions] had Zimri turned on Phineas and [in self-defense] had he killed Phineas, he would not have been out to death on his account, for lo, [Phineas then] was in the position of being a pursuer."

VII.

A.   "And Moses said to the judges of Israel, Slay every one his men that were joined to Baal Peor" (Num. 25:5).

B.   The tribe of Simeon went to Zimri b. Salu and said to him, "Lo, the judges are judging capital cases, and you sit silent."

C.   What did he do? He went and called together twenty-four thousand Israelites and went to Kozki and said to her, "Listen to me [and have sexual relations with me]."

D.   She said to him, "I am a royal princess, and father has told me, 'Listen [I have sexual relations] only with the greatest man among them.'"

E.   He said to her, "Even I am the prince of a tribe, and not only so, but [my tribe]is greater than his [Moses'], for he is second in order of birth, and I am third in order of birth."

F.   He took her by her forelock and brought her to Moses. He said to him, "Ben Armam, is this woman forbidden or permitted? And if you should rule that she is forbidden, as to the daughter of Jethro, who permitted you to marry her?"

G.   Moses forgot the law, and all of them broke out in tears, as it is written, "And they were weeping before the door of the tabernacle of the congregation" (Num. 25:6).

H.   And it is written, "And Phineas, son of Eleazar, son of Aaron the priest, saw" (Num. 25:7).

I.   What did he see?

J.   Said Rab, "He saw the deed and then remembered the law." He said to him, "O brother of the father of my father, have you not taught us as you came down from Mount Sinai, 'He who has sexual relations with an Aramaean woman -- zealots beat him up on the spot' [M. 9:6A-B]?"

K.   He said to him, "The one who reads the letter should be the one to serve as agent [to carry out its orders] [So, do it.]."

L.   Samuel said, "He saw that, 'There is no wisdom, understanding, or counsel against the Lord' (Prov. 21:30). In any circumstance in which there is a profanation of the Name [of God], people are not to defer to the master [but are to correct the situation immediately]."

M.   R. Isaac said R. Eleazar said, "He saw that an angel came and destroyed some of the people."

N.   "And he rose up out of the midst of the congregation and took a spear in his hand" (Num. 25:7).

O.   On this basis we learn that people may not enter the school house carrying weapons.

P.   He took off the spear-head and put it in his garment and was [82B] leaning on the stock. He went along as if leaning on his staff. When he came to the tribe of Simeon, he said, "Where do we find that the tribe of Levi is greater than the tribe of Simeon? [Let me do it too!]"

Q.   They said, "Let him too do what he needs to do. The people who kept separate now have permitted the matter too."

R.   Said R. Yohanan, "Six miracles were done for Phineas:

S.   "First, that Zimri should have taken out his penis from the woman and he did not do so [leaving Phineas free to act];

T.   "another, that he should have spoken out [for help] but he did not speak out;

U.   "a third, that Phineas got his spear right through the penis of the man and the vagina of the woman'

V.   "fourth, that they did not fall off the spear;

W.   "fifth, that an angel came and raised up the lintel [so he could carry them out on his spear];

X.   "and sixth, that an angel came and destroyed the people [so they paid no attention to what Phineas had done]."

Y.   "Phineas came and cast them down before the Omnipresent, and said, 'Lord of the world, on account of these should twenty-four thousand Israelites die?'

Z.   "For it is said, 'And those that died in the plague were twenty-four thousand' (Num. 25:9).

AA.   "Thus it is written, 'Then Phineas stood up and executed judgment' (Ps. 106:30)."

BB.   Said R. Eleazar, "'And he prayed' is not written, but rather, 'And he argued with ...,' teaching that it was as if he made an argument with his Maker [about punishing them]."

CC.   The ministering angels wanted to push him aside. He said to them, "Let him be. He is a zealot, son of a zealot, he is one who seeks to turn away anger, son of one who seeks to turn away anger."

DD.   The other tribes began to tear him down, "Do you see this son of Puti [Putiel]. For the father of his mother fattened [PTM] calves for idolatry, and he has himself killed the head of a tribe of Israel."

EE.   Scripture came along and spelled out his genealogy: "Phineas, son of Eleazar, son of Aaron the priest" (Num. 25:11).

FF.   Said the Holy One, blessed be he, to Moses, "[When you see him], greet him in peace first, as it is written, 'Wherefore say, Behold, I give to him my covenant of peace' (Num. 25:12).

GG.   "And this act of atonement is worthy that it should continue to make atonement forever."

VIII.

A. Said R. Nahman said Rab, "What is the meaning of the verse of Scripture, 'A greyhound, a hegoat also, and a king, against whom there is no rising up' (Prov. 30:31)?

B. "Four hundred twenty-four acts of sexual relations did that wicked man have that day.

C. "Phineas waited for him until he grew weak, for he did not know that 'a king, against whom there is no rising up' is [God]."

D. In a Tannaite teaching it is taught:

E. He had sexual relations sixty times, until he became like an addled egg, and she became like a furrow filled with water."

F. Said R. Kahana, "And her 'seat' was a _seah_ [in size]."

G. R. Joseph taught on Tannaite authority, "Her womb-opening was a cubit."

IX.

A. Said R. Sheshet, "Her name was not Cosbi but Shewilani, daughter of Zur.

B. "Why was she called Cozbi? Because she violated her father's instructions [in having sexual relations with someone as unimportant as Zimri]."

C. Another explanation of Cozbi:

D. She said to her father, "Devour (_kosbi_) this people for me."

E. So it is in line with what people say, "What does Shewilani want among the reeds of the lake, what does Shewilani want among the peeling rushes? Did she embrace her mother?"

X.

A. Said R. Yohana n, "Zimri had five names: Zimri, son of Salu; Saul, son of the Canaanite woman; and Shelumiel, son of Zurishaddai.

B. "'Zimri,' because he became like an addled egg.

C. "'Son of Salu'because he outweighed the sins of his family;

D. "'Saul,' because he lent himself to sin;

E. "'Son of the Canaanite woman,' because he acted like a Canaanite.

F. "But what was his real name? It was Shelumiel, son of Zurishaddai."

XI.

A. A priest who performed the rite in a state of uncleanness [M. 9:6C]:

B. R. Aha, son of R. Huna, asked R. Sheshet, "Is a priest who performed an act of service while in a state of uncleanness liable to the death penalty at the hands of heaven, or is he not liable to the death penalty at the hands of heaven?"

C. He said to him, "You have learned to repeat the following passage of the Mishnah: A priest who performed the rite in a state of uncleanness -- his brothers, the priests, do not bring him to court. But the young priests take him outside the courtyard and break his head with clubs [M. 9:6C-E].

D. "Now if you think that he is liable to the death penalty at the hands of heaven, then they should let him be, and let him be put to death at the hands of heaven.

E. "Then what is the upshot? He is not liable [to death at the hands of heaven]."

F. But is there any action which the All-Merciful has treated as exempt from penalty, and on account of which we should go and inflict the death penalty?

G. And is there none? And lo, have we not learned in the Mishnah:

H. He who was floged and did the same deed and was flogged again -- if he did it yet a third time, the court puts him in prison and feeds him barley until his belly explodes [M. 9:5A-B]?

I. Here the All-Merciful has treated him as exempt from penalty, but we put him to death.

J. [That poses no problem], for has not R. Jeremiah said R. Simeon b. Laqish said, "We deal with a case in which the flogging was administered in a case in which the penalty is extirpation, for the man was subject to the death penalty"?

K. But lo, there is the case of one who steals a sacred vessel [M. 9:6A]!

L. [That too is no problem], for has not R. Judah said, "We deal with utensils used for the cult, and there is an allusion to [the death penalty for stealing them] in that which is written, 'That they come not to see how the holy things are stolen, lest they die' (Num. 4:20)."

M. And lo, there is the case of one who curses using the name of an idol [M. 9:6A]!

N. Lo, did not R. Joseph repeat on Tannaite authority, "'May the charm slay the enchanter'"? It is because he appears to commit blasphemy.

O. And lo, there is he who has sexual relations with an Aramaean woman [M. 9:6A]?

P. Lo, in that same case R. Kahana in a dream was made to recite a verse of Scripture, and this reminded Rab of the law [IIIA-G].

Q. An objection was raised:

R. He pours out oil over a meal-offering, he who mixes meal with the oil, he who breaks meal-offering cakes into pieces, he who salts meal-offering, he who waves it, he who brings it near [opposite the southwest corner of the alter], he who arranges the bread on the table, he who trims the lamps, he who takes the handful of meal-offering, he who receives the blood [none of which actions completes the sacrificial rite] outside of the Temple is exempt [from all penalty]. They are not liable on account of such actions [83A] either because of being a non-priest or because of uncleanness or because of lacking the proper vestments or because of having unwashed hands and feet [M. Zeb. 14:3F-I].

S. Lo, if such a one had burned incense [and so completed an act of service], he would have been liable. Now is this not liable to the death penalty?

T. No, it is liable to violating an admonition [not to do so].

U. And is that the case also for a non-priest, that he is merely subject to violating an admonition?

V. And is it not written, "And the non-priest who comes near shall be put to death" (Num. 18:7)?

W. Each item on the list is subject to its own rule [and for the one who is unclean, on violates a prohibition, but for the one who is a non-priest, the death penalty applies].

X. Does it then follow that pouring and mingling [oil for the meal-offering] are not violations of a negative commandment?

Y.   But has it not been taught on Tannaite authority:

Z.   Whence in Scripture do we find an admonition [that an unclean priest] nor pour or mingle [oil]?

AA. As it is written, "They shall be holy to their God and not profane the name of their God" (Lev. 21:6). [Freedman, p. 550, n. 9: This is referred to the performance of one of these acts of service while unclean.]

BB. It is merely on the authority of rabbis, and the verse provides an additional support.

CC. An objection was raised on the basis of the following:

DD. And these are the ones who are subject to the death penalty: an unclean priest who performed an act of service [T. Zeb. 12:17].

EE. That indeed refutes the view of R. Sheshet.

XII.

A.   Reverting to the body of the cited text:

B.   And these are the ones who are subject to the death penalty:

C.   He who eats untithed food, and a non-priest, an unclean person, who ate heave-offering, and an unclean priest who ate clean heave-offering,

D.   and a non-priest, one in the status of Tebul Yom, one lacking priestly vestments, one whose rites of atonement were not yet complete, and one with unwashed hands and feet, and those with unkempt hair, and those who were drunk, who served [at the altar] --

E.   all of them are subject to the death penalty.

F.   But an uncircumcised [priest] and a priest in mourning, and one who was sitting down [while at the altar], lo, these are subject to warning.

G.   "A blemished priest [who performed a sacrificial rite] is subject to the death penalty," the words of Rabbi.

H.   And sages say, "He is subject to the penalty for transgressing a negative commandment."

I.   He who deliberately carried out an act of sacrilege --

J.   Rabbi says, "He is subject to the death penalty."

K.   And sages say, "He is subject to the penalty for transgressing a negative commandment," [T. Zeb. 12:17A-I].

L.   He who eats untithed food: Whence in Scripture do we find proof [of the fact that such a one is subject to the death penalty]?

M.   It is in accord with what Samuel said in the name of R. Eleazar, "How do we know of one who eats untithed food that he is subject to the death penalty?

N.   "It is in accord with the following verse of Scripture: 'And they shall not profane the holy things of the children of Israel, which they shall offer to the Lord' (Lev. 22:15).

O.   "Scripture speaks of what they are going to offer up to the Lord [heave-offering or priestly rations] [and this is in the future, hence, what is going to be designated from the produce, and the produce at this point therefore is liable to tithing and not yet tithed].

P. "And we establish an analogy between two laws, in the framing of both of which there is reference to 'profanation.' [Reference is to (Lev. 22:9: 'They shall therefore keep my ordinance, lest they bear sin for it and die therefore, if they profane it,' alluding to the eating of priestly rations by a priest who is unclean (Freedman, p. 551, n. 6)].

Q. "Just as, in that other setting, the penalty is death, so here it is death."

R. But might we not derive the penalty from the appearance of a reference to "profanation" both here and with regard to what is leftover from sacrificial meat beyond the point at which one is supposed to eat that meat?

S. [Such a proof would be as follows:] Just as in that case, [as specified at Lev. 19:6-8] the penalty is extirpation, so here too it should be extirpation.

T. [We may reject that possibility on the basis of this argument:] It is more reasonable to derive the law from the matter of the penalty for violating the sanctity of the priestly rations, for the two matters have in common the following points: both are raised up, both are subject to the same rule outside of the Holy Land, both are remitted, both are given in the plural, both are produce of the land, both are subject to the same rule as regards improper priestly intention regarding their disposition, and both are subject to the same rule in regards what is left over [and not to be eaten after a certain point]. [That is, in neither case do the rules apply outside of the Holy Land; the prohibitions in both cases can be annulled, while that concerning what is left over of the offering cannot be annulled; the laws governing priestly intention and the disposition of what is left over do not apply either to what is untithed or to priestly rations].

U. But to the contrary, [we may argue in a different way]: One should derive the governing analogy from the case of leftover sacrificial meat, for they share in the traits of being unfit as food and not being subject to remission through the taking of a cultic bath. [In respect to both untithed produce and leftover sacrificial meat, one cannot eat the substance; a priest who is clean, by contrast, may eat priestly rations. The prohibition of untithed produce and leftover sacrificial meat is not affected by a cultic bath.]

V. The common traits [shared by untithed produce and priestly rations] are more numerous [and therefore the proper analogy for the one is to be drawn from the other].

W. Rabina said, "The use of the plural with reference to 'profanation' [linking untithed produce and priestly rations] presents a preferable [basis for analogy]."

X. **An unclean priest who ate clean heave-offering:** Whence in Scripture do we find proof [of the fact that such a one is subject to the death penalty]?

Y. It is in line with what Samuel said, "How do we know on the basis of Scripture that an unclean priest who ate clean heave-offering is subject to the death penalty at the hands of heaven?

Z. "Since it is written, 'Therefore they shall keep my ordinance, lest they bear sin for it and die on that account if they profane it' (Lev. 22:9)."

AA. That statement speaks of what is clean, but not of what is unclean.

BB. For Samuel said R. Eleazar said, "How do we know that an unclean priest who ate unclean priestly rations is not subject to the death penalty?

CC. "As it is said, 'And die on that account, if they profane it' (Lev. 22:9). [83B]. That excludes [unclean priestly ration], that is already profaned [and cannot be made more profane]."

DD. **A non-priest who ate heave-offering:**

EE. Rab said, "A non-priest who ate heave-offering is flogged."

FF. R. Kahana and R. Assi said to Rab, "But should not the master rule that he is subject to the death penalty.

GG. "For it is written, 'There shall no stranger eat of the holy thing [and die on that account]' (Lev. 22:10)?"

HH. "'I the Lord sanctify them' interrupts the matter. [Freedman, p. 552, n. 5: Consequently the penalty of death stated in Lev. 22:9 does not apply to the prohibition at Lev. 22:10.]"

II. They raised an objection: **"And these are the ones who are subject to the death penalty...A non-priest who ate heave-offering [T. Zeb. 12:17B]."**

JJ. Is teaching on Tannaite authority what you raise in contradiction to Rab?! Rab himself enjoys Tannaite status and differs [from the view expressed by the teaching on the same status, as he has every right to do].

KK. A non-priest who served at the altar: As it is written, "And the stranger who comes nigh shall be put to death" (Num. 18:7).

LL. An unclean person who served at the altar:

MM. The answer derives from the inquiry addressed by R. Hiyya bar Abin to R. Joseph, "How on the basis of Scripture do we know that an unclean priest who served at the altar is subject to the death penalty?

NN. "Since it is written, 'Speak to Aaron and to his sons, that they separate themselves from the holy things of the children of Israel and that they not profane my holy name' (Lev. 22:2). [Freedman, p. 553, n. 3: The reference is to abstention from sacrificial service during their uncleanness.]

OO. "We then establish an analogy on the basis of the use of the word 'profanation' both here and with regard to heave-offering.

PP. "Just as in the case of heave-offering, violation of the law produces the death penalty, so here too violation of the law produces the death penalty."

QQ. But why not derive the meaning of the word 'profanation' from its use with reference to leftover sacrificial meat [not eaten in the specified span of time]. Then the result would be that, just as in that case, the penalty is extirpation, so too here the penalty is extirpation.

RR. It is more reasonable to derive the meaning of the word from its use with reference to heave-offering, for in common in both matters are the considerations of the bodily unfitness [of the person involved], uncleanness, use of the immersion-pool, and use of the plural.

.

SS.   Quite to the contrary, it would be better to derive the sense of the word from its use with respect to leftover sacrificial meat. For to both matters apply the considerations of sanctity, conduct of the rite within the Temple court, the matter of the disqualifying affect of a priest's improper intention, and the issue of the rules governing leftover sacrificial meat themselves.

TT.   The use of the plural with reference to "profanation" presents a preferable basis for analogy.

UU.   **One in the status of a Tebul Yom [who had immersed that day but who had to wait for sunset to complete the rite of purification] who served at the altar:**

VV.   How on the basis of Scripture do we know that fact?

WW.   It accords with what has been taught on Tannaite authority:

XX.   R. Simai says, "Whence in Scripture do we find an indication that if a priest awaiting sunset for the completion of his rite of purification performed an act of service, he has profaned [the cult]?

YY.   "Scripture says, 'They shall be holy to their God and not profane the name of their God' (Lev. 21:6).

ZZ.   "If [because we have already proved the matter on another basis] that verse cannot refer to an unclean priest who served at the altar, for we have derived the fact from the reference to 'that they separate themselves' (Lev. 22:2), apply it to he matter of a priest's serving at the altar on the day on which he has immersed but prior to sunset.

AAA. "And we further derive the sense of 'profane' here from the sense of 'profane' with reference to heave-offering.

BBB. "Just as in that matter, the death penalty is invoked, so here too the death penalty is invoked."

CCC. **One lacking priestly vestments:**

DDD. How on the basis of Scripture do we know that fact?

EEE. Said R. Abbahu said R. Yohanan (and some attribute it to the name of R. Eleazar b. R. Simeon) "'And you shall put coats on them and you shall gird them with girdles...[and the priest's office shall be theirs...]' (Ex. 29:9).

FFF. "When their garments are upon them, their status as priests applies to them. When their garments are not on them, their status as priests does not apply to them, and they are deemed non-priests, and a master has said, '**A non-priest who served at the altar is subject to the death penalty.**'"

GGG. **One whose rites of atonement were not yet complete:**

HHH. How on the basis of Scripture do we know [that such a one is subject to the death penalty]?

III. Said R. Huna, "It is because Scripture has said, 'And the priest shall make an atonement for her and she shall be clean' (Lev. 12:8).

JJJ. "'And she shall be clean' -- indicates that before she had been unclean.

KKK. "And a master has stated, '**An unclean person who served at the altar is subject to the death penalty.**'"

LLL.   And one with unwashed hands and feet:

MMM.   How on the basis of Scripture do we know that fact?

NNN.   Scripture states, "And when they go into the tabernacle of the congregation, they shall wash with water, so that they do not die" (Ex. 30:20).

OOO.   And those who were drunk:

PPP.   For it is written, "Do not drink wine or strong drink...lest you die" (Lev. 10:9).

QQQ.   And those with unkempt hair:

RRR.   For it is written, "Neither shall they shave their heads nor suffer their locks to remain unshorn" (Ez. 44:20).

SSS.   And thereafter: "Neither shall they drink wine" (Ez. 44:21).

TTT.   The matter of unkempt hair is thus made comparable to the matter of wine-drinking.

UUU.   Just as ministering while drunk is penalized by death, so ministering with unkempt hair is subject to the death penalty.

VVV.   But an uncircumcised priest, a priest in mourning, and one who was sitting down while at the altar -- lo, these are subject to warning [but not to the death penalty]:

WWW.   How on the basis of Scripture do we know that that is the case for the Uncircumcised priest?

XXX.   Said R. Hisda, "This matter we did not derive from the Torah of Moses, our master, until Ezekiel, son of Buzi, came and taught it to us:

YYY.   "'No stranger, uncircumcised in heart [84A] or uncircumcised in flesh, shall enter my sanctuary' (Ez. 44:20)."

ZZZ.   How do we know that this is the case for the priest in mourning [who has not yet buried his deceased]?

AAAA.   As it is written, "Neither shall [the high priest in mourning] go out of the sanctuary, yet shall he not profane the sanctuary of his God" (Lev. 21:12).

BBBB.   Lo, another priest [than the high priest] who did not go forth has profaned the rite [and therefore he is required to deal with his deceased].

CCCC.   Said R. Ada to Raba, "And let us derive the sense of the word 'profane' from the meaning of the word 'profane' as used with reference to heave-offering?

DDDD.   "Just as in that case, the penalty is death, so here too the penalty should be death."

EEEE.   [He replied,] "But is the prohibition of the priest in mourning stated explicitly in the cited verse of Scripture? It derives, rather, by inference [from the explicit reference to the high priest]. And in respect to any matter which derives only by inference, one does not construct a further argument by analogy."

FFFF.   How on the basis of Scripture do we know that one who performs a rite while sitting down [is not subject to the death penalty]?

GGGG.   Said Raba said R. Nahman, "Scripture has said, 'For the Lord your God has chosen him out of all your tribes, to stand to minister' (Deut. 18:5).

HHHH.   "I have chosen him for standing, and not for sitting."

IIII.   "A blemished priest who performed a sacrificial rite is subject to the death penalty," the words of Rabbi. And sages say, "He is subject to the penalty for transgressing a negative commandment" [T. Zeb. 12:17G-H].

JJJJ.   What is the Scriptural basis for the position of Rabbi?

KKKK.   Since it is written, "Only he shall not go in to the veil nor come near the altar, because he has a blemish, that he not profane my sanctuaries? (Lev. 21:23).

LLLL.   We then derive the sense of the word "profane" as it is used here from the meaning of the word when used with reference to heave-offering. Just as, in that context, the penalty is death, so here too, the penalty is death.

MMMM.   But why not derive the sense of the work "profanation" from its use with respect to left-over sacrificial meat?

NNNN.   Just as in that case, the penalty is extirpation, so here too the penalty should be extirpation..

OOOO.   It is more reasonable to derive the meaning of the work from its use with reference to heave-offering, for in that case, as in the present one, we have the shared trait that what is invalid is the body of the priest himself, and so we derive the rule from a parallel case of bodily invalidity.

PPPP.   to the contrary, he should derive the rule from the law governing left-over sacrificial meat, for in both cases, we have the considerations of sanctification, conduct of the rite within the Temple court, the priest's capacity to invalidate the rite through an improper intention, and the rule of not eating left-over sacrificial meat.

QQQQ.   Rather, one should derive the analogy [hence the penalty] from the case of an unclean priest who served at the altar, in which case we derive the rule governing the invalidity of the priest's body from another case in which the priest's body is invalid, as well as from the fact that there are the shared considerations, in both matters, of holiness, conduct of the rite inside the Temple, the matter of the priest's invalidating the offering through improper intention, and, finally, the consideration of the rules governing left-over sacrificial meat.

RRRR.   And rabbis [who ignore these proofs and regard it as merely a negative prohibition]?

SSSS.   Scripture says, "...and die on that account" (Lev. 22:9) [with respect to an unclean priest who ate heave-offering], meaning for that particular sin, but not for the sin of serving at the altar when one is blemished.

TTTT.   He who deliberately carried out an act of sacrilege -- Rabbi says, "He is subject to the death penalty." And sages says, "He is subject to the penalty for transgressing a negative commandment" [T. Zeb. 12:17I-K]:

UUUU.   What is the scriptural basis for the position of Rabbi?

VVVV.   Said R. Abbahu. "One derives the meaning of the law by analogy based on the use of the word 'sin' both here and in the matter of heave-offering. [Here: 'if a soul commits a trespass and sin through ignorance in the holy things of the Lord'

(Lev. 5:15), and, with respect to heave-offering, 'Lest they bear sin for it and die on that account' (Lev. 22:9).]

WWWW. "Just as in that case, the penalty is death, so here the penalty is death."

XXXX. And rabbis say, "Scripture has said, '...on that account...' (Lev. 22:9) -- and not on account of an act of sacrilege."

XIII.

A. A non-priest who served in the Temple [M. 9:6F]:

B. It has been taught on Tannaite authority:

C. Ishmael says, "Here it is said, 'And the non-priest who comes near shall be put to death' (Num. 18:7), and elsewhere, 'Whosoever comes anything near to the tabernacle of the Lord shall die' (Num. 17:28).

D. "Just as in the latter case [the rebellion of Korah and the subsequent plague], it is death at the hands of heaven, so here it is death at the hands of heaven" [= M. 9:6H].

E. R. Aqiba says, "Here it is said, 'And the non-priest who comes near shall be put to death' (Num. 18:7), and elsewhere, 'And that prophet or that dreamer of dreams shall be put to death' (Deut. 18:6).

F. "Just as there it is by stoning, so here too it is by stoning."

G. R. Yohanan b. Nuri says, "Just as in that case it is by strangling, so here it is by strangling."

H. What is at issue between R. Ishmael and R. Aqiba?

I. R. Aqiba takes the view that we derive the sense of the work, "shall be put to death" from the meaning of the word "shall be put to death" as it occurs elsewhere, and not from the meaning of the word "shall die."

J. And R. Ishmael maintains that we derive the rule governing an ordinary person from the rule governing another ordinary person, and we do not derive the rule governing an ordinary person from the rule governing a prophet.

K. And R. Aqiba?

L. If someone has enticed [a town to commit idolatry], you have no greater evidence that one is an ordinary person than that [for such a one cannot be regarded as a prophet].

M. What is at issue between R. Aqiba and R. Yohanan b. Nuri?

N. At issue is the dispute involving R. Simeon and rabbis.

O. For it has been taught on Tannaite authority:

P. A prophet who enticed [a town to commit idolatry] is subject to the death penalty inflicted by stoning.

Q. R. Simeon says, "It is through strangulation."

R. But we have learned in the Mishnah: R. Aqiba says, "He is put to death by strangling" [M. 9:5G].

S. There are two Tannaite authorities on the view of R. Aqiba.

T. The Mishnah before us is R. Simeon's view of R. Aqiba's rule, and the other Tannaite tradition [holding that a non-priest who served at the altar is put to death through stoning] and deriving that view from the analogy [to the false prophet] represents rabbis' view of R. Aqiba's opinion.

Our attention is drawn, first of all, to the splendid and satisfying exegesis of the Tosefta-passage at unit XII. This sort of sustained composition shows the powers of Bavli's authors at their best. The claim that their fundamental approach to their work lay in the exegesis of authoritative materials at hand finds full validation in the elegant unit before us. When we revert to the Mishnah-passage, we have no reason to compare unfavorably the exegetical efforts devoted to the principal document. The explanation of clauses of the Mishnah-paragraph's language takes up units I, II, III, supplemented at IV, V. The theme of the action of zealots, M. 9:6B, accounts for the explanation at unit VI, and then the extensive treatment of the locus classicus of zealotry, the case of Zimri, units VII-X. Units XI, XIII deal with the remainder of the Mishnah-paragraph.

10:1 A–C

A. These are the ones who are to be strangled:

B. [84B] he who hits his father and his mother [Ex. 21:15]; he who steals an Israelite [Ex. 21:16, Deut. 24:7]; an elder who defies the decision of a court, a false prophet, a prophet who prophesies in the name of an idol;

C. He who has sexual relations with a married woman, those who bear false witness against a priest's daughter and against one who has sexual relations with her.

I.

A. He who hits his father and his mother: How on the basis of Scripture do we [know that such a one is strangled]?

B. It is in accord with the following verse of Scripture: "And he who hits his father or mother shall surely be put to death" (Ex. 21:15).

C. And any reference without further specification to "death" that is made in Scripture means only strangulation.

D. But might I say that the one who smites the parents is liable only if he actually kills them.

E. Do you imagine that he would have to kill them? If he killed anyone else, he would be decapitated, while if he killed his father, would it be through strangulation [that is not likely. The same penalty would have to apply, and hence at issue here cannot be killing the parent, but only hitting him or her].

F. That poses no problem to him who maintains that strangulation is the less severe mode of execution.

G. But in the view of him who has said that strangulation is the more severe mode of execution, what is to be said?

H. Since it is written, "He who smites a man so that he dies shall surely be put to death" (Ex. 21:12), and it also is written, "Or in enmity smote him with his hand that he die" (Num. 35:21), it bears the implication that, in any passage in which there is reference to smiting, without further specification, the implication is not that the one has killed the other. [Hence, here too, the son has not killed the parent but only hit him or her.]

II.

A. It was necessary for Scripture to state, "He who smites a man" (Ex. 21:12), and it also was necessary for Scripture to state, "Who kills any soul" (Num. 35:30).

B. For if the All-Merciful had written, "He who smites a man that he die" (Ex. 21:12), I might have maintained that that rule pertains to smiting by an adult, who is subject to the obligation to carry out the commandments, but it would not apply to smiting by a minor, who is not.

C.   Accordingly, the All-Merciful found it necessary to state, "Whoso kills any soul" (Num. 35:30).

D.   Had the All-Merciful written only, "Whose kills any soul" (Num. 35:30), I might have concluded that under the law are included even such classifications as abortions or foetuses produced at eight months of conception. [But they are not included.]

E.   It was therefore necessary to make both statements.

III.

A.   And might I propose that [one who smites his parents is put to death] even though he does not make a bruise on them?

B.   Wherefore do we learn in the Mishnah: He who hits his father and his mother is liable only if he will make a lasting bruise on them [M. 10:1D]?

C.   Scripture has said, "And he who kills a beast [shall restore it] but he who kills a man [shall be put to death]" (Lev. 24:21). [This creates an analogy.]

D.   Just as he who smites a beast is liable only if he inflicts a bruise, as it is written, "soul" in that connection [at Lev. 24:18], so he who smites a man is liable only if he inflicts a bruise.

E.   To this proof R. Jeremiah objected, "How then deal with the following: If one injured the beast by loading stones on it, [and in this case there is no physical bruise], in such a case also is the person who injured the beast not liable to make it up? [Surely he is liable!]"

F.   Rather, since the reference [to soul] cannot speak of the soul of a beast, for if one injured the ox with heavy stones, he remains liable to make it up, apply the reference to the soul of a man. [Then it would mean, just as claimed, that one is liable only if he makes a wound.]

G.   If so, what need do I have for the analogy [constructed above, C-D]?

H.   It accords with what was taught by the house of Hezekiah [at 79B, with respect to whether we differentiate, in the case of injury to beasts, between doing so deliberately and accidentally].

I.   That poses no problems to him who accords with that which was taught on Tannaite authority for the house of Hezekiah.

J.   But for the one who does not accord with what was taught on Tannaite authority for the house of Hezekiah, what use is there for the analogy.

K.   Just as one who hits a beast in order to cure it is exempt [from paying damages], so he who hits a man in order to cure him is exempt from having to pay damages.

IV.

A.   For the question was raised:

B.   What is the law on a son's letting blood for his father?

C.   R. Mattena said, "'And you shall love your neighbor as yourself' (Lev. 19:18). [The son surely may do so, since he would do the same for himself.]"

D. R. Dimi bar Hinena said, "'He who smites a man ... he who smite smites a beast ...': Just as the one who smites a beast for purposes of healing is exempt, so one who smites a man for purposes of healing is exempt."

E. Rab would not allow his son to take a thorn out of his flesh.

F. Mar, son of Rabina, would not allow his son to open a boil for him, lest he make a bruise and so be guilty of inadvertently violating a prohibition.

G. If so, then even an outsider also should be prohibited [for a person may not wound someone else].

H. If so, it would be an inadvertent violation of a mere prohibition, while in the case of his son, it is the inadvertent violation of a law penalized by strangulation.

I. And lo, we have learned in the Mishnah: [One may handle] a small needle for removing a thorn [M. Shab. 17:2G].

J. And should one not take account of the possibility that the needle will make a bruise, in which case there will be a matter of inadvertent violation of a law for which [a deliberate violation is penalized by] stoning?

K. In the case [of the Sabbath] the person does damage, [which is not penalized on the Sabbath, even when done deliberately].

L. That poses no problem to the one who maintains that one who does damage on the Sabbath is exempt from all penalty.

M. But in the view of him who says that he is liable, what is there to be said?

N. And whom have you heard who takes the view that one who does damage by inflicting a wound is liable [for violating the Sabbath]?

O. It is R. Simeon!

P. [85A] But R. Simeon also is the one who said, "Any form of labor which is done not for its normal purpose leaves one exempt from having violated the Sabbath." [Freedman, p. 560, n. 5: When a thorn is extracted and wound made, even intentionally, no punishment is involved, because the purpose of the work is extraction, not wounding.]

V.

A. The following question was addressed to R. Sheshet: "What is the law on appointing a son to be an agent of a court as to his own father, to inflict a flogging on him or to curse him?"

B. He said to them, "And have they permitted an outsider to do so except for the honor owing to heaven? It is a superior obligation, and here too, the honor owing to Heaven is a superior obligation. [So a son may act for the court.]"

C. An objection was then raised:

D. Now if in the case of one whom it is a religious duty to smite [namely, one specified by a court as subject to flogging], it is a religious duty in point of fact not to smite [in that a son may not be agent of a court to flog his own father],

E. one whom it is a religious duty not to smite, is it not a matter of logic that it is a religious duty not to smite such a one [namely, one's father]?

F.   Is the sense, then, not that in both instances we deal with a religious duty, but one refers to one's son, the other to an outsider? [Thus, as is clear, if one who is subject to flogging may not be flogged by his son as agent of the court, how much the more so may one who is not subject to a flogging, not be flogged by his son.] [Freedman, p. 561, n. 2: Thus by ad majus reasoning, a formal prohibition is deduced against a son's striking his father. For Ex. 21:15 merely prescribes the punishment; but it is a general principle that no punishment can be inflicted unless a prohibition is either stated or deduced from elsewhere. On this interpretation Sheshet's ruling is contradicted.]

G.   No, in both this case and that case there is no difference between one's son and an outsider. But there is no problem, for the one statement speaks of a case in which it is a religious duty, and the other speaks of a case in which it is not a religious duty.

H.   And this is the sense of the passage:

I.   Now if in a case in which there is a religious duty to be done, for it is a religious duty to inflict the flogging, it still is a religious duty not to inflict a flogging [in any but the prescribed manner, e.g., with too many lashes],

J.   in a case in which no religious duty is involved, in which it is not a religious duty to flog, is it not a matter of reason that it is a religious duty not to inflict a flogging? [So what the teaching at hand tells us is that one may flog only at the order of a court.]

K.   Come and take note:

L.   he who was being taken out to be executed, and his son came along and hit him and cursed him -- the son is liable. If another party came along and hit him and cursed him, the other party is exempt.

M.   And we reflected on the matter, asking what the difference is between one's son and a third party.

N.   And R. Hisda said, "We deal with a case in which the court forces the man to go forth and he does not wish to go forth [so the court may not have the son come along and drive the man to his execution, and this contradict's Sheshet's judgment]."

O.   R. Sheshet interprets the passage to speak of a case in which the court is not forcing the man to go forth.

P.   If so, another party also [should be liable for reviling the condemned man].

Q.   [So far as] the other party in this case is concerned, the condemned man is already a dead man. [But the son has to honor the man even after death.]

R.   And did not R. Sheshet say, "If people humiliated a sleeping man and he died [in his sleep], they nonetheless are liable." [Why should mistreating the condemned man be treated any differently?]

S.   With what sort of a case do we deal here?

T.   It is a case in which one hit the condemned man with a blow which is not worth a perutah [so that is why there is no penalty for the third party's action].

U.   But did not R. Ammi say R. Yohanan said, "If one smote [another party] with a blow that is not worth a perutah, he is nonetheless flogged"?

V. What is the sense of "exempt" stated earlier? One is exempt from having to pay a financial reparation.

W. Would it then follow that his son is liable for monetary compensation?! [But what would he pay, since the injury is not worth a perutah!]

X. Rather, [he is liable] in accord with the law that applies to him [which is, in the case of the son, the death penalty].

Y. Then [the stranger should be exempt from the law] applying to him, [which is flogging] [so what is the difference between the act of the son and the act of a third party]?

Z. Rather, as to the outsider [who hits the condemned man], the reason that he is exempt is because Scripture has said, "You shall not curse a prince among your people" (Ex. 22:27), which applies to one who carries on in the manner of your people. [Freedman, p. 562, n. 7: But to transgress is not fitting for "your people," and hence the prohibition against cursing does not apply to such a case.]

AA. Now that settles the matter of the curse, but how do we know that that is the case of the actual blow?

BB. We draw an analogy between hitting and cursing.

CC. If so, then the son also should be subject to the same rule.

DD. It accords with what R. Phineas said, "We deal with a case in which he repented." So here too, we deal with a case in which the criminal repented.

EE. If so, then the outsider also [should be prohibited from cursing or hitting the condemned man]. [So, again, what is the difference between the son and the outsider?]

FF. Said R. Mari, "'Among your people' means 'among those who are permanently established among your people [and not a condemned criminal, who may be cursed]."

GG. If so, his son also [should be allowed to curse or hit him]!

HH. [85B] The same rule after death applies [that the son may not curse the father].

II. What is the upshot of the matter?

JJ. Said Rabbah bar R. Huna, and so a Tannaite authority of the house of R. Ishmael taught, "In all cases a son may not serve as an agent of a court in flogging or cursing his father, except in the case of one who entices a town to apostasy, in which case it is written, Neither shall you spare nor conceal him' (Deut. 13:9)."

The entire opening discussion deals only with the matter of hitting the father or mother. Unit I proves that the penalty is strangulation, as M. 10:1A states. Unit II carries forward the exegesis begun in Unit I. Unit III then takes up a speculative question, relevant in a general way to the Mishnah-paragraph, and units IV and V take up further speculative questions along the same lines.

10:1 D-G

D. He who hits his father and his mother is liable only if he will make a lasting bruise on them.

E.   This rule is more strict in the case of the one who curses than the one who hits them.

F.   For the one who curses them after they have died is liable.

G.   But the one who hits them after they have died is exempt.

I.

A.   Our rabbis have taught on Tannaite authority:

B.   "His father or his mother he has cursed" (Lev. 20:9).

C.   This applies even after they have died.

D.   For one might have thought [to the contrary] that since one is liable for hitting them and also liable for cursing them, just as one who hits them is liable only if he does so while they are alive, so the one who curses them is liable only if he does so while they are alive.

E.   And furthermore there is an argument a fortiori:

F.   If in the case of one who hits his parents, in which the law treats [a parent] "who is not of your people" as equivalent to one who is "of your people," [so that if the father is a condemned criminal, one still must not hit him], and yet one is not liable after the death of the parents [for hitting them], in the matter of cursing, in which the law has not treated [a parent] who has not conducted himself as if he were "one of your people" as equivalent to one who has conducted himself as if he is "one of you people," is it not a matter of logic that one should not be liable if he curses the parents after death?

G.   Accordingly, Scripture [is required to] state, "He has cursed his father or his mother" (Lev. 20:9), and this applies to the time after they have died [so one is liable on that account as well].

H.   This interpretation poses no problems to the principle of R. Jonathan, who regards as superfluous the verse, "His father or his mother he has cursed."

I.   But in the view of R. Josiah, what is there to be said? [He makes use of the verse at hand for another purpose entirely, as we shall now see.]

J.   For it has been taught on Tannaite authority:

K.   "'[For any man that curses his father or his mother shall surely be put to death; his father and his mother she has cursed; his blood shall be upon him' (Lev. 20:9).]' Why does Scripture say 'any man'?

L.   "It serves to encompass a daughter, one of undefined sexual traits, and one who exhibits the traits of both sexes.

M.   "'Who curses his father or his mother' -- I know only that the law covers his father and his mother. How do I know that it covers his father but not his mother, or his mother but not his father?

N.   "Scripture says, 'His father and his mother he has cursed; his blood shall be upon him' (Lev. 20:9), that is, 'he has cursed his father,' 'he has cursed his mother,'" the words of R. Josiah.

O.   R. Jonathan says, "The verse bears the implication that it speaks of the two of them simultaneously, and it bears the implication that it speaks of each by himself or herself, unless the text explicitly treats the two of them together."

P.   How then does [Josiah] prove the present matter?

Q.   He derives it from the verse, "And he who curses his father or his mother shall surely be put to death" (Ex. 21:17).

R.   And the other? [How does Jonathan interpret the same verse]?

S.   He requires that verse to encompass within the law a daughter, one of undefined sexual traits, and one who exhibits the sexual traits of both sexes.

T.   And why should he not derive that fact from the usage cited above ["Any man ..."]?

U.   The Torah speaks in the language of ordinary people, [and the usage bears no exegetical consequences whatsoever].

V.   And should not the framer of the passage teach in addition: "A more strict rule applies to one who hits parents than to one who curses them, for in the case of hitting them the law has treated in the same way a parent who does not conduct himself as "among your people" and the one who conducts himself as "among your people," which is not the case for one who curses parents. [A parent who is a condemned criminal may be cursed by a son, as we saw earlier.]

W.   The framer of the passage takes the view that we do draw an analogy between hitting and cursing, [so the latter also is forbidden, even in the case of a parent who does not conduct himself properly].

II.

A.   May we say that the dispute at hand follows the course of the Tannaite dispute which follows?

B.   For one Tannaite authority teaches:

C.   As to a Samaritan, you are commanded against smiting him, but you are not commanded against cursing him. [The two are not treated as comparable.]

D.   And another Tannaite authority holds:

E.   You are not commanded either against cursing him or against hitting him.

F.   Now if we take the view that all parties hold that the Samaritans are true proselytes is not at issue this simple proposition:

G.   one party holds that we draw an analogy between hitting and cursing, and the other party maintains that we do not draw an analogy between hitting and cursing?

H.   No, all parties take the view that we do not draw an analogy between hitting and cursing.

I.   Here then what is at issue?

J.   One party holds that Samaritans are true converts [so they are not to be hit], and the other party maintains that they converted merely because of fear of lions [in the Land of Israel] [so there is no precept against harassing them].

K.   If that is all that is at issue, then what is the sense of the Tannaite teaching on the same passage:

L.   And a Samaritan's ox is in the status of ownership of an Israelite's ox.

M.   Rather, does that not bear the implication that at issue is whether or not we draw the stated analogy?

N.   It does indeed prove the matter.

Unit I provides a proof-text for the proposition of the Mishnah, and this proof is subjected to a careful inspection and articulation. Unit II continues the foregoing by introducing what are alleged to be parallel materials.

10:1 H-P

H.   He who steals an Israelite [B2] is liable only when he will have brought him into his own domain.

I.   R. Judah says, "Only if he will have brought him into his own domain and will have made use of him,

J.   "as it is said, 'And if he deal with him as a slave or sell him' (Deut. 24:7)."

K.   He who steals his son --

L.   R. Ishmael, son of R. Yohanan b. Beroqah, declares him liable.

M.   And sages declare him exempt.

N.   [If] he stole someone who was half slave and half free --

O.   R. Judah declares him liable.

P.   And sages declare him exempt.

I.

A.   Does not the first of the two Tannaite authorities [at M. 10:1H-I] require utilization [of the victim as a prerequisite to liability for kidnapping]?

B.   [Of course he does, but,] said R. Aha, son of Raba, "It is utilization of the victim to the extent of work less than a perutah in value that is at issue between the two authorities."

II.

A.   R. Jeremiah raised this question, "If one stole and sold a person while he was sleeping, what is the law?

B.   "If one sold a woman for the sake of enslaving the foetus, what is the law?

C.   "Do we maintain that there is an aspect of utilization in such a procedure, or do we not maintain that there is an aspect of utilization in such a procedure?"

D.   And why not solve the problem by maintaining that there is no aspect of utilization whatsoever [in these actions]?

E.   No, it is necessary to raise the issue, so far as the one who was asleep is concerned, to take account of a case in which the kidnapper leaned on the victim,

F.   [and,] in the case of a woman, to take account of a case in which the kidnapper used the woman as a screen [against the wind, and if she is pregnant, she makes that much better a screen].

G.   Does this constitute a mode of utilization or not?

H.   What is the law?

I.   The question stands over [there being no clear basis for an answer].

III.

A.   Our rabbis have taught on Tannaite authority:

B.   "If a man be found stealing any of his brethren of the children of Israel" (Deut. 24:7):

C.   I know only that the law applies to a man who stole someone.

D.   How do I know that the law applies to a woman's doing so?

E.   Scripture says, "And any one who steals a man" (Ex. 21:16).

F.   I know only that the law applies to a man who stole either a woman or a man, and to
      a woman who stole a man [as specified at Ex. 21:16].

G.   How do I know that a woman who stole a woman [is covered by the law]?

H.   Scripture states, "Then that thief shall die" (Deut. 24:7) -- under all circumstances
      [without regard to the gender of the thief or the victim].

IV.

A.   It has further been taught on Tannaite authority:

B.   "If a a man be found stealing any of his brethren" (Deut. 24:7):

C.   **All the same are the one who steals a man and the one who steals a woman, a
      proselyte, a freed slave, and a minor. One is liable [on any of these counts].**

D.   **If one stole someone but did not sell him, sold him but he is yet within his domain,
      he is exempt [from liability].**

E.   **If he sold him to his father or his brothers or to any of his relatives, he is liable.**

F.   **He who steals slaves is exempt [T. B.Q. 8:1A-I].**

G.   [86A] A Tannaite authority repeated this statement before R. Sheshet.

H.   He said to him, "I repeat [the matter as follows:] 'R. Simeon says, "['If a man be
      found stealing a person] from his brethren' [means that one is liable only if] he
      removes the victim from the domain of his brothers.'"

I.   "And do you say that he is _liable_? Rather, repeat the matter on Tannaite authority
      as '_exempt_.'"

J.   But what is the problem? Perhaps the version at hand is that of R. Simeon as
      against views of rabbis.

K.   Do not let that possibility come to mind, for R. Yohanan has stated, "An unassigned
      teaching of the Mishnah represents the view of R. Meir, an unassigned teaching in
      the Tosefta represents the view of R. Nehemiah, an unassigned teaching in the Sifra
      represents the view of R. Judah, an unassigned opinion in the Sifre represents the
      view of R. Simeon, and all of them express their views in line with those of R.
      Aqiba. [The passage at hand, given anonymously in the Sifre, therefore must stand
      for the view of Simeon.]"

V.

A.   He who steals his son [M. 10:1K]:

B.   What is the scriptural basis for the view of rabbis?

C.   Said Abayye, "Scripture has said, 'If a man be found ...' (Deut. 24:7) -- excluding a
      case in which the victim is located [with the kidnapper to begin with]."

D.   Said R. Pappa to Abayye, "Then how do you deal with the following: 'If a man be found with a woman married to a husband' (Deut. 22:22)? Here too do you maintain: 'If ... be found ...' -- so excluding a case in which the woman is commonly found with the lover? For example, [a woman] in the house of Mr. So-and-so, in which women are ordinarily located. In such a case, too, will you regard the man as exempt from all penalty!?"

E.   He said to him, "I refer to the passage, '... and he be found in his hand ...' (Ex. 21:16). [Freedman, pp. 567-8, n. 7. This is redundant and therefore shows that the law applies only to a person who is found in his captor's hand as a result of abduction, and not to one who was to be found in his hand before too.]'

F.   Said Raba, "Therefore Scripture-teachers and Mishnah-reciters for [young] rabbis fall into the category of those who have [their charges] in their hand and would be exempt [were they to kidnap them]."

VI.

A.   If he stole someone who was half slave [M. 10:1N]:

B.   We have learned in the Mishnah: R. Judah says, "Slaves do not receive payment for being humiliated" [M. B.Q. 8:3G].

C.   What is the scriptural basis for the position of R. Judah?

D.   Scripture has said, "When men strive together, a man with his brother" (Deut. 25:11) [yielding compensation for humiliation in the fight].

E.   [Scripture thus assigns compensation for humiliation] to one who is subject to bonds of brotherhood, excluding a slave, who is not subject to bonds of brotherhood.

F.   And rabbis?

G.   He indeed does fall into the category of "brother" so far as keeping the religious duties is concerned.

H.   In the present case how does R. Judah interpret matters?

I   He takes the view that the reference to stealing "any of his brothers" [at Deut. 24:7] serves to exclude slaves.

J.   " ... of the children of Israel" serves to exclude one who is half-slave and half-free.

K.   "Of the children of Israel" likewise serves to exclude one who was half-slave and half-free, so you have one exclusionary clause followed by another exclusionary clause, and in the case of one exclusionary clause followed by another exclusionary clause, the sole outcome is to encompass [what is putatively excluded].

L.   And rabbis?

M.   " ... of his brethren ..." serving to eliminate slaves is an interpretation that they do not find persuasive. For lo, he indeed is one's brother so far as keeping the religious duties are concerned.

N.   [Then the sense of] " ... children of Israel ...," " ... of the children of Israel ...," [in their view is such that] one serves to exclude a slave, and the other serves to exclude one who is half-slave and half-free.

VII.

A.   Where in Scripture do we find an admonition against kidnapping [since Deut. 24:7 and Ex. 21:16 state only the penalty for doing so]?

B. R. Josiah said, "It is from, 'You shall not steal' (Ex. 20:15)."

C. R. Yohanan said, "It is from, 'They shall not be sold as a slave is sold' (Lev. 25:42)."

D. And there is no dispute between them, for one authority takes into account the admonition against stealing, and the other takes into account the prohibition of selling.

VIII.

A. Our rabbis have taught on Tannaite authority:

B. "You shall not steal" (Ex. 20:15):

C. Scripture speaks of kidnapping persons.

D. You say that it speaks of kidnapping persons. But perhaps it speaks of stealing money.

E. Do you then say so? Go and derive the matter from the thirteen principles by which the Torah is interpreted, including the one that says that a matter is interpreted in its own context.

F. [In the present passage], of what subject does the Scripture speak? It deals with crimes against persons.

G. So here too the commandment takes up capital crimes [such as violating the Sabbath or murder, and so too, kidnapping].

IX.

A. Further teaching on Tannaite authority:

B. "You shall not steal" (Ex. 20:15):

C. Scripture speaks of stealing money.

D. You say that it speaks of stealing money, but perhaps it speaks only of stealing persons?

E. Do you say so? Go and derive the matter from the thirteen principles by which the Torah is interpreted, including the one that says that a matter is interpreted in its own context.

F. [In the present passage], of what subject does the Scripture speak? It speaks of crimes against property [such as envy and false witness].

G. So here too the commandment takes up property crimes.

X.

A. It has been stated on Amoraic authority:

B. If [one set of] witnesses said that there had been a kidnapping and [another set of] witnesses said that there had been a sale of a kidnap-victim, and [both] were proved a conspiracy of perjurers --

C. Hezekiah said, "They are not put to death."

D. R. Yohanan said, "They are put to death."

E. Hezekiah accords with what R. Aqiba said, for he said, "'[At the testimony of two witnesses or at the testimony of three witnesses shall] the matter [be established]' (Deut. 19:15) -- the whole of the matter, not part of it. [The two witnesses must testify to the entire crime, not only to part of the crime (Freedman, p. 569, n. 11)]." [Hence the witnesses to only part of the matter are not put to death.]

F.   And R. Yohanan rules in accord with the position of rabbis, who maintain, "' ... the matter ...,' -- and even part of the matter."

G.   But Hezekiah concedes that the second set of witnesses against a wayward and incorrigible son were proved to be a conspiracy of perjurers, they are put to death, for the first set of witnesses have the power to claim, [86B] "It was to see that he was flogged that we came to court [and on the basis of our testimony, he would have been flogged. Only if he then transgressed a second time, to which the later witnesses testify, would he be put to death.] Accordingly, the second set of witnesses are the ones who inflict on the son the complete penalty [of execution, and the former set of witnesses have no part in the matter]."

H.   To this allegation R. Pappa objected, "If that is the case, then witnesses to the sale also should be subject to the death penalty, since the witnesses to the theft have the power to claim, 'It was to see that he was flogged that we came to court, [and not to have him put to death]'"

I.   And should you claim that Hezekiah takes the view that, in such a case, the kidnapper is not flogged [for merely stealing the person] lo, it has been stated on Amoraic authority:

J.   As to witnesses to a kidnapping of a person, who were proved to be a conspiracy for perjury,

K.   Hezekiah and R. Yohanan: one said, "They are flogged," and the other said, "They are not flogged."

L.   And in that connection we maintained, "One should draw the conclusion that Hezekiah is the one who said that they are flogged, since it is Hezekiah who has ruled that they are not put to death.

M.   "For so far as R. Yohanan is concerned, since he has maintained that they are put to death, he has in hand a violation of a negative commandment that is subject to the admonition against committing a crime that, in fact, is punishable by the death penalty inflicted by a court, and in the case of any violation of a negative commandment that is subject to the admonition involving a death penalty at the hands of a court, there is no further penalty of flogging."

N.   If, therefore, the accused would not have been flogged [in accord with the principle just now stated], how can the witnesses against him be flogged? [Clearly, from Yohanan's viewpoint, they cannot be flogged. Thus we have shown that Hezekiah would have the false witnesses flogged. It follows that kidnapping produces the penalty of flogging, and the witnesses would under certain circumstances only be flogged.]

O.   Rather, said R. Pappa, "In the case of witnesses to the sale of the victim, who are proved a conspiracy for perjury, all parties concur that such witnesses are put to death.

P.   "Where there is a dispute, it concerns witnesses to the abduction.

Q.   "Hezekiah said, 'They are not put to death, for the act of kidnapping stands by itself, and the act of sale is treated by itself.'

R. "And R. Yohanan said, 'They are put to death, because the abduction is the beginning of the act of sale.'

S. "And R. Yohanan concedes in the case of the first set of witnesses against the wayward and incorrigible son who were proved to be a conspiracy for perjury, that they are not put to death, for, since they have the power to claim, 'It was to inflict a flogging on him that we came to court,' [they have not conspired to kill the accused and so they are not made victim to that penalty]."

T. Said Abayye, "All concur in one matter concerning the wayward and incorrigible son, all concur in a second matter regarding him, and there is a dispute in yet a third matter.

U. "All concur in one matter concerning a wayward and incorrigible son, that the first set of witnesses [proved perjurers] is not put to death, because they have the power to claim, 'It was to inflict a flogging on him that we came to court.'

V. "All concur in yet another matter concerning the wayward and incorrigible son, with respect to the second set of witnesses, that they are put to death [should they be proved a conspiracy of perjurers], for the first set of witnesses have the power to claim, 'We came to inflict a flogging on him, and these others are the ones who committed against the accused the entirety of the act of perjury.

W. "And there is a dispute concerning a third matter having to do with the wayward and incorrigible son: If two witnesses say, 'In our presence, he stole [the food],' and two witnesses say, 'In our presence he ate it,' [each set attests half of the offense]. Freedman, p. 571, n. 4: Hence according to Hezekiah, who agrees with Aqiba's dictum, 'the whole matter but not half the matter,' they are exempt; but in R. Yohanan's view, based on that of the rabbis, 'the matter and even half the matter,' they are liable.]"

XI.

A. Said R. Assi, "Witnesses against one on account of selling someone, who were proved to form a conspiracy for perjury, are not put to death.

B. "For they have the power to claim, '[The one who sold him may say,' "I sold my own slave"' [Freedman, p. 571, n. 5: Hence he was not liable to death on their evidence, and therefore they in turn are also exempt.]"

C. Said R. Joseph, "In accord with which authority is this tradition in the name of R. Assi?

D. "It accords with R. Aqiba, who has said, '"A matter ..." and not part of a matter.'"

E. Said Abayye to him, "But would they, on the view of rabbis, be put to death? Lo, he gives a reason, 'Since ...,' Rather, you may even say that the statement accords with rabbis' view, and it pertains to a case in which no witnesses to the kidnapping came to court."

F. If that is the fact, then what value is there in making such an obvious statement?

G. It was to deal with a case in which, later on, such witnesses [to the actual kidnapping] came, and even so, [the same ruling applies]. [Freedman, p. 572, n. 3: On the combines testimonies the accused was convicted. Yet, if the first witnesses of the sale were falsified, they are not punished, since they can plead, "We did not know that others would testify to the kidnapping."]

H.   Nonetheless, what need is there to make such an obvious statement?

I.   It was indeed necessary, to deal with a case in which the witnesses made surreptitious gestures to one another.

J.   What might you have ruled? Such gestures are to be taken into account.

K.   So we are informed [by Assi] that a surreptitious gesture has no standing whatsoever.

As usual, we move from the simplest exegesis of the Mishnah-passage, with special attention to scriptural proofs for its propositions, to rather complex theoretical problems. In the present case, unit I clarifies the intent of one of the authorities at hand, M. 10:1H-I. Unit II raises a theoretical issue continuous with unit I. Unit III then introduces the scriptural foundations for the topic as a whole. Work on this same matter continues at unit IV. Units V and VI take up the exposition of sentences of the Mishnah-paragraph, in order. Unit VII then turns to the scriptural basis for an admonition, as distinct from a penalty, in the present crime. Units VIII-IX continue the same matter. My sense is that units VII-IX set up the important theoretical exercise that follows, since units X-XI, a protracted statement, simple fact that the act at hand involves both capital and property offenses, and that is the very point of the exegetical exercises that precede. So the composition is made up of units VII-XI, an artfully constructed theoretical exercise.

10:2

A.   An elder who defies the decision of a court [M. 10:1B]

B.   as it is said, "If there arise a matter too hard for you in judgment, between blood and blood, between plea and plea" (Deut. 17:8) --

C.   there were three courts there.

D.   One was in session at the door gate of the Temple mount, one was in session at the gate of the courtyard, and one was in session in the hewn-stone chamber.

E.   They come to the one which is at the gate of the Temple mount and say, "Thus I have explained the matter, and thus my colleagues have explained the matter.

F.   "Thus I have ruled in the matter, and thus my colleagues have ruled."

G.   If they had heard a ruling, they told it to them, and if not, they come along to that court which was at the gate of the courtyard.

H.   And he says, "Thus I have explained the matter, and thus my colleagues have explained the matter.

I.   "Thus I have ruled in the matter [lit.: taught], and thus my colleagues have ruled."

J.   If they had heard a ruling, they told it to them, and if not, these and those come along to the high court which was in the hewn-stone chamber,

K.   from which Torah goes forth to all Israel,

L.   as it is said, "From that place which the Lord shall choose" (Deut. 17:12).

M.   [If] he went back to his town and again ruled just as he had ruled before, he is exempt.

N.   But if he instructed [others] to do it in that way, he is liable,

O.   as it is said, "And the man who does presumptuously" (Deut. 17:12).

P.   He is liable only if he will give instructions to people actually to carry out the deed [in accord with the now-rejected view].

Q.   A disciple of a sage who gave instruction to carry out the deed [wrongly] is exempt.

R.   It turns out that the strict ruling concerning him [that he cannot give decisions] also is a lenient ruling concerning him [that he is not punished if he does give decisions].

I.

A.   Our rabbis have taught on Tannaite authority:

B.   "If a thing be outstandingly difficult for you" [Freedman](Deut. 17:8):

C.   [87A] Scripture speaks of an outstanding figure on a court [and not a disciple].

D.   "You" -- this refers to a counsellor, and so it is said, "There is one come out from you, who imagines evil against the Lord, a wicked counsellor" (Nahum 1:11).

E.   "A thing" -- refers to a law.

F.   "In judgment" -- refers to a ruling based on an influential argument.

G.   "Between blood and blood" -- refers to the difference among the types of blood produced by a menstruating woman, a woman in childbirth, and a person suffering flux.

H.   "Between ruling and ruling" -- whether capital cases, property cases, or cases involving a flogging.

I.   "Between plague spot and plague spot" -- refers to a diseased spot in a human being, a house, and clothing.

J.   "Matters" -- refers to decisions on devoted objects and pledges of valuations as well as sanctification of objects to the Temple.

K.   "Contentions" -- this speaks of the ordeal of the accused wife, the breaking of the neck of a heifer on the occasion of discovery of a neglected corpse, and decisions on the declaration of purification of a person suffering from saraat.

L.   "In your gates" -- this refers to gleanings, forgotten sheaves, and the corner of the field.

M.   "Then you shall arise" -- from the session of the court.

N.   "And go up" -- this teaches that the house of the sanctuary is higher than the rest of the Land of Israel, and the Land of Israel is higher than all other lands.

O.   "To the place" -- this teaches that the place [in which the high court meets] is the decisive factor [in the authority of that court].

P.   Now it is perfectly true that the house of the sanctuary is higher than the Land of Israel, for it is written, "And you shall go up" (Deut. 17:8).

Q.   But how on the basis of Scripture does one know that the Land of Israel is higher than all other lands?

R.   As it is written, "Therefore, behold the days are coming, says the Lord, that they shall no more say, 'The Lord lives, which brought up the children of Israel out of the Land of Egypt;' but, 'the Lord lives, who brought up and led the seed of the house of Israel out of the north country and from all other countries whether I have driven them and they shall dwell in their own land' (Jer. 23:7-8)."

II.

A.   "A presumptuous sage is liable only on account of a ruling concerning a matter, the deliberate violation of which is subject to the penalty of extirpation, and the inadvertent violation of which is subject to the penalty of bringing a sin-offering," the words of R. Meir.

B.   R. Judah says, "It involves a matter, the principle of which derives from the teachings of the Torah, and the elaboration of which derives from the teachings of scribes."

C.   R. Simeon says, "It involves even the most minor detail among the details contributed by scribes."

D.   What is the scriptural basis for the position of R. Meir?

E.   He derives an analogy based on the meaning of the word "matter" as it occurs in two passages. In one passage it is written, "If there arises a matter too hard for you in judgment" (Deut. 17:8). And in a second passage it is written, "[And if the whole congregation of Israel sin through ignorance,] the matter being hidden from the eyes of the assembly" (Lev. 4:13).

F.   Just as, in this latter passage, "matter" refers to a rule, the deliberate violation of which is punishable by extirpation, and the inadvertent violation of which is punishable through the bringing of a sin-offering, so the word "matter" in the present context refers to a matter, the deliberate violation of which is subject to the penalty of extirpation, and the inadvertent violation of which is subject to the penalty of bringing a sin-offering.

G.   And R. Judah?

H.   "According to the Torah which they shall teach you" (Deut. 17:11) -- a matter that involves both Torah and what [scribes] shall teach you.

I.   And R. Simeon?

J.   "[And you shall do according to the sentence] which they of that place shall show you" (Deut. 17:10) -- even the most minor detail.

III.

A.   Said R. Huna bar Hinena to Raba, "Explain to me the teaching on Tannaite authority [of unit I] in accord with the view of R. Meir [about what is at issue, that is, distinctions based on types of penalty]."

B.   Said Raba to R. Pappa, "Go out and explain it to him."

C.   "'If a thing be outstandingly difficult for you' (Deut. 17:8) -- Scripture speaks of an outstanding figure on a court. This refers to a counsellor" -- who knows how to intercalate years and designate the appearance of the new moon.

D.   As we have learned in the Mishnah: <u>They gave testimony that they intercalate the year at any time in Adar.</u>

E.   <u>For they had said, "Only up to Purim."</u>

F.   <u>They gave testimony that they intercalate the year conditionally [M. Ed. 7:7F-H].</u>

G.   [If the presumptuous elder should reject the ruling of the high court], then, if it is to the one side, he will permit the use of leaven on Passover, and, if it is to the other side, he will also permit the use of leaven on Passover.

H.   "'A thing' -- refers to a law."

I.   This refers to the law of the eleventh day. [Freedman, p. 577, n. 2: According to Biblical Law, a <u>niddah</u> (menstruating woman) can cleanse herself when seven days have passed from the beginning of her menstrual flow, provided it ceased on the seventh day before sunset. During the following eleven days, which are called the eleven days between menses, she cannot become a <u>niddah</u> again, it being axiomatic that a discharge of blood in that period is not a sign of <u>niddah</u>, but <u>may</u> be symptomatic of gonorrhoea. A discharge on one or two days within the eleven days renders her unclean, and she is forbidden cohabitation until the evening of the following day, and must wait for the third to see whether another discharge will follow, rendering her a <u>zabah</u>, or not. Should another discharge follow on the third day, she becomes unclean as a <u>zabah</u>, and cannot become clean until seven days have passed without any issue at all. Should she, however, discharge on the tenth, eleventh, and twelfth days, she is not a <u>zabah</u>, for the twelfth day commences a new period wherein the issue of blood may make her a <u>niddah</u>.]

J.   For it has been taught on Amoraic authority:

K.   As to the tenth day,

L.   R. Yohanan said, "The tenth day is in the category of the ninth day."

M.   R. Simeon b. Laqish said, "The tenth day is in the category of the eleventh day."

N.   R. Yohanan said, "The tenth day is in the category of the ninth day, for just as the ninth day requires watchfulness [to see whether there is a discharge of blood on that day], so the tenth day requires watchfulness [for the same reason]."

O.   R. Simeon b. Laqish said, "The tenth day falls into the category of the eleventh day, just as the eleventh day does not require watchfulness [on account of a discharge of blood], so the tenth likewise does not require watchfulness." [Freedman, p. 577-8, n. 6: Thus, in R. Johanan's opinion, there is only one traditional <u>halachah</u> with respect to the eleventh day, viz., that a blood discharge thereon does not necessitate observation, and this is the only thing in which it differs from the preceding ten days. But if there was a discharge on the tenth, observation is necessary on the eleventh just as on the other days. But according to Resh Lakish it differs in two respects: (i) that a discharge thereon necessitates no further observation, and (ii) that it does not become an observation day on account of the tenth day's discharge. Hence there were two <u>halachoth</u> for that day. This explains the use of the plural in this passage. Now to revert to the main subject, in the opinion of R. Johanan, if a woman had a discharge on the tenth, cohabitation on the eleventh is <u>Biblically</u>

forbidden on pain of extinction, whilst according to Resh Lakish it is prohibited only be a Rabbinical ordinance, not by Biblical law; thus this too conforms to R. Meir's requirements.

P. "'In judgment' -- refers top a ruling based on an inferential argument."

Q. [87B] [This is illustrated by the inferential argument concerning a man's incest with his daughter produced by a woman whom he has raped.

R. For Raba said, "R. Isaac bar Abodimi said, "'The proof [that incest in such a case is punishable] derives from the common use of the word 'they' in two pertinent passages and also the common use of the word "wickedness" in two related passages.'"

S. "'Between blood and blood' -- refers to the difference among the types of blood produced by a menstruating woman, a woman in childbirth, and a person suffering flux."

T. "Blood produced by a menstruating woman" concerns the dispute of Aqabia b. Mehallel and rabbis.

U. For we have learned in the Mishnah:

V. Blood which is yellow ---

W. Aqabia b. Mehallel declares it unclean.

X. And sages declare it clean [M. Nid. 2:6E-G].

Y. "A woman in childbirth" refers to the dispute of Rab and Levi.

Z. For it has been stated on Amoraic authority: Rab said, "All blood comes from a single source, and the Torah has declared it unclean [for the first fourteen days after childbirth] and clean for the next sixty-six days."

AA. Levi said, "It comes from two different sources. When the source of the clean blood is closed, the source of the unclean blood is opened, and when the source of the clean blood is closed, the source of the clean blood is opened."

BB. "The blood of a person suffering flux."

CC. This refers to the dispute of R. Eliezer and R. Joshua, for we have learned in the Mishnah:

DD. [If] a woman was in hard travail for three days during the eleven days.

EE. and [if] she enjoyed a respite for twenty-four hours and [then] gave birth --

FF. "lo, this one is one who has given birth as a Zabah [while in the status of one who has a flux]," the words of R. Eliezer.

GG. R. Joshua says, "A night and a day, like the eve of the Sabbath and its day."

HH. For she has had relief from the pain and not from the blood [M. Nid. 4:4B-F].

II. "'Between ruling and ruling' -- whether capital or property cases or cases involving a flogging."

JJ. "Property cases:"

KK. This refers to the dispute of Samuel and R. Abbahu.

LL. For Samuel said, "If two judges decided a case, their decision is valid, but they are called a presumptuous court."

MM. And R. Abbahu said, "In the view of all parties their decision is not valid." [Freedman, pp. 579-580, n. 3: Extinction may be involved therein in the following way: -- If as a result of their decision money was withdrawn from A to B, on Samuel's view, it rightfully belongs to B: on R. Abbahu's, it does not. Now if B married a woman with this money as kiddushin, according to Samuel the marriage is valid, and cohabitation with another man is punishable by death or extinction in the absence of witnesses; but according to R. Abbahu, the kiddushin is invalid, for if one marries a woman with money or goods not belonging to him, his act is null. Hence, if the Beth din accepted Samuel's view, whilst the rebellious elder accepted R. Abbahu's, he declares a married woman free to others. Now further, if another man C also married the same woman, in Samuel's opinion the second marriage is invalid, and if B subsequently died, she is a free woman. But on R. Abbahu's view this second marriage is valid, since the first was null. Hence, if the Beth din ruled as R. Abbahu, and the rebellious elder as Samuel, he declares her free from C, when in reality she is married to him.]

NN. "Capital cases:"

OO. This refers to the dispute between Rabbi and rabbis.

PP. For it has been taught on Tannaite authority:

QQ. Rabbi says, "'And you shall give life for life' (Ex. 21:23).

RR. "This refers to a monetary compensation.

SS. "You say it refers to monetary compensation, but perhaps it means only that one literally takes a life?

TT. "Here there is reference to 'giving,' and elsewhere there is a reference to 'giving' [at Ex. 21:22].

UU. "Just as 'giving' in the latter passage refers to monetary compensation, so 'giving' in the former passage also refers to monetary compensation."

VV. "Or cases involving a flogging" -- this refers to the dispute between R. Ishmael and rabbis.

WW. For we have learned in the Mishnah:

XX. Cases involving flogging are judged by a court made up of three judges.

YY. In the name of R. Ishmael they have said, "A court made up of twenty three judges" [M. San. 1:2A-B].

ZZ. "'Between plague spot and plague spot' -- referring to a diseased spot in a human being, a house, and clothing:"

AAA. "Plague spots in a human being" refers to the dispute of R. Joshua and rabbis.

BBB. For we have learned in the Mishnah:

CCC. For they have said, If the bright spot preceded the white hair, he is unclean, and if the white hair preceded the bright spot, he is clean.

DDD. And if there is doubt, he is unclean.

EEE. And R. Joshua was doubtful [M. Nid. 4:11F-H].

FFF. What is the meaning of "doubtful"?

GGG. Said Raba, "If it is subject to doubt, the man is ruled to be clean."

HHH.   "A diseased spot in a house" refers to the dispute of R. Eleazar b. R. Simeon and rabbis.

III.   For we have learned in the Mishnah:

JJJ.   R. Eleazar b. R. Simeon says, "Until [a spot the size of] two split beans will apear on two stones -- on two walls in the corner.

KKK.   "Its length is two split beans, and its width a split bean" [M. Neg. 12:3G-H].

LLL.   What is the scriptural basis for the view of R. Eleazar b. R. Simeon?

MMM.   It is written, "wall," and it is further written, "Walls" (at Lev. 14:37, 39). Where do we find one wall as two? It is at the angle.

NNN.   "A diseased spot in clothing:"

OOO.   This refers to the dispute between R. Nathan b. Abetolomos and rabbis.

PPP.   For it has been taught on Tannaite authority:

QQQ.   R. Nathan b. Abetolomos says, "How do we know [88A] that when there is a spreading of disease-signs in clothing, [if it covers the entire garment], it is ruled to be clean?

RRR.   "The words 'baldness on the back of the head' and baldness on the front of the head are stated in respect to man, and 'baldness on the back' and 'baldness on the front' are mentioned in connection with clothing.

SSS.   "Just as is in the former case, if the baldness spread throughout the whole, the man is clean, so here too, if the baldness spread throughout the whole, the garment is clean."

TTT.   "'Matters' refers to decision on devoted objects, pledges of valuations, as well as sanctification of objects to the Temple:"

UUU.   "Pledges of valuations" refers to the dispute of R. Meir and rabbis, as we have learned on Tannaite authority:

VVV.   He who pledges the Valuation of an infant less than a month old --

WWW.   R. Meir says, "He pays his value [since there is no Valuation in Scripture]."

XXX.   And sages say, "He has not made a statement of any consequence at all [and pays nothing]" [cf. B. Arakhin 5a/1:1HIA-C].

YYY.   " ... decisions on devoted objects:"

ZZZ.   This refers to the dispute of R. Judah b. Beterah and rabbis.

AAAA.   For we have learned in the Mishnah:

BBBB.   R. Judah b. Betera says, "What is declared herem without further explanation is for the repair of the Temple house,

CCCC.   "since it is said, 'Every devoted thing is most holy to the Lord' (Lev. 27:28)."

DDDD.   And sages say, "What is declared herem without further explanation is for the priests,

EEEE.   "since it is said, As a field devoted to the possession thereof shall be the priest's (Lev. 27:21).

FFFF.   "If so, why is it said, And every devoted thing is most holy to the Lord?

GGGG.   "That it applies to Most Holy Things and to Lesser Holy Thing" [M. Ar. 8:6B-G].

HHHH.   " ... as well as sanctification of objects to the Temple:"

IIII. This refers to the dispute of R. Eliezer b. Jacob and rabbis, for it has been taught on Tannaite authority:

JJJJ. R. Eliezer b. Jacob says, "The valuation even of a hook that has been declared sanctified requires the assessment of a court of ten judges so that it may be redeemed [by the payment of a monetary equivalent to the value of the hook]."

KKKK. "'Contentions' -- this speaks of the ordeal of the accused wife, the breaking of the neck of a heifer on the occasion of discovery of a neglected corpse, and decisions on the declaration of purification of a person suffering from saraat:"

LLLL. "The ordeal of the accused wife" refers to the dispute of R. Eliezer and R. Joshua, for we have learned in the Mishnah:

MMMM. He who expresses jealousy to his wife [concerning her relations with another man (Num. 5:14) --

NNNN. R. Eliezer says, "He expresses jealousy before two witnesses, and he imposes on her the requirement of drinking the bitter water on the testimony of a single witness or even on his own evidence [that she has been alone with the named man]."

OOOO. R. Joshua says, "He expresses jealousy before two witnesses, and he requires her to drink the bitter water before two witnesses" [M. Sot. 1:1A-C].

PPPP. "The breaking of the neck of a heifer ..." refers to the dispute between R. Eliezer and R. Aqiba, for we have learned in the Mishnah:

QQQQ. From what point did they measure?

RRRR. R. Eliezer says, "From his belly-button."

SSSS. R. 'Aqiba says, "From his nose."

TTTT. R. Eliezer b. Jacob says, "From the place at which he was turned into a corpse -- from his neck" [M. Sot. 9:4A-D].

UUUU. "Decisions on the purification of a person suffering from saraat" refers to the dispute of R. Simeon and rabbis, for we have learned in the Mishnah:

VVVV. If he did not have a thumb, a big toe, [or] a right ear he can never have purification.

WWWW. R. Eliezer says, "One puts it [the blood] on their place."

XXXX. R. Simeon says, "If he put it on the left [side instead of the right], he has carried out his obligation" [M. Neg. 14:9E-G].

YYYY. "'In your gates' -- this refers to gleanings, forgotten sheaves, and the corner of the field:"

ZZZZ. As we have learned in the Mishnah:

AAAAA. "Two sheaves [of grain which are left side-by-side in a field] are [subject to the restrictions of] the forgotten sheaf.

BBBBB. "But three [sheaves left side-by-side in a field] are not [subject to the restrictions of] the forgotten sheaf.

CCCCC. "Two piles of olives or carob-[fruit which are left side-by-side in a field] are [subject to the restrictions of] the forgotten sheaf.

DDDDD. "But three [such piles left side-by-side in a field] are not [subject to the restrictions of] the forgotten sheaf.

EEEEE.   But concerning all of them, the House of Shammai say, "Three [measures of produce left side-by-side in a field] belong to the poor, while four [measures] belong to the householder" [M. Pe. 6:5A-D, L (Brooks)].

FFFFF.   " ... and the corner of the field:"

GGGGG.   This refers to the dispute of R. Ishmael and rabbis.

HHHHH.   For it has been taught on Tannaite authority:

IIIII.   The religious duty of designating a corner of the field for the poor involves separating standing grain.

JJJJJ.   If one did not designate the portion out of standing grain, he should designate it out of grain in sheaves.

KKKKK.   This should be done before he smoothed the stack.

LLLLL.   If he had first smoothed the stack of grain, he should separate tithe and give it to [the poor man].

MMMMM.   In the name of R. Ishmael they said, "One may separate [the share of the poor] even from the dough [of grain that has been processed]."

IV.

A.   There were three courts there [M. 10:2C]:

B.   [With reference to M. 10:2E-F], said R. Kahana, [If] he says, "'[I heard it] from tradition, and they say, '[We heard it] from tradition,' he is not put to death.

C.   "[If] he says, 'Thus matters appear to me [on this basis of reasoning],' and they say, 'Thus matters appear to us [on the basis of reasoning],' he is not put to death.

D.   "And all the more so [if] he says, 'I heard it from tradition,' and they say, 'Thus matters appear to us,' he is not put to death.

E.   "[He is put to death] only if he says, 'Thus it appears to me,' while they say, '[We have heard] on the basis of tradition.'

F.   "You may know that that is the case, for lo, they did not put Aqabia b. Mehallel to death."

G.   But R. Eleazar says, "Even if he says, '[I heard] from tradition,' and they say, 'Thus matters appear to us,' he is put to death, so as to prevent dissension in Israel.

H.   "And should you say, On what account did they not put Aqabiah b. Mehallel to death, it was because he did not teach the law as a matter of practical conduct [but only as a theory].

I.   "You may know that that is the case, for lo, we have learned in the Mishnah: Thus I have explained the matter and thus my colleagues have explained the matter, thus I have taught and thus my colleagues have taught [M. 10:2H-I].

J.   "Is this not a case in which he said, '[I heard it] on the basis of tradition,' and they say, 'Thus matters appear to us'?"

K.   No, it is a case in which he says, "Thus it appears to me,'" and they say, "[Thus have we heard] in tradition."

L.   Come and take note:

M.   R. Josiah said, "Three things did Zeira tell me in the name of the men of Jerusalem: 'A husband who retracted his expression of jealousy -- his expression of jealousy is null [88B]. A disobedient son whom the father and mother wished to forgive is forgiven. A rebellious elder whom a court wished to forgive is forgiven. Now when I came to my colleagues in the south, they concurred with me in two items, but as to the rebellious elder they did not concur with me, so as not to permit the increase of dissention in Israel."

N.   This constitutes a valid refutation [of Kahana's position and support of Eleazar's].

V.

A.   It has been taught on Tannaite authority:

B.   Said R. Yose, "At first there were dissensions in Israel only in the court of seventy in the hewn-stone chamber in Jerusalem.

C.   "And there were other courts of twenty-three in the various towns of the land of Israel, and there were other courts of three judges each in Jerusalem, one on the Temple mount, and one on the Rampart.

D.   "[If] someone needed to know what the law is, he would go to the court in his town.

E.   "[If] there was no court in his town, he would go to the court in the town nearest his.

F.   "If they had heard the law, they told him. If not, he and the most distinguished member of that court would come on to the court which was on the Temple mount.

G.   "If they had heard the law, they told them. And if not, they and the most distinguished member of that group would come to the court which was on the Rampart.

H.   "If they had heard, they told them, and if not, these and those would go to the high court which was in the hewn-stone chamber.

I.   "The court which was in the hewn-stone chamber, even though it consists of seventy-one members, may not fall below twenty-three.

J.   "[If] one of them had to go out, he looks around to see whether there would be twenty-three left [after he departs]. If there would be twenty-three left he goes out, and if not, he does not go out --

K.   "unless there would be twenty-three left.

L.   "And there they remained in session from the time of the daily whole-offering of the morning until the time of the daily whole-offering at twilight.

M.   "On Sabbaths and on festivals they came only to the study-house which was on the Temple mount.

N.   "[If] a question was brought before them, if they had heard the answer, they told them.

O.   "if not, they stand for a vote.

P.   "[If] those who declare unclean turn out to form the majority, they declared the matter unclean. [If] those who declare the matter clean form the majority, they declared the matter clean.

Q.   "From there did the law go forth and circulate in Israel.

R.   "From the time that the disciples of Shammai and Hillel who had not served their masters as much as was necessary became numerous, dissensions became many in Israel.

S.   "And from there they send for and examine everyone who is wise, prudent, fearful of sin, and of good repute, in whom people found pleasure.

T.   "They make him a judge in his town.

U.   "Once he has been made a judge in his town, they promote him and seat him on the Rampart's court, and from there they promote him and seat him in he court of the hewnstone chamber [T. San. 7:1B-U].

VI.

A.   They sent from there, "Who is someone who will inherit the world to come?

B.   "It is one who is meek and humble, who bends when he comes and and bends when he goes out, who always is studying the Torah, but does not take pride in himself in on that account."

C.   Rabbis gazed at R. Ulla bar Abba.

VII.

A.   If he went back to his town and again ruled [just as he had ruled before he is exempt] [M. 10:2M]:

B.   Our rabbis have taught on Tannaite authority:

C.   He is liable only if he will act in accord with the instruction that he has given, or unless he instructs others to do so and they act in accord with his instruction [T. San. 14:12].

D.   Now there is no problem with the case of his teaching others who act in accord with his instruction.

E.   To begin with, he was not subject to the death penalty, but now [after the court has ruled] he is indeed subject to the death penalty.

F.   But if he should act in accord with his own instruction, [that is a different matter, for] to begin with, also, he was subject to the death-penalty.

G.   There is [to continue the exposition], moreover, no problem if the original ruling had to do with the prohibition of eating forbidden fat or blood, for to begin with he was not subject to the death penalty, while now he is subject to the death penalty.

H.   But in a case in which he had given instruction concerning matters on account of which the court inflict the death penalty, to begin with he was subject to the death penalty [and it is not only now that the court has made its ruling].

I.   [No, that is not a problem, for] to begin with he required admonition [against teaching as he did; barring admonition, he would not be subject to the death penalty], while now, he does not require admonition [and is subject to the death penalty in any event].

J.   Then as to the case of one who incites [a whole town to commit idolatry], who does not require an admonition at all, what is to be said?

K.   If, [prior to the consultation with the high court], he had given reason for his action, we might have accepted it from him, but now even if he gave a reason, we should not accept it from him.

The magnificent exposition of unit I at unit III should not distract attention from other impressive traits of systematic exegesis of the fine composition before us. Unit I provides an explanation for the proof-text of Scripture cited by the Mishnah itself. Unit II then defines the matter at issue in the Mishnah-paragraph. Then unit III spells out the materials of unit I, in light of one of the three positions of unit II. That the whole is a unity cannot be doubted, a wonderful piece of composition. All of the matters spelled out involve the disjunctive penalty specified by Meir, though this requires explicit exposition only at a few points. Unit IV then brings us to M. 10:2E-F. Unit V presents the Tosefta's expansion of M. 10:2G-L. I take it that unit VI is meant to expand upon who gets appointed to the court. Unit VII then proceeds to M. 10:2M. So the entire passage is laid out as a systematic exposition of the Mishnah.

10:3

A. A more strict rule applies to the teachings of scribes than to the teachings of Torah.

B. He who, in order to transgress the teachings of the Torah, rules, "There is no requirement to wear phylacteries," is exempt.

C. [But if,] in order to add to what the scribes have taught, [he said,] "There are five partitions [in the phylactery, instead of four], he is liable.

I.

A. Said R. Eleazar, said R. Oshaia, "The liability applies only to a case in which the principle derives from the teachings of the Torah, the amplification derives from words of scribes, there is a possibility of adding, but if, should there be addition, it constitutes diminution.

B. "The only example of such a matter is the case of the phylacteries. [Freedman, p. 587, n. 6: The fundamental law of wearing phylacteries is biblical. By rabbinic interpretation, the phylactery for the head must contain four compartments, with inscriptions in each. Hence it is possible to rule that it should consist of a greater number. But if this is done, the phylactery is unfit, so that the addition amounts to subtraction of its fitness]."

C. This [A] accords with the principle of R. Judah [at B. San. 87A, above, who holds that at issue must be both a teaching of the Torah and an amplification based on views of scribes].

D. But [as against B] there is the matter of the palm-branch [waved on the festival of Tabernacles], in which the principle of the matter derives from the teaching of the Torah [Lev. 23:40], and the amplification, from the teaching of scribes there is a possibility of adding, but if, should there be addition, it constitutes diminution in the case of the palm-branch.

E. What is the basic thesis of the present proposal? Is it that it is not necessary to bind together the several components of the palm-branch [that is, the palm with the citron and myrtle]? Then this part is distinct from that [Freedman, p. 588, n. 5: so that the combination is quite valid]. [Adding further will make no difference.]

F. If we take the view that the palm-branch does have to be bound together, then the [palm-branch] persists in being invalid [as soon as an additional species, beyond the three required, is bound together with the others]. [Freedman, p. 588, n. 6: But in the case of phylacteries, when four compartments are made, the head-phylactery is valid, while only when a fifth is added, does it become invalid.]

G. [so this matter of the palm-branch does not constitute a further example to illustrate the conditions set forth at the outset.]

H. And lo, there is the case of show-fringes, in which case the principle derives from a teaching of the Torah, while the amplification of the matter derives from teachings of scribes, and there is a possibility of adding, but if, should there be an addition [of a thread], it constitutes diminution.

I. But what theory do we espouse in the case of show-fringes? If we take the view that the upper knot [on the show-fringes] does not derive from the requirement of the Torah, then this knot stands apart from that knot. [Freedman, p. 588, n. 10: The fringes are inserted through a hole and knotted near the edge of the garment. It is disputed whether this is really necessary by biblical law. If not, then even when made, the threads or fringes are regarded as hanging apart and distinct. Conse-quently, if five instead of four threads were inserted and knotted, four fulfill the precept, while the fifth may be disregarded entirely, without rendering the rest invalid.]

J. And if we take the view that [89A] the upper knot does derive from the requirement of the Torah, then to begin with the show-fringes are invalid.

K. [This same argument may now apply to the phylacteries, namely,] if so, in the case of phylacteries also, if one made four cubicles and then added a fifth and set it beside the four, [we also may say] that this one is regarded as distinct from the others. And if to begin with one made five cubicles [instead of four], then to begin with the phylactery was invalid [as soon as it was made],

L. for has not R. Zira said, "In the case of a cubicle that is open to the next [the phylactery is unfit,]" [Freedman, p. 588, n. 12: not having been made according to rule, which requires that each compartment shall be entirely shut off from the next, so it is not a case of phylacteries have been rendered unfit, but of something that was never a phylactery to begin with.]

M. [Freedman supplies from the Munich MS: This must be taught only in the case of one who made a frontlet of four compartments, and then added a fifth thereto and joined it. (By this addition the original is impaired,) even as Raba said, "If the outset compartment does not look upon space, it is invalid..."]

The Talmud provides ample illustration of the Mishnah's principle.

10:4

A. "They put him to death not in the court in his own town or in the court which is in Yabneh, but they bring him up to the high court in Jerusalem.

B.   "And they keep him until the festival, and they put him to death on the festival,

C.   "as it is said, 'And all the people shall hear and fear and no more do presumptuously' (Deut. 17:13)," the words of R. Aqiba.

D.   R. Judah says, "They do not delay the judgment of this one, but they put him to death at once.

E.   "And they write messages and send them with messengers to every place:

F.   'Mr. So-and-so, son of Mr. So-and-so, has been declared liable to the death penalty by the court.'"

I.

A.   Our rabbis have taught on Tannaite authority:

B.   "They put him to death not in the court in his own town or in the court which is in Yabneh, but they bring him up to the high court in Jerusalem. And they keep him until the festival, and they put him to death on the festival, as it is said, 'And all the people shall hear and fear and no more do presumptuously' (Deut. 17:13)," the words of R. Aqiba [M. 10:4A-C].

C.   Said R. Judah to him, "And is it said, 'They shall see and fear'? What is stated is only, 'They shall hear and fear..'

D.   "So why delay the judgment of this one? Rather they put him to death at once, and they write messages and send them with messengers to every place:

E.   "'Mr. So-and-so has been declared liable to the death penalty by the court'" [M. 10:4D-F].

II.

A.   Our rabbis have taught on Tannaite authority:

B.   The condemnation of four classes of criminals requires public announcement:

C.   one who entices [a town to apostacy], a wayward and incorrigible son, a rebellious elder, and witnesses who have been proved to form a conspiracy for perjury.

D.   And in the case of all of them [except for the fourth], it is written, "And all the people ...," or, "and all Israel ...."

E.   But in the case of a conspiracy of perjurers, it is written, "And those that remain shall hear and fear" (Deut. 19:20),

F.   for not every body is fit to be a witness, [so the admonition is not to all Israel].

Unit I provides a light gloss to the Mishnah's formulation, giving an answer to the exegetical argument, and unit II likewise amplifies matters.

10:5-6

A.   A false prophet [M. 10:1B],

B.   one who prophesies concerning something which he has not actually heard or concerning something which was not actually said to him,

C.   is put to death by man.

D. But he who holds back his prophesy, he who disregards the words of another prophet, or the prophet who transgresses his word words

E. is put to death by heaven,

F. as it is said, "I will require it of him" (Deut. 18;19).

M.10:5

A. He who prophesies in the name of an idol [M.10:1B5], and says, "Thus did such-and-such an idol say to me,"

B. even though he got the law right, declaring unclean that which in fact is unclean, and declaring clean that which in fact is clean.

C. He who has sexual relations with a married woman [M.10:1C1]

D. as soon as she has entered the domain of the husband in marriage, even though she has not had sexual relations with him

E. he who has sexual relations with her - lo, this one is put to death by strangling.

F. And those who bear false witness against a priest's daughter and against one who has sexual relations with her [M. 10:1C2,3] --

G. for all those who bear false witness first suffer that same mode of execution,

H. except for those who bear false witness against a priest's daughter and her lover.

M.10:6

I.

A. Our rabbis have taught on Tannaite authority:

B. Three [false prophets] are put to death by man, and three are put to death by heaven.

C. He who prophesies concerning something which he has not actually heard or concerning something which was not actually said to him [M. 10:5B],

D. and one who prophesies in the name of an idol -- such as these are put to death by man.

E. But he who holds back his prophecy, he who disregards the words of another prophet, or the prophet who transgreses his own words is not to death by heaven [M. 10:5D-F].

F. What is the source of this rule?

G. Said R. Judah said Rab, "It is because Scripture has said, 'But the prophet who shall presume to speak a word in may name' (Deut. 18:20) -- this refers to a prophet who prophesies concerning something which he has not actually heard.

H. "'Which I have not commanded him to speak' (Deut. 18:20) -- but lo, I have indeed commanded his fellow, [and accordingly], this refers to one who prophesies concerning something which was not actually said to him [but to someone else].

I. "'Or shall speak in the name of other gods' (Deut. 18:20) -- this refers to one who prophesies in the name of an idol.

J.   "And it is written, 'Even that prophet shall die' (Deut. 18:20), and in the case of a death penalty specified in the Torah which is left undefined, it is only through strangulation.

K.   "But he who holds back his prophecy, he who disregards the words of another prophet, or the prophet who transgresses his own words is put to death by heaven,

L.   "For it is written, 'And it shall come to pass that whoever will not hearken...' (Deut. 18:19).

M.   "In regard to such a person applies the statement, 'Who will not listen to my words.'

N.   "And it is written, 'I shall require it of him' (Deut. 18:19) -- meaning, [he is put to death] by heaven."

II.

A.   One who prophesies concerning something which he has not actually heard [M. 10:5B].

B.   For example, Zedekiah b. Chenaanah [T. San. 14:14A-B],

C.   for it is written, "And Zedekiah, the son of Chenaanah, had made him horns of iron" (1 Kgs. 22:11).

D.   What ought he have done? For it was the spirit of Naboth that had confused him!

E.   For it is written, "And the Lord said, Who shall persuade Ahab that he may go up and fall at Ramoth-Gilead? And there came forth a spirit and stood before the Lord and said, I will persuade him...and the Lord said, You shall persuade him and prevail also, go forth and do so" (1 Ks. 22:20ff.)?

F.   Said R. Judah, "What is the meaning of 'go forth'? It is 'go forth' from my vicinity."

G.   What is the meaning of "spirit"?

H.   Said R. Yohanan, "It was the spirit of Naboth, the Jezreelite."

I.   [Reverting to the question of what else Zedekiah might have done, we answer:] He might have checked out [the predictions of the other prophets].

J.   That accords with what R. Isaac said.

K.   For R. Isaac said, "The same message reaches many prophets, but no two prophets prophesy in the same wording.

L.   "Obadiah said, 'The pride of your heart has deceived you' (Ob. 1:3), while Jeremiah said, 'Your terribleness has deceived you and the pride of your heart' (Jer. 49:16), [and both referred to Edom, but expressed themselves differently.]"

M.   [And returning to the argument against Zedekiah:] Since all of these prophets together spoke in the same way, it indicated that they had nothing at all to say [that God had delivered to them as his message].

N.   But perhaps [Zedekiah] did not know about this statement of R. Isaac.

O.   Jehoshaphat was there, and he spoke to them, for it is written, "And Jehoshaphat said, Is there not here a prophet of the Lord besides, that we may inquire of him?" (1 Kgs. 22:7).

P.   [Ahab] said to him, "Lo, there are all of these [prophets]."

Q.   "I have received a teaching from the house of my father's father that the same message reaches many prophets, but no two prophets prophesy in the same wording."

III.

A. He who prophesies concerning something which was not actually said to him [M. 10:5B]:

B. for example, Hananiah b. Azor [T. San. 14:14D].

C. For Jeremiah was standing in the upper market, and saying, "Thus says the Lord of hosts, Behold I will break the bow of Elam" (Jer. 49:35).

D. Now Hanahiah constructed an argument a fortiori on his own, "If concerning Elam, who came only to help Babylonia, the Holy One, blessed be he, has said, 'Behold, I will break the bow of Elam,' the Chaldeans themselves, how much the more so [will the Lord break their bow]."

E. He came along to the lower market and said, "Thus says the Lord of hosts, the God Israel, saying, I have broken the yoke of the kingdom of Babylon: (Jer. 28:2).

F. Said R. Pappa to Abayye, "[But this does not constitute violating the rule, for] that message also had not been given to his fellow [Jeremiah]."

G. He said to him, "Since an argument a fortiori has been made available as an exegetical tool, it is as if it had been stated to him.

H. "Accordingly, this falls into the category of saying something that had not been said to him [but had been said to his fellow prophet]."

IV.

A. He who prophesies in the name of an idol [I:D]:

V.

A. He who holds back his prophecy [M. 10:5D]:

B. for example Jonah b. Amittai [T. San. 14:15B].

VI.

A. He who disregards the words of another prophet [M. 10:5D]:

B. for example [89B] the friend of Micah,

C. as it is written, "And a certain man of the sons of the prophets said to his fellow in the word of the Lord, Smite me I pray you, and the man refused to smite him" (1 Kgs. 20:35).

D. And it is further written, "And he said to him, Because you have not obeyed [the voice of the Lord, behold as soon as you have departed from me, a lion will kill you]" (1 Kgs. 20:36).

VII.

A. Or the prophet who transgresses his own words [M. 10:5D]:

B. for example, Iddo, the prophet [T. San. 15:15E],

C. as it is written, "For so it was charged me by the word of the Lord, [saying, Eat not bread not drink water nor turn again by the same way that you come]" (1 Kgs. 13:9).

D. "And [the prophet] said to him, I am a prophet also as you are [and an angel spoke to me by the work of the Lord, saying, Bring him back with you to your house that he may eat bread and drink water" (1 Kgs. 13:18).

E. "So he went back with him," and "When he was gone, a lion met him by the way and slew him" (1 Kgs. 13:24).

VIII.

A. A Tannaite authority repeated before R. Hisda, "He who holds back his prophecy is flogged."

B. He said to him, "He who eats dates out of a sieve is flogged! Who warned [the prophet who withheld his prophecy, since no one could have known about that fact]? [No admonition, no flogging!]"

C. Said Abayye, "His fellow prophets."

D. "How did they know about it?"

E. Said Abayye, "For it is written, 'Surely the Lord will do nothing unless he reveals his secret to his servants, the prophets, (Amos 3:7)."

F. "But perhaps [the heavenly messengers] retracted?"

G. "If it were the case that they had retracted, they would have informed all the other prophets."

H. "And lo, there is the case of Jonah, in which heaven had retracted [its decision], but they had not notified Jonah."

I. "To begin with, Jonah was told that Tenveh would be turned, but he was not informed whether it was for good or for bad."

IX.

A. He who disregards the wods of another prophet [M. 10:5D]:

B. How does one know [that the other is a prophet], so that he should be punished?

C. [The other] gives him a sign.

D. And lo, there is the case of Micah, who did not give a sign, and yet [the other prophet] was punished.

E. In a case in which one was already well established as a prophet, the law is different.

F. For if you do not take that view, then in the case of Abraham at Mount Moriah, how could Isaac have listened to Abraham, and in the case of Elijah at Mount Carmel, how could the people have relied on him, so as [in both cases] to make an offering outside of the Temple?

G. It must follow that in a case in which one was already well established, the law is different.

X.

A. "And it came to pass after these words that God tested Abraham" (Gen. 22:1):

B. What is the meaning of "after"?

C. Said R. Yohanan in the name of R. Yose b. Zimra, "It was after the words of Satan.

D. "For it is written 'And the child grew and was weaned [and Abraham made a great feast the same day that Isaac was weaned' (Gen. 21:8).

E. "Said Satan to the Holy One, blessed be he, 'Lord of the world, as to this old man, you have shown him grace by giving him the fruit of the womb at one hundred years. Now of the entire meal that he has made, he did not have a single pigeon or a single dove to offer before you.'

F. "He said to him, 'Has he done anything at all except to honor his son? [But] if I were to say to him, "Sacrifice your son before me," he would sacrifice him immediately.'

G. "Forthwith: 'And God tested Abraham' (Gen. 22:1)."

H. "And he said, Take, I pray you, your son" (Gen. 22:2).

I. Said R. Simeon b. Abba, "The word 'I pray you' bears the meaning only of supplication.

J. "The matter may be compared to the case of a mortal king, against whom many wars were fought. He had one powerful leader, who won all his battles.

K. "After a while a very difficult war was waged against him.

L. "He said to him, 'By your leave, stand up for me in this war too, so that people will not say that, as to the earlier wars, they really did not add up to much.'

M. "So the Holy One, blessed be he, said to Abraham, 'I tried you in a number of trials and you stood up to all of them. Now stand up for me in this trial as well, so that people will not say that, as to he earlier trials, they really did not add up to much."

N. "Your son" (Gen. 22:2) -- "I have two sons."

O. "Your only son (Gen. 22:2) -- "This one is an only son for his mother, and that one is an only son for his mother."

P. "Whom you loved" (Gen. 22:2) -- "I love them both."

Q. "Isaac" (Gen. 22:2).

R. Why all this?

S. So that he should not be confused.

T. Satan met him on the way and said to him, "If we try to commune with you, will you be grieved? ... Behold you have instructed many, and you have strengthened weak hands. Your words have held up him who was falling, and you have strengthened feeble knees. But now it is come upon you, and you faint" (Job 4:2-5).

U. He said to him, "I will walk in my integrity." (Ps. 26:2).

V. He said to him, "But should not your fear by your confidence" (Job 4:6).

W. He said to him, "Remember, I pray you, whoever perished, being innocent?" (Job 4:6).

X. Since [Satan] saw that he would not listen to him, he said to him, "Now a thing was secretly brought to me" (Job 4:12).

Y. "This I have heard from the other side of the curtain: 'The lamb is for a burnt-offering (Job 4:7) -- and Isaac is not for a burnt-offering."

Z. This is the penalty paid by a liar, that even when he tells the truth, people do not pay any attention to him.

AA. [Explaining, "After these words" (Gen. 22:1):] said R. Levi, "After the words between Ishmael and Isaac.

BB. "Ishmael said to Isaac, 'I am greater than you in the performance of religious duties, for you were circumcized on the eighth day, while I was circumcized in the thirteenth year.'

CC. "He said to him, 'And on account of one limb are you going to put me down? If the Holy One, blessed be he, were to say to me, 'Sacrifice yourself before me,' I should sacrifice myself immediately.'

DD. "'And God tried Abraham' (Gen. 22:1)."

XI.

A.   [With reference to M. 10:6A-B], our rabbis have taught on Tannaite authority:

B.   **A prophet who enticed [people to commit idolatry] is put to death through stoning.**

C.   R. Simeon says, "It is through strangulation"

D.   **Those who entice a whole town to commit idolatry are put to death through stoning.**

E.   R. Simeon says, "Through strangulation" [cf. T. San. 11:5D].

F.   What is the scriptural basis for the position of rabbis?

G.   They establish an analogy between the matter of the false prophet and the one who enticed a town to commit idolatry on the basis of the common usage of the word "enticement" in both cases [for the prophet, at Deut. 13:6, and for the one who enticed the town to commit idolatry, at Deut. 13:11].

H.   Just as, in the latter case, the penalty is death through stoning, so in the present case, the penalty is death through stoning.

I.   And R. Simeon? The penalty is death is ascribed to such a one, and in any case in which in the Torah death is prescribed without further specification, it is is through strangulation.

J.   **Those who entice a whole town to commit idolatry are put to death through stoning:**

K.   What is the scriptural basis for the position of rabbis?

L.   [As before], they establish an analogy between the matter of the one who entices the town to commit idolatry and the prophet who enticed [people to commit idolatry], based on the common use of the word enticement.

M.   And R. Simeon? He derives the penalty applicable to the one who entices the town to commit idolatry from the penalty applicable to the prophet on the basis of the use of the word "enticement" in common to both.

N.   And why not derive the proof from the case of one who entices a community to commit idolatry [at which, at Deut. 13:11, the penalty of stoning is explicitly prescribed]?

O.   We draw an analogy from the case of one who entices the community at large from the case of one who entices the community at large, and we do not derive an analogy concerning the one who entices the community at large from the instance of one who entices an individual.

P.   On the contrary, we should derive an analogy for the penalty applying to a common person from the penalty that applies to another such common person, and we should not establish an analogy concerning a common person from the rule that applies to a prophet!

Q.   And R. Simeon?

R.   Since one has enticed [a community to commit idolatry], you have no more solid grounds than that for regarding one as a common person!

S.   Said R. Hisda, "[90A] The dispute concerns the case of one who uprooted the very principle that idolatry is forbidden, or who in part confirmed and in part annulled the principle of idolatry.

T.   "For the All-Merciful has said, '[To entice you]..from the way [which the Lord your God commanded you to walk in]' (Deut. 13:6) -- that is, even part of the way.

U.   "But as to one who uprooted the very principle of other religious opinions in the opinion of all parties is put to death through strangulation, and as to one who upholds part and annuls part of any of the other commandments, all parties concur that such a one is exempt."

V.   R. Hamnuna objected, "'[Because he has spoken ... to entice you from the way which the Lord your God has commanded you] to walk' -- this refers to commandments concerning positive deeds.

W.   "'...in it' -- this refers to commandments concerning things not to do.

X.   "Now if you take that view that at issue is idolatry, where do you find a commandment concerning a duty actually to carry out a deed in connection with idolatry?"

Y.   "R. Hisda explained, "[You do indeed find such a positive commandment: 'And you shall overthrow their altars' (Deut. 12:3)."

Z.   R. Hamnuna said, "The dispute concerns one who uproots the very principle of the law, whether with respect to idolatry or any other religious duties, or the partial fulfillment and the partial nullification of idolatry.

AA.   "For the All-Merciful has said, '...from the way...' (Deut. 13:6) -- even part of the way.

BB.   "But if one a one confirms in part and annuls in part the matter of all other commandments, all parties concur that he is exempt."

CC.   Our rabbis have taught on Tannaite authority:

DD.   He who prophesies in such a way as to uproot a teaching of the Torah is liable.

EE.   [If he prophesies so as] to confirm part and annul part [of a teaching of the Torah],

FF.   R. Simeon declares him exempt.

GG.   But as for idolatry, even if one says, "Today serve it and tomorrow annul it," all parties concur that he is liable.

HH.   Abayye reasons matters in accord with the view of R. Hisda and deals with the matter at hand in accord with the view of R. Hisda, and Raba reasons matters in accord with the view of R. Hamnuna and interprets the matter at hand with the view of R. Hamnuna.

II.   Abayye reasons matters in accord with the view of R. Hisda and deals with the matter at hand in accord with the view of R. Hisda:

JJ.   As to him who prophesies in such a way as to uproot a teaching of the Torah, all parties concur that he is put to death through strangulation.

KK.   If he so prophesies as to confirm part and annul part, R. Simeon declares him exempt, and that is the view also of rabbis.

LL.   And as to a matter of idolatry, even if he said, "Today serve it and tomorrow annul it," he is liable.

MM.   Each will condemn him to the death penalty in accord with his established position [so rabbis have him stoned, Simeon has him strangled.]

NN.   Raba reasons matters in accord with the view of R. Hamnuna and interprets the matter at hand in accord with the view of R. Hamnuna:

OO.   He who prophesies as to uproot a teaching of the Torah, whether it concerns idolatry or any of the other religious duties, it is liable.

PP.   Each will condemn him to the death penalty in accord with his established position.

QQ.   If he so prophesies as to confirm part and annul part of another religious duties.

RR.   R. Simeon declares him exempt, and that is the view of rabbis. [Freedman, p. 599, n.b. 1: In Hamnuna's view, Simeon is particularly mentioned to show that he is exempt even from strangulation, a more lenient death than stoning, hence certainly from stoning].

SS.   And as idolatry, even if he says, "Today serve it and tomorrow annul it," he is liable.

TT.   Each will condemn him to the death penalty in accord with his established position.

XII.

A.   Said R. Abbahu said, R. Yohanan, "In any matter, if a prophet should say to you, 'Violate the teachings of the Torah,' obey him, except for the matter of idolatry.

B.   "For even if he should make the sun stand still for you in the middle of the firmament, do not listen to him."

C.   It has been taught on Tannaite authority:

D.   R. Yose the Galilean says, "The Torah reached the ultimate depth of idolatry, therefore the Torah have [the false prophet] rule over it,

E.   "so that even if he should make the sun stand still for you in the midst of the firmament, you should not obey him."

F.   It has been taught on Tannaite authority:

G.   Said R. Aqiba, "Heaven forfend that the Holy One blessed be he should make the sun stand still in behalf of those who violate his will.

H.   "But it would be like one such as Hananiah, son of Azur, who to begin with had been a true prophet but in the end became a false prophet."

XIII.

A.   And those who bear false witness against a priest's daughter...[M. 10:F]:

B.   What is the source in Scripture of this rule?

C.   Said R. Aha, son of R. Iqa, "It is in accord with that which has been taught on Tannaite authority:

D.   "R. Yose says, 'What is the meaning of the verse of Scripture, "Then you shall do to him as he had thought to have done to his brother" (Deut. 19:19)?

E.   "'Since all those in the Torah who are proved to be a conspiracy of perjury, those who prove them to be perjured and lovers are treated as they are [that is, as are the perjured witnesses, so to the death they sought to impose on the women and the lovers to that of the women they had dishonored (Freedman, p. 600, n. 1)].

F.   "'In the case of the priest's daughter, however, she is executed by burning, but her lover is not executed by burning.

G.   "'As to perjured witnesses against her, therefore, I do not know whether they are linked to him or to her [and so made to suffer the death they had conspired to bring upon her or upon him].

H.   "'When Scripture says, "to have done to his brother," it teaches, "to his brother and not to his sister" [Freedman, p. 600, n .3: He is executed by her paramour's death, not her own]."'

The Talmud once more follows the Mishnah's topics, systematically and in order. Unit I deals with M. 10:5B-F; units II-IV with M. 10:5B, units V-IX with M. 10:5D. The reference at IX F accounts for the inclusion of unit X. Unit XI then moves on to M. 10:6A-B. Unit XII deals with the theme at hand, the false prophet. Then unit XIII takes up M. 10:6F. So the work is orderly and sensible.

CHAPTER THREE
BAVLI SANHEDRIN CHAPTER ELEVEN

11:1-2

A. All Israelites have a share in the world to come,

B. as it is said, "your people also shall be all righteous, they shall inherit the land forever; the branch of my planting, the work of my hands, that I may be glorified" (Is. 60:21).

C. And these are the ones who have no portion in the world to come:

D. He who says, the resurrection of the dead is a teaching which does not derive from the Torah, and the Torah does not come from Heaven; and an Epicurean.

E. R. Aqiba says, "Also: He who reads in heretical books,

F. "and he who whispers over a wound and says, 'I will put none of the diseases upon you which I have put on the Egyptians, for I am the Lord who heals you' (Ex. 15:26)."

G. Abba Saul says, "Also: He who pronounces the divine Name as it is spelled out."

M. 11:1

A. Three kings and four ordinary folk have no portion in the world to come.

B. Three kings: Jeroboam, Ahab, and Manasseh.

C. R. Judah says, "Manasseh has a portion in the world to come,

D. "since it is said, 'And he prayed to him and he was entreated of him and heard his supplication and brought him again to Jerusalem into his kingdom' (2 Chr. 33:13)."

E. They said to him, "To his kingdom he brought him back, but to the life of the world to come he did not bring him back."

F. Four ordinary folk: Balaam, Doeg, Ahitophel, and Gehazi.

M. 11:2

I.

A. Why all this [that is, why deny the world to come to those listed]?

B. On Tannaite authority [it was stated], "Such a one denied the resurrection of the dead, therefore he will not have a portion in the resurrection of the dead.

C. "For all the measures [meted out by] the Holy One, blessed be he, are in accord with the principle of measure for measure."

D. For R. Samuel bar Nahmani said R. Jonathan said, "How do we know that all the measures [meted out by] the Holy One, blessed be he, accord with the principle of measure for measure?

E.   "As it is written, 'Then Elisha said, Hear you the word of the Lord. Thus says the Lord, Tomorrow about this time shall a measure of fine flour be sold for a shekel, and two measures of barley for a sekel in the gates of Samaria' (2 Kgs. 7:1).

F.   "And it is written, 'Then a lord on whose hand the king leaned answered the man of God and said, Behold, if the Lord made windows in heaven, might this thing be? And he said, Behold, you shall see it with your eyes, but shall not eat thereof' (2 Kgs. 7:2).

G.   [90B] "And it is written, 'And so it fell unto him; for the people trod him in the gate and he died' (2 Kgs. 7:20).

H.   But perhaps it was Elisha's curse that made it happen to him, for R. Judah said Rab said, "The curse of a sage, even for nothing, will come about"?

I.   If so, Scripture should have said, "They trod upon him and he died." Why say, "They trod upon him in the gate"?

J.   It was that on account of matters pertaining to [the sale of wheat and barley at] the gate [which he had denied, that he died].

II.

A.   How, on the basis of the Torah, do we know about the resurrection of the dead?

B.   As it is said, "And you shall give thereof the Lord's heave-offering to Aaron the priest" (Num. 18:28).

C.   And will Aaron live forever? And is it not the case that he did not even get to enter the Land of Israel, from the produce of which heave-offering is given?

D.   Rather, this teaches that he is destined once more to live, and the Israelites will give him heave-offering.

E.   On the basis of this verse, therefore, we see that the resurrection of the dead is a teaching of the Torah.

III.

A.   A Tannaite authority of the house of R. Ishmael [taught], "' ... to Aaron ...,' 'like Aaron. [That is to say,] just as Aaron was in the status of an associate [who ate his produce in a state of cultic cleanness even when not in the Temple], so his sons must be in the status of associates."

B.   Said R. Samuel bar Nahmani said R. Jonathan, "How on the basis of Scripture do we know that people do not give heave-offering to a priest who is in the status of an ordinary person [and not an associate]?

C.   "As it is said, 'Moreover he commanded the people who lived in Jerusalem to give the portion of the Levites, that they might hold fast to the Torah of the Lord' (2 Chr. 31:4).

D.   "Whoever holds fast to the Torah of the Lord has a portion, and whoever does not hold fast to the Torah of the Lord has no portion.:

E.   Said R. Aha bar Ada said R. Judah, "Whoever hands over heave-offering to a priest who is in the status of an ordinary person is as if he throws it in front of a lion.

F.   "Just as, in the case of a lion, it is a matter of doubt whether he will tear at the prey and eat it or not do so,

G. "so in the case of a priest who is in the status of an ordinary person, it is a matter of doubt whether he will eat it in a condition of cultic cleanness or eat it in a condition of cultic uncleanness."

H. R. Yohanan said, "[if one gives it to an improper priest], he also causes him to die, for it is said, 'And ... die therefore if they profane it' (Lev. 22:9).

I. The Tannaite authority of the house of R. Eliezer B. Jacob [taught], "One also gets him involved in the sin of guilt [of various kinds], for it is written, 'Or suffer them to bear the iniquity of trespass when they eat their holy things' (Lev. 22:16)."

IV.

A. It has been taught on Tannaite authority:

B. R. Simai says, "How on the basis of the Torah do we know about the resurrection of the dead?

C. "As it is said, 'And I also have established my covenant with [the patriarchs] to give them the land of Canaan' (Ex. 6:4).

D. "'With you' is not stated, but rather, 'with them,' indicating on the basis of the Torah that there is the resurrection of the dead."

V.

A. Minim asked Rabban Gamaliel, "How do we know that the Holy One, blessed be he, will resurrect the dead?'

B. He said to them, "It is proved from the Torah, from the Prophets, and from the Writings." But they did not accept his proofs.

C. "From the Torah: for it is written, 'And the Lord said to Moses, Behold, you shall sleep with your fathers and rise up' (Deut. 31:16)."

D. They said to him, "But perhaps the sense of the passage is, 'And the people will rise up' (Deut. 31:16)?"

E. "From the Prophets: as it is written, 'Thy dead men shall live, together with my dead body they shall arise. Awake and sing, you that live in the dust, for your dew is as the dew of herbs, and the earth shall cast out its dead' (Is. 26:19)."

F. "But perhaps that refers to the dead whom Ezekiel raised up."

G. "From the Writings, as it is written, 'And the roof of your mouth, like the best wine of my beloved, that goes down sweetly, causing the lips of those who are asleep to speak' (Song 7:9)."

H. "But perhaps this means that the dead will move their lips?"

I. That would accord with the view of R. Yohanan.

J. For R. Yohanan said in the name of R. Simeon b. Yehosedeq, "Any authority in whose name a law is stated in this world moves his lips in the grave,

K. "as it is said, 'Causing the lips of those that are asleep to speak.'"

L. [The minim would not concur in Gamaliel's view] until he cited for them the following verse: "'Which the Lord swore to your fathers to give to them' (Deut. 11:21) -- to them and not to you, so proving from the Torah that the dead will live."

M. And there are those who say that it was the following verse that he cited to them: "'But you who cleaved to the Lord you God are alive, everyone of you this day'

(Deut. 4:4). Just as on this day all of you are alive, so in the world to come all of you will live."

VI.

A.   Romans asked R. Joshua b. Hananiah, "How do we know that the Holy One will bring the dead to life and also that he knows what is going to happen in the future?"

B.   He said to them, "Both propositions derive from the following verse of Scripture:

C.   "As it is said, 'And the Lord said to Moses, Behold you shall sleep with you fathers and rise up again, and this people shall go awhoring ...' (Deut. 31:16)."

D.   "But perhaps the sense is, '[the people] will rise up and go awhoring'

E.   He said to them, "Then you have gained half of the matter, that God knows what is going to happen in the future."

VII.

A.   It has also been stated on Amoraic authority:

B.   Said R. Yohanan in the name of R. Simeon b. Yohai, "How do we know that the Holy One, blessed be he, will bring the dead to life and knows what is going to happen in the future?

C.   "As it is said, 'Behold, you shall sleep with you fathers, and ... rise again ... (Deut. 31:16)."

VIII.

A.   It has been taught on Tannaite authority:

B.   Said R. Eliezer b. R. Yose, "In this matter I proved false the books of the minim.

C.   "For they would say, 'The principle of the resurrection of the dead does not derive from the Torah.'

D.   "I said to them , 'You have forged your Torah and have gained nothing on that account.

E.   "'For you say, "The principle of the resurrection of the dead does not derive from the Torah."

F.   "'Lo, Scripture says, "[Because he has despised the Lord of the Lord ...] that soul shall be cut off completely, his iniquity shall be upon him" (Num. 15:31).

G.   ""'... shall be utterly cut off ...," in this world, in which case, at what point will "... his iniquity be upon him ..."?

H.   "'Will it not be in the world to come?'"

I.   Said R. Pappa to Abayye, "And might one not have replied to them that the words 'utterly ...' '... cut off ...,' signify the two worlds [this and the next]?"

J.   [He said to him,] "They would have answered, 'The Torah speaks in human language [and the doubling of the verb carries no meaning beyond its normal sense]'"

IX.

A.   This accords with the following Tannaite dispute:

B.   "'That soul shall be utterly cut off' -- 'shall be cut off' -- in this world, 'utterly' -- in the world to come," the words of R. Aqiba.

C.   Said R. Ishmael to him, "And has it not been said, 'He reproaches the Lord, and that soul shall be cut off' (Num. 15:31). Does this mean that there are three worlds?

D. "Rather: '... it will be cut off ...,' in this world, '... utterly ...,' in the world to come, and 'utterly cut off ...,' indicates that the Torah speaks in ordinary human language."

E. Whether from the view of R. Ishmael or of R. Aqiba, what is the meaning of the phrase, "His iniquity shall be upon him"?

F. It accords with that which has been taught on Tannaite authority:

G. Is it possible that that is the case even if he repented?

H. Scripture states, "His iniquity shall be upon him."

I. I have made the statement at hand only for a case in which "his iniquity is yet upon him" [but not if he repented].

X.

A. Queen Cleopatra asked R. Meir, saying, "I know that the dead will live, for it is written, 'And [the righteous] shall blossom forth out of your city like the grass of the earth' (Ps. 72:16).

B. "But when they rise, will they rise naked or in their clothing?"

C. He said to her, "It is an argument a fortiori based on the grain of wheat.

D. "Now if a grain of wheat, which is buried naked, comes forth in many garments, the righteous, who are buried in their garments, all the more so [will rise in many garments]."

XI.

A. Caesar said to Rabban Gamaliel, "You maintain that the dead will live. But they are dust, and can the dust live?"

B. [91A] His daughter said to him, "Allow me to answer him.

C. "There are two potters in our town, one who works with water, the other who works with clay. Which is the more impressive?"

D. He said to her, "The one who works with water."

E. She said to him, "If he works with water, will he not create even more out of clay?"

XII.

A. A Tannaite authority of the house of R. Ishmael [taught], "[Resurrection] is a matter of an argument a fortiori based on the case of a glass utensil.

B. "Now if glassware, which is the work of the breath of a mortal man, when broken, can be repaired,

C. "A mortal man, who is made by the breath of the Holy One, blessed be he, how much the more so [that he can be repaired, in the resurrection of the dead]."

XIII.

A. A min said to R. Ammi, "You say that the dead will live. But they are dust, and will the dust live?"

B. He said to him, "I shall draw a parable for you. To what may the matter be compared?

C. "It may be compared to the case of a mortal king, who said to his staff, 'Go and build a great palace for me, in a place in which there is no water or dirt [for bricks].

D.   "They went and built it, but after a while it collapsed.

E.   "He said to them, 'Go and rebuild it in a place in which there are dirt and water [for bricks].'

F.   "They said to him, 'We cannot do so.'

G.   "He became angry with them and said to them, 'In a place in which there is neither water nor dirt you were able to build, and now in a place in which there are water and dirt, how much the more so [should you be able to build it].'

H.   "And if you [the min] do not believe it, go to a valley and look at a rat, which today is half-flesh and half-dirt and tomorrow will turn into a creeping thing, made all of flesh. Will you say that it takes much time? Then go up to a mountain and see that today there is only one snail, but tomorrow it will rain and the whole of it will be filled with snails."

XIV.

A.   A min said to Gebiha, son of Pesisa, [a hunchback,] "Woe for you! You are guilty! For you say that the dead will live. Those who are alive die, and will those who are dead live?"

B.   He said to him, "Woe for you! You are guilty! For you say that the dead will not live. [Now if we] who were not [alive before birth] now live, will not those who do live all the more so [live again]?"

C.   He said to him, "Have you then called me guilty? If I stood up, I could kick you and straighten out your hump."

D.   He said to him, "If you could do that, you would be a physician, a specialist who collects enormous fees."

XV.

A.   Our rabbis have taught on Tannaite authority:

B.   On the twenty-four of Nisan the tax-farmers were dismissed from Judea and Jerusalem.

C.   When the Africans came to trial with Israel before Alexander of Macedonia, they said to him, "The land of Canaan belongs to us, for it is written, 'The land of Canaan, with the coasts thereof' (Num. 34:2), and Canaan was the father of these men."

D.   Said Gebiha, son of Pasisa, to sages, "Give me permission, and I shall go and defend the case with them before Alexander of Macedonia. If they should win out over me, say, 'You won over a perfectly common person of our group,' and if I should win out over them, say to them, 'It is the Torah of Moses that overcame you.'"

E.   They gave him permission, and he went and engaged in debate with them. He said to them, "From whence do you bring proof?"

F.   They said to him, "From the Torah."

G.   He said to them, "I too shall bring you proof only from the Torah, for it is said, 'And he said, Cursed be Canaan, a servant of servants shall he be to his brothers' (Gen. 9:25).

H.   "Now if a slave acquires property, for whom does he acquire it? And to whom is the property assigned?

I.   "And not only so, but it is quite a number of years since you have served us."

J.   Said King Alexander to them, "Give him an answer."

K.   They said to him, "Give us a span of three days time." He gave them time.

L.   They searched and did not find an answer. They forthwith fled, leaving their fields fully sown and their vineyards laden with fruit, and that year was the Sabbatical Year. [So the Israelites could enjoy the produce in a time in which they most needed it.]

XVI

A.   There was another time, [and] the Egyptians came to lay claim against Israel before Alexander of Macedonia. They said to him, "Lo, Scripture says, 'And the Lord gave the people favor in the sight of the Egyptians, and they lent them gold and precious stones' (Ex. 12:36). Give us back the silver and gold that you took from us."

B.   Said Gebiha, son of Pasisa, to sages, "Give me permission, and I shall go and defend the case with them before Alexander of Macedonia. If they should win out over me, say, 'You won over a perfectly common person of our group,' and if I should win out over them, say to them, 'It is the Torah of Moses, our master, that overcame you.'"

C.   They gave him permission, and he went and engaged in debate with them. He said to them, "From whence do you bring proof?"

D.   They said to him, "From the Torah."

E.   He said to them , "I too shall bring you proof only from the Torah, for it is said, 'Now the sojourning of the children of Israel, who dwelt in Egypt, was four hundred and thirty years' (Ex. 12:40).

F.   "Now pay us the salary of six hundred thousand people whom you enslaved in Egypt for four hundred and thirty years."

G.   Said Alexander of Macedonia to them, "Give him an answer."

H.   They said to him, "Give us time, a span of three days."

I.   He gave them time. They searched and found no answer. They forthwith fled, leaving their fields sown and their vineyards laden with fruit, and that year was the Sabbatical Year.

XVII.

A.   There was another time, [and] the children of Ishmael and the children of Keturah came to trial with the Israelites before Alexander of Macedonia. They said to him, "The land of Canaan belongs to us as well as to you, for it is written, 'Now these are the generations of Ishmael, son of Abraham' (Gen. 25:12), and it is written, 'And these are the generations of Isaac, Abraham's son' (Gen. 25:19). [Both Ishmael and Isaac have an equal claim on the land, hence so too their descendants]."

B.   Said Gebiha, son of Pasisa, to sages, "Give me permission, and I shall go and defend the case with them before Alexander of Macedonia. If they should win out over me, say, 'You won over a perfectly common person of our group,' and if I should win out over them, say to them, 'It is the Torah of Moses, our master, that overcame you.'"

C. They gave him permission, and he went and engaged in debate with them. He said to them, "From whence do you bring proof?'

D. They said to him, "From the Torah."

E. He said to them, "I too shall bring you proof only from the Torah, for it is said, 'And Abraham gave all that he had to Isaac. But to the sons of the concubines which Abraham had Abraham gave gifts' (Gen. 25:5-6).

F. "In the case of a father who gave a bequest to his sons while he was yet alive and sent them away from one another, does any one of them have a claim on the other? [Certainly not.]"

G. What were the gifts [that he gave]?

H. Said R. Jeremiah bar Abba, "This teaches that he gave them [the power of utilizing the divine] Name [for] unclean [purposes]."

XVIII.

A. Antoninus said to Rabbi, "The body and the soul both can exempt themselves from judgment.

B. "How so? The body will say, 'The soul is the one that has sinned, for from the day that it left me, lo, I am left like a silent stone in the grave.'

C. "And the soul will say, 'The body is the one that sinned. For from the day that I left it, lo, I have been flying about in the air like a bird.'"

D. He said to him, "I shall draw a parable for you. To what may the matter be likened? To the case of a mortal king who had a lovely orchard, and in it were [91B] luscious figs. He set in it two watchmen, one crippled and one blind.

E. "Said the cripple to the blind man, 'There are lucious figs that I see in the orchard. Come and carry me, and let us get some to eat. The cripple rode on the blind man and they got the figs and ate them. After a while the king said to them, 'Where are the luscious figs?'

F. "Said the cripple, 'Do I have feet to go to them?'

G. "Said the blind man, 'Do I have eyes to see?'

H. "What did the king do? He had the cripple climb onto the blind man, and he inflicted judgment on them as one.

I. "So the Holy One, blessed be he, brings the soul and places it back in the body and judges them as one, as it is said, 'He shall call to the heavens from above and to the earth, that he may judge his people' (Ps. 50:4).

J. "'He shall to call to the heavens from above' -- this is the soul.

K. "'And to the earth, that he may judge his people' -- this is the body."

XIX.

A. Said Antoninus to Rabbi, "Why does the sun rise in the east and set in the west?"

B. He said to him, "If thing were opposite, you would still ask me the same thing!"

C. He said to him, "This is what I meant to ask you: Why does it set in the west?"

D. He said, "To give a greeting to its maker, as it is written, 'And the host of the heavens make obeisance to you' (Neh. 9:6)..."

E. He said to him, "Then let it go half way through the firmament, pay its respects, and then ascend from there [eastward]."

F.   "It is because of workers and wayfarers [who need to know when the day is over]."

XX.

A.   Said Antoninus to Rabbi, "At what point is the soul placed in man? Is it at the moment that it is decreed [that the person shall be born] or when the embryo is formed?"

B.   He said to him, "From the moment when it is formed."

C.   He said to him, "Is it possible that a piece of flesh should keep for three days of it is not salted and not become rotten?

D.   "Rather, it should be from the time at which it is decreed [that the person should come into being."

E.   Said Rabbi, "This is something that Antoninus taught me, and a verse of Scripture supports his view, for it is said, 'And your decree has preserved my soul' (Job 10:12)."

XXI.

A.   And Antoninus said to Rabbi, "At what point does the impulse to do evil take hold of a man? Is it from the moment of creation or from the moment of parturition?"

B.   He said to him, "It is from the moment of creation."

C.   He said to him, "If so, the fetus will kick its mother's womb and escape. Rather, it is from the moment of parturition."

D.   Said Rabbi, "This is something that Antoninus taught me, and a verse of Scripture supports his view, for it is said, 'At the door [of the womb] sin lies in wait' (Gen. 4:7)."

XXII.

A.   R. Simeon b. Laqish contrasted [these two verses]: "It is written, 'I will gather them ... with the blind and the lame, the woman with child and her that trail travails with child together' (Jer. 31:8), and it is written, 'Then shall the lame man leap as a hart and the tongue of the dumb sing, for in the wilderness shall waters break out and streams in the desert' (Is. 35:6). How so [will the dead both retain their defects and also be healed]?

B.   "They will rise [from the grave] bearing their defects and then be healed."

XXIII.

A.   Ulla contrasted [these two verses]: "It is written, 'He will destroy death forever and the Lord God will wipe away tears from all faces' (Is. 25:9), and it is written, 'For the child shall die a hundred years old ... there shall no more thence an infant of days' (Is. 65:20).

B.   "There is no contradiction. The one speaks of Israel, the other of idolators."

C.   But what do idolators want there [Freedman, p. 612, n. 9: in the reestablished state after the resurrection]?

D.   It is to those concerning whom it is written, "And strangers shall stand and feed your flocks, and the sons of the alien shall be your plowmen and your vinedressers" (Is. 61:5)."

XXIV.

A. R. Hisda contrasted [these two verses]: "It is written, 'Then the moon shall be confounded and the sun ashamed, when the Lord of hosts shall reign' (Is 24:23), and it is written, 'Moreover the light of the moon shall be as the light of seven days' (Is 30:26).

B. "There is no contradiction. The one refers to the days of the Messiah, the other to the world to come."

C. And in the view of Samuel, who has said, "There is no difference between the world to come and the days of the messiah, except the end of the subjugation of the exilic communities of Israel"?

D. There still is no contradiction. The one speaks of the camp of the righteous, the other the camp of the Presence of God.

XXV.

A. Raba contrasted [these two verses]: "It is written, 'I kill and I make alive' (Deut. 32:"39) and it is written, 'I wound and I heal' (Deut. 32:39). [Freedman, p. 613, n. 4, 5: The former implies that one is resurrected just as he was at death, thus with blemishes, and the other implies that at the resurrection all wounds are healed].

B. "Said the Holy One, blessed be he, 'What I kill I bring to life,' and then, 'What I have wounded I heal.'"

XXVI.

A. Our rabbis have taught on Tannaite authority: "I kill and I make alive" (Deut. 32:39).

B. Is it possible to suppose that there is death for one person and life for the other, just as the world is accustomed [now]?

C. Scripture says, "I wound and I heal" (Deut. 32:39).

D. Just as wounding and healing happen to one person, so death and then resurrection happen to one person.

E. From this fact we derive an answer to those who say, "There is no evidence of the resurrection of the dead based on the teachings of the Torah."

XXVII.

A. It has been taught on Tannaite authority:

B. R. Meir says, "How on the basis of the Torah do we know about the resurrection of the dead?

C. "As it is said, 'Then shall Moses and the children of Israel sing this song to the Lord' (Ex. 15:1).

D. "What is said is not 'sang' but 'will sing,' on the basis of which there is proof from the Torah of the resurrection of the dead.

E. "Along these same lines: 'Then shall Joshua build an altar to the Lord God of Israel' (Josh. 8:30).

F. "What is said is not 'built' but 'will build,' on the basis of which there is proof from the Torah of the resurrection of the dead.

G. Then what about this verse: "Then will Solomon build a high place for Chemosh, abomination of Moab" (1Kgs. 11:7)? Does it mean that he will build it? Rather, the

Scripture treats him as though he had built it [even though he had merely thought about doing so]

XXVIII.

A. Said R. Joshua b. Levi, "How on the basis of Scripture may we prove the resurrection of the dead?

B. "As it is said, 'Blessed are those who dwell in your house, they shall ever praise you, selah' (Ps. 84:5).

C. "What is said is not 'praised you' but 'shall praise you,' on the basis of which there is proof from the Torah of the resurrection of the dead."

D. And R. Joshua b. Levi said, "Whoever recites the song [of praise] in this world will have the merit of saying it in the world to come,

E. "as it is said, 'Happy are those who dwell in you house, they shall ever praise you, selah' (Ps. 84:5)."

F. Said R. Hiyya b. Abba said R. Yohanan, "On what basis do we know about the resurrection of the dead from Scripture."

G. "As it says, 'Your watchman shall lift up the voice, with the voice together they shall sing (Is. 52:8).'"

H. What is said is not 'sang' but 'will sing' on the basis of which there is proof from the Torah of the resurrection of the dead.

I. Said R. Yohanan, "In the future all the prophets will sing in unison, as it is written, 'Your watchman shall lift up the voice, with the voice together they shall sing (Is. 57:8).'"

XXX.

A. Said R. Judah said Rab, "Whoever withholds a teaching of law from a disciple is as if he steals the inheritance of his fathers from him,

B. "for it is said, 'Moses commanded us Torah, even the inheritance of the congregation of Jacob' (Deut. 33:4).

C. "It is an inheritance destined for all Israel from the six days of creation."

D. Said R. Hana bar Bizna said R. Simeon the Pious, "Whoever withholds a teaching of law from a disciple is cursed even by the fetuses in their mothers' womb, as it is said, 'He who withholds grain [92A] will be cursed by the embryo' (Prov. 11:26), for the word at hand can only mean 'embryo,' as it is written, 'And one embryo shall be stronger than the other people' (Gen. 25:23) [referring to Jacob and Esau in the womb]

E. "And the cited word can only mean 'cursing,' as it is written, 'How shall a curse whom God has not cursed?' (Num. 23:8).

F. "And the word for grain speaks only of 'the Torah,' as it is written, 'Nourish yourselves with grain lest he be angry' (Ps. 2:12)."

G. Ulla bar Ishmael says, "They pierce him like a sieve, for here it is written, 'The people will pierce him,' (Prov. 11:26), and the word means pierce in the verse, 'And he pierced a hole in the lid of it' (2 Kgs. 12:10)."

H.   And Abayye said, "He will be like a fuller's trough [so perforated as a drainage plank]."

I.   An if he does teach a law, what is his reward?

J.   Said Raba said R. Sheshet, "He will merit blessings like those that came to Joseph, as it is said, 'But blessing shall be upon the head of the one who sells' (Prov. 11:26).

K.   "And the one who sells speaks only of Joseph, as it is said, 'And Joseph was the governor over the land, and he was the one who sells to all the people of the land' (Gen. 47:6)."

XXXI.

A.   Said R. Sheshet, "Whoever teaches Torah in this world will have the merit of teaching it in the world to come,

B.   "as it is said, 'And he who waters shall water again too' (Prov. 11:25)."

XXXII.

A.   Said Raba, "How on the basis of the Torah do we find evidence for the resurrection of the dead?

B.   "As it is said, 'Let Reuben live and not die' (Deut. 33:6).

C.   "'Let Reuben live' in this world, and 'not die', in the world to come."

D.   Rabina said, "Proof derives from here: 'And many of them that sleep in the dust of the earth shall awake, some to everlasting life, and some to shame and everlasting contempt.' (Den. 12:2)."

E.   R. Ashi said, "Proof derives from here: 'But go your way till the end be, for you shall rest and stand in your lot at the end of days' (Dan. 12:13)."

XXXIII.

A.   Said R. Eleazar, "Every authority who leads the community serenely will have the merit of leading them in the world to come, as it is said, 'For he who has mercy on them shall lead them, even by springs of water shall he guide them' (Is. 49:10)."

B.   And said R. Eleazar, "Great is knowledge, for it is set between two names [lit. letters] [of God], as it is written, 'For a God of knowledge is the Lord' (1 Sam. 2:3)."

C.   And said R. Eleazar, "Great is the sanctuary, for it is set between two names [of God], as it is written, 'You have made for yourself, O Lord, a sanctuary, O Lord, your hands have established it' (Ex. 15:17)."

D.   To this view R. Ada Qarhinaah objected, "Then how about the following: Great is vengeance, for it is set between two names [of God], as it is written, 'O God of vengeance, O Lord, O God of Vengeance, appear' (Ps. 94:1)."

E.   He said to him, "In context, that is quite so, in line with what Ulla said."

F.   For Ulla said, "What purpose is served by these two references to 'appear'? One speaks of the measure of good, the other, the measure of punishment."

G.   And said R. Eleazar, "In the case of any man who has knowledge it is as if the house of the sanctuary had been built in his own time, for this [knowledge] is set between two names of [God], and that [the Temple] likewise is set between two names of [God]."

H. And said R. Eleazar, "Any man in whom there is knowledge in the end will be rich, for it is said, 'And by knowledge shall the chambers befilled with all precious and pleasant riches' (Prov. 24:4)."

I. And said R. Eleazar, "It is forbidden to have pity on any man in whom there is no knowledge, as it is said, 'For it is a people of no understanding; therefore he that made them will not have mercy upon them, and he that formed them will show them no favor' (Is. 27:11)."

J. And said R. Eleazar, "Whoever gives his bread to someone who does not have knowledge in the end will be afflicted with sufferings, for it is said, 'They who eat your bread have laid a wound under you, there is no understanding in him' (Obad. 1:7), and the word for 'wound' can mean only suffering, as it is written, 'When Ephraim saw his sickness and Judah his suffering' [using the same word] (Hos. 5:13)."

K. And said R. Eleazar, "Any man who has no knowledge in the end will go into exile, as it is said, 'Therefore my people have gone into exile, because they have no knowledge' (Is. 5:13)."

L. And said R. Eleazar, "Any house in which words of Torah are not heard by night will be eaten up by fire, as it is said, 'All darkness is hid in his secret places; a fire not blown shall consume him; he grudges him that is left in his tabernacle' (Job 20:26).

M. "The word for 'grudges' means only a disciple of a sage, as it is written, 'And in those left [using the same root] whom the Lord shall call' (Joel 3:5). [Freedman, p. 616, n. 12: The first part of the verse, 'all darkness is hid ...,' is interpreted as, his secret places are not illumined by the study of the law; the last part, 'he grudges ...,' as, he looks with disfavor upon any student who enters his house for a meal]."

N. And said R. Eleazar, "Whoever does not give a benefit to disciples of sages from his property will see no blessing ever, as it is said, 'There is none who remains to eat it, therefore shall he not hope for prosperity' (Job 20:21).

O. "The word for 'remain' refers only to a disciple of a sage, as it is written, 'And in those left whom the Lord shall call' (Joel 3:5)."

P. And said R. Eleazar, "Anyone who does not leave a piece of bread on his table will never see a sign of blessing, as it is said, 'There be none of his food left, therefore shall he not hope for his prosperity'(Job 20:21)."

Q. But has not R. Eleazar said, "Whoever leaves pieces of bread on his table is as if he worships an idol, as it is said, 'That prepare a table for God and that furnish the drink offering to Meni' (Is. 65:11)"?

R. There is no contradiction, in the one case [the latter] a complete loaf is left alongside, and in the other case [the former], no complete loaf is left [with the crumbs].

S. And said R. Eleazar, "Whoever goes back on what he has said is as if he worships an idol.

T. "Here it is written, 'And I seem to him as a deceiver' (Gen. 27:12), and elsewhere it is written, 'They [idols] are vanity and the work of deceivers' (Jer. 10:15)."

U. And said R. Eleazar, "Whoever stares at a woman's sexual parts will find that his 'bow' is emptied out, as it is said, 'Shame shall empty you bow [of strength]' (Hab. 3:9)."

V. And said R. Eleazar, "One should always accept [things] and so endure."

W. Said R. Zira, "We too also have learned on Tannaite authority:

X. "As to a room without windows, people are not to open windows for it to examine whether or not it is afflicted with a plague-sign [M. Neg. 2:3]. [Thus the possible signs will be missed because of the obscurity of the room. Likewise humility protects one's life.]"

Y. That makes the case.

XXXIV.

A. Said R. Tabi said R. Josiah, "What is the meaning of this verse of Scripture: 'The grave and the barren womb and the earth that is not filled by water' (Prov. 30:16).

B. "What has the grave to do with the womb?

C. It is to say to you, just as the womb takes in and gives forth, so Sheol takes in and gives forth.

D. "And is it not an argument a fortiori? If in the case of the womb, in which they insert [something] in secret, the womb brings forth in loud cries, Sheol, into which [bodies] are placed with loud cries, is it not reasonable to suppose that from the grave people will be brought forth with great cries?

E. On the basis of this argument there is an answer to those who say that the doctrine of the resurrection of the dead does not derive from the Torah."

XXXV.

A. A Tannaite authority of the house of Elishah [taught], "The righteous whom the Holy One, blessed be he, is going to resurrect will not revert to dust,

B. "for it is said, 'And it shall come to pass that he that is left in Zion and he that remains in Jerusalem shall be called holy, even everyone that is written among the living in Jerusalem, (Is. 4:3).

C. "Just as the Holy One lives forever, so they shall live forever.

D. [92B] "And if you want to ask, as to those years in which the Holy One, blessed be he, will renew his world, as it is said, 'And the Lord alone shall be exalted in that day' (Is. 2:11), during that time what will the righteous do?

E. "The answer is that the Holy One, blessed be he, will make them wings like eagles, and they will flutter above the water, as it is said, 'Therefore will not fear, when the earth be moved and the mountains be carried in the midst of the sea' (Ps. 44:3).

F. "And if you should say that they will have pain [in all this], Scripture says, 'But those who wait upon the Lord shall renew their strength, they shall mount up with wings as eagles, they shall run and not be weary, they shall walk and not be faint' (Is. 40:31).

G. And should we derive [the opposite view] from the dead whom Ezekiel resurrected?

H. He accords with the view of him who said that, in truth, it was really a parable.

I. For it has been taught on Tannaite authority:

J.   R. Eliezer says, "The dead whom Ezekiel resurrected stood on their feet, recited a song, and they died."

K.   What song did they recite?

L.   "The Lord kills in righteousness and revives in mercy" (1 Sam. 2:6).

M.   R. Joshua says, "They recited this song, 'The Lord kills and makes live, he brings down to the grave and brings up' (1 Sam. 2:6)."

N.   R. Judah says, "It was true it was a parable."

O.   Said to him R. Nehemiah, "If it was true, then why a parable? And if a parable, why true? But in truth it was a parable."

P.   R. Eliezer, son of R. Yose the Galilean, says, "The dead whom Ezekiel resurrected went up to the Land of Israel and got married and produced sons and daughters."

Q.   R. Judah b. Betera stood up and said, "I am one of their grandsons, and theses are the phylacteries that father's father left me from them."

R.   And who were the dead whom Ezekiel resurrected?

S.   Said Rab, "They were the Ephraimites who reckoned the end of time and erred, as it is said, 'And the sons of Ephraim, Shuthelah and Bared his son and Tahath his son and Eladah his son and Tahath his son. And Zabad his son and Shuthelah his son and Ezzer and Elead, whom the men of Gath that were born in the land slew' (1 Chr. 7:20-21). And it is written, 'And Ephraim their father mourned many days and his brethren came to comfort him' (1 Chr. 7:22)."

T.   And Samuel said, "They were those who denied the resurrection of the dead, as it is said, 'Then he said to me, Son of man, these bones are the whole house of Israel; behold, they say, Our bones are dried and our hope is lost, we are cut off for our parts' (Ez. 37:11)."

U.   Said R. Jeremiah, 'These were the men who had not a drop of religious duties to their credit, as it is written, 'O you dry bones, hear the word of the Lord' (Ez. 37:4)."

V.   R. Isaac Nappaha said, "They were the men who had covered the sanctuary entirely with abominations and creeping things, as it is said, 'So I went in and saw, and behold, every form of creeping things and abominable beasts and all the idols of the house of Israel, portrayed upon the wall round about' (Ez. 8:10).

W.   "While [in the case of the dry bones] it is written, 'And caused me to pass by them round about' (Ez. 37:2). [Freedman, p. 620, n. 1: The identification is based on the use of 'round about' in both narratives. In his view even those who in their despair surrender themselves to abominable worship are not excluded from the bliss of resurrection.]"

X.   R. Yohanan said, "They were the dead in the valley of Dura."

Y.   And said R. Yohanan, "From the river Eshel to Rabbath is the valley of Dura. For when Nebuchadnezzar, that wicked man, exiled Israel, there were young men who outshone the sun in their beauty. Chaldean women would see them and reach orgasm [from the mere gaze]. They told their husbands and their husbands told the king. The king ordered them killed. Still, the wives would reach orgasm [merely from laying eyes on the corpses]. The king gave an order and they trampled [the corpses beyond all recognition]."

XXXVI.

A.   Our rabbis have taught on Tannaite authority:

B.   When Nebuchadnezzar, the wicked man, cast Hananiah, Mishael, and Azariah, into the fiery furnace, the Holy One, blessed be he, said to Ezekiel, "Go and raise the dead in the valley of Dura."

C.   When he had raised them, the bones came and smacked that wicked man in his face. He said, "What are these things?"

D.   They said to him, "The friend of these is raising the dead in the valley of Dura."

E.   He then said, "'How great are his signs, and how mighty his wonders. His kingdom is an everlasting kingdom, and his dominion is from generation to generation' (Dan. 3:23)."

F.   Said R. Isaac, "May liquid gold pour into the mouth of that wicked man.

G.   "For had not an angel come and slapped his mouth shut, he would have attempted to shame [by the excellence of his composition] all the songs and praises that David had recited in the book of Psalms."

XXXVII.

A.   Our rabbis have taught on Tannaite authority:

B.   Six miracles were done on that day, and these are they:

C.   the furnace floated, the furnace split open, the foundations crumbled, the image was turned over on its face, the four kings were burned up, and Ezekiel raised the dead in the valley of Dura.

D.   And all of the others were a matter of tradition, but the [miracle of the] four kings is indicated in a verse of Scripture: "Then Nebuchadnezzar the king sent to gather together the princes, the governors, and the captains, the judges, the treasurers, the counsellors, the sheriffs, and all the rulers of the provinces [to come to the dedication of the image]" (Dan. 3:2),

E.   and it is written, "There are certain Jews ..." (Deut. 3:2),

F.   and also: "And the princes, governors, and captains, and the king's counsellors, being gathered together, saw these men, upon whom the fire had no power" (Dan. 3:27).

XXXVIII.

A.   A Tannaite authority of the house of R. Eliezer b. Jacob [taught], "Even in time of danger a person should not pretend that he does not hold his high office,

B.   "For it is said, 'Then these men were bound in their coats, their hose, and their other garments' (Dan. 3:21). [Freedman, p. 621, n. 8: These were garments specially worn by men in their exalted position, and they did not doff them though cast into the furnace.]"

XXXIX.

A.   Said R. Yohanan, "[93A] The righteous are greater than ministering angels.

B.   "For it is said, 'He answered and said, Lo, I see four men loose, walking in the midst of the fire, and they are not hurt, and the form of the fourth is like the son of God' (Dan. 3:25) [Freedman, p. 621, n. 9: Thus the angel is mentioned last, as being least esteemed]."

XL.

A.   Said R. Tanhum bar Hanilai, "When Hananiah, Mishael, and Azariah went out of the fiery furnace, all the nations of the world came and slapped the enemies of Israel [that is, Israel] on their faces.

B.   "They said to them, 'You have a god such as this, and yet you bow down to an idol!'

C.   "Forthwith they said this verse, 'O Lord, righteousness belongs to you, but to us shamefacedness, as at this day' (Dan. 9:7).:

XLI.

A.   Said R. Samuel bar Nahmani said R. Jonathan, "What is the meaning of the verse of Scripture, 'I said, I will go up to the palm tree, I will take hold of the boughs thereof' (Song 7:9)?

B.   "'I said I will go up to the palm tree' refers to Israel.

C.   "But now 'I grasped' only one bough, namely, Hananiah, Mishael and Azariah."

XLII.

A.   And said R. Yohanan, "What is the meaning of the verse of Scripture, 'I saw by night, and behold a man riding upon a red horse, and he stood among the myrtle trees that were in the bottom' (Zech. 1:8).?

B.   What is the meaning of, 'I saw by night'?

C.   "The Holy One blessed be he, sought to turn the entire world into night.

D.   "'And behold, a man riding' -- 'man' refers only to the Holy One, blessed be he, as it is said, 'The Lord is a man of war, the Lord is his name' (Ex. 15:3).

E.   "'On a red horse' -- the Holy One, blessed be he, sought to turn the entire world to blood.

F.   "When, however, he saw Hananiah, Mishael, and Azariah, he cooled off, as it is said, 'And he stood among the myrtle trees that were in the deep.'

G.   "The word for 'myrtle trees' speaks only of the righteous as it is written, 'And he brought up the myrtle' (Est. 2:7) [another name of Esther].

H.   "And the word for 'deep' speaks only of Babylonia, as it is said, 'That says to the deep, be dry, and I will dry up your rivers' (Is. 44:27) [Freedman, p. 622, n. 11: To Babylon, situated in a hollow].

I.   "Forthwith, those who were filled with [red] anger turned pale, and those who were red turned white [in serenity]."

J.   Said R. Pappa, "Those proves that a white horse in a dream is a good sing."

XLIII.

A.   The rabbis [Hananiah, Mishael, and Azariah] -- where did they go?

B.   Said Rab, "They died through the working of the evil eye."

C.   And Samuel said, "They drowned in spit."

D.   And R. Yohanan, said, "They went up to the land of Israel, got married, and produced sons and daughters."

E.   This accords with a Tannaite dispute on the same issue:

F.   R. Eliezer says, "They died through the working of the evil eye."

G.   R. Joshua says, "They drowned in spit.

H. And sages say, "They went up to the land of Israel, got married, and produced sons and daughters, as it is said, 'Hear now, Joshua, the high priest, and your fellows who sit before you, for they are men wondered at' (Zech. 3:8).

I. "Who are men who are wondered at? One must say, This refers to Hananiah, Mishael, and Azariah."

J. And where did Daniel go?

K. Said Rab, "To dig a large well at Tiberias."

L. And Samuel said, "To buy fodder."

M. R. Yohanan said, "To buy pigs in Alexandria, Egypt."

N. Can this be true?

O. And have we not learned in the Mishnah:

P. Todos the physician said, "A cow or a pig does not leave Alexandria, Egypt, out of which they do not cut its womb, so that it will not breed" [M. San. 4:4].

Q. He brought little ones, to which they gave no thought.

XLIV.

A. Our rabbis have taught on Tannaite authority:

B. There were three who were involved in that scheme [to keep Daniel out of the furnace]: the Holy One, blessed be he, Daniel, and Nebuchadnezzar.

C. The Holy One, blessed be he, said, "Let Daniel leave here, so that people should not say that they were saved on account of Daniel's merit [and not on their own merit]."

D. Daniel said, "Let me get out of here, so that through me the verse will not be carried out, 'The graven images of their gods you shall burn with fire' (Dan. 7:25). [They may make a god of me.]'

E. Nebuchadnezzar said, "Let Daniel get out of here, lest people say that [the king] has burned up his god [Daniel] in fire."

F. And how do we know that [Nebuchadnezzar] worshipped [Daniel]?

G. As it is written, "Then the king Nebuchadnezzar fell upon his face and worshippped Daniel" (Dan. 2:46).

XLV.

A. Thus says the Lord of hosts, the God of Israel, of Ahab, son of Kolaiah, and of Zedekiah, son of Maaseiah, who prophesy a lie to you in my name" (Jer. 29:21).

B. And it is written, "And of them shall be taken up a curse by all the captivity of Judah who are in Babylonia, saying, The Lord make you like Zedekiah and like Ahab, whom the king of Babylonia roasted in fire" (Jer. 29:22).

C. What is said is not "whom he burned in fire" but "whom he roasted in fire."

D. Said R. Yohanan in the name of R. Simeon b. Yohai, "This teaches that he turned them into pop corn."

XLVI.

A. "Because they have committed villainy in Israel and have committed adultery with their neighbors' wives" (Jer. 29:23):

B. What did they do?

C. They went to Nebuchadnezzar's daughter. Ahab said to her, "Thus said the Lord, 'Give yourself to Zedekiah.'"

D.   And Zedekiah said, "Thus said the Lord, 'Give yourself to Ahab.'"

E.   She went and told her father. He said to her, "The god of these men hates lewdness. When they come to you, send them to me."

F.   When they came to her, she sent them to her father. He said to them, "Who said this to you?"

G.   They said, "The Holy One, blessed be he."

H.   "But lo, I asked Hananiah, Mishael, and Azariah, and they said to me, 'It is forbidden.'"

I.   They said to him, "We too are prophets like them. To them the message was not given, to us [God] gave the message."

J.   He said to him, "I want to test you in the same manner I tested Hananiah, Mishael, and Azariah."

K.   They said to him, "They were three, and we are two."

L.   He said to them, "Choose anyone you like to go with you."

M.   They said to him, "Joshua, the high priest." They were thinking, "Joshua, whose merit is great, will protect us."

N.   They seized them and tossed them into the fire. They were roasted. As to Joshua, the high priest, his clothing was singed.

O.   For it is said, "And he showed me Joshua, the high priest, standing before the angel of the Lord" (Zech. 3:1), and it is written, "'And the Lord said to Satan, the Lord rebuke you, O Satan" (Zech. 3:2).

P.   [Nebuchadnezzar] said to [Joshua], "I know that you are righteous. But what is the reason that the fire had any power whatsoever over you? Over Hananiah, Mishael, and Azariah the fire had no power at all."

Q.   He said to him, "They were three, and I am only one."

R.   He said to him, "Lo, Abraham was only one."

S.   "But there were no wicked men with him, and the fire was not given power to burn him, while in my case, I was joined with wicked men, so the fire had the power to burn me."

T.   This is in line with what people say, "If there are two dry brands and one wet one, the dry ones kindle the wet one."

U.   Why was he punished in this way?

V.   Said R. Pappa, "Because his sons had married wives who were not fit for marriage into the priesthood and he did not object, as it is said, 'Now Joshua was clothed with filthy clothing' (Zech. 3:3).

W.   "Now was it Joshua's way to dress in filthy garments? Rather this teaches that his sons had married women who were not worthy to marry into the priesthood, and he did not object."

XLVII.

A.   Said R. Tanhum, "In Sepphoris, bar Qappara interpreted the following verse: 'These six [grains] of barley gave he to me' (Ruth 3:17).

B.   "What are the six of barley? If we should say that they were actually six of barley, was it the way of Boaz to give out a gift of only six barley grains?

C.   "[93B] Rather it must have been six <u>seahs</u> of barley?

D.   "And is it the way of a woman to carry six <u>seahs</u>?

E.   "Rather, this formed an omen to her that six sons are destined to come forth from her, each of whom would receive six blessings, and these are they: David, the Messiah, Daniel, Hananiah, Mishael, and Azariah.

F.   "David, as it is written, 'Then answered one of the servants and said, Behold I have seen the son of Jesse, the Bethlehemite, who is cunning in playing and a mighty, valiant man, and a man of war, and understanding in matters, and a handsome man, and the Lord is with him' (1 Sam. 16:18). [Freedman, p. 626, n. 1: The six epithets, <u>viz.</u>, cunning in playing, mighty, valiant, etc., are regarded as blessings applicable to each of the six persons mentioned]."

G.   And said R. Judah said Rab, "The entire verse was stated by Doeg only as vicious gossip.

H.   "'Cunning in playing' -- skillful in asking questions;

I.   "'a mighty valiant man' -- skillful in answering them;

J.   "'a man of war' -- skillful in the battle of Torah-learning;

K.   "'understanding in matters' -- understanding in learning one thing from another;

L.   "'and a comely person' -- who argues for his position with considerable reasons;

M.   "'and the Lord is with him' -- the law everywhere follows his opinion.

N.   "'And in all regards,' he said to him, 'my son Jonathan is his equal.'

O.   "When he said, 'The Lord is with him' -- something which did not apply to himself -- he was humbled and envied him.

P.   "For of Saul it is written, 'And wherever he turned about, he vexed them' (1 Sam. 14:47), while of David it is written, 'And wherever he turned about he prospered.'"

Q.   How do we know that this was Doeg?

R.   It is written here, "then one of the servants answered," meaning, "one who was distinguished from the other young men," and there it is written, "Now a man of the servants of Saul was there that day, detained before the Lord, and his name was Doeg, an Edomite, head herdmen that belonged to Saul" (1 Sam. 21:8). [Freedman, p. 626, n. 8: Thus "a man" that is, "one distinguished" is the epithet applied to Doeg.]

S.   [Reverting to Bar Qappara's statement:] "The Messiah, as it is written, 'And the spirit of the Lord shall rest upon him, the spirit of wisdom and understanding, the spirit of counsel and might, the spirit of knowledge of the fear of the Lord, and shall make him of quick understanding in the fear of the Lord' (Is. 11:2-3)."

T.   And R. Alexandri said, "The use of the words 'for quick understanding' indicates that he loaded him down with good deeds and suffering as a mill [which uses the same letters] is loaded down."

U.   [Explaining the same word, now with reference to the formation of the letters of the word to mean "smell,"] said Raba, "[The Messiah] smells and judges, for it is written, 'And he shall judge not after the sight of his eyes nor reprove after the hearing of his ears, yet with righteousness shall he judge the poor' (Ex. 11:3-4)."

V.   Bar Koziba ruled for two and a half years. He said to rabbis, "I am the Messiah."

W. They said to him, "In the case of the Messiah it is written that he smells a man and judges. Let us see whether you can smell a man and judge."

X. When they saw that he could not smell a man and judge, they killed him.

Y. [Reverting again to Bar Qappara's statement:] "Daniel, Hananiah, Mishael, and Azariah, as it is written, 'In whom there was no blemish, but well favored, skillful in all wisdom, and cunning in knowledge, understanding science, and such as had ability in them to stand in the king's palace, and whom they might teach the learning and the tongue of the Chaldeans' (Dan. 1:4)."

Z. What is the meaning of, "In whom there was no blemish" (Dan. 1:4)?

AA. Said R. Hama bar Hanina, "Even the scar made by bleeding was not on them."

BB. What is the meaning of, "And such as had ability in them to stand in the king's palace" (Dan. 1:3)?

CC. Said R. Hama in the name of R. Hanina, "This teaches us that they restrained themselves from laughing and chatting, from sleeping, and they held themselves in when they had to attend to the call of nature, on account of the reverence owing to the king."

XLVIII.

A. "Now among these were of the children of Judah, Daniel, Hananiah, Mishael, and Azariah" (Dan. 1:6):

B. Said R. Eleazar, "All of them came from the children of Judah."

C. And R. Samuel bar Nahmani said, "Daniel came from the children of Judah, but Hananiah, Mishael, and Azariah came from the other tribes."

XLIX.

A. "And of your sons which shall issue from you, which you shall beget, shall they take away, and they shall be eunuchs in the palace of the king of Babylonia" (2 Kgs. 20:18):

B. What are these "eunuchs"?

C. Rab said, "Literally, eunuchs."

D. And R. Hanina said, "The sense is that idolatry was castrated [i.e. made sterile] in their time."

E. In the view of him who has said that idolatry was castrated in their time, that is in line with the verse of Scripture, "And there is no hurt in them" (Dan. 3:25).

F. But in the view of him who says that "eunuch" is in its literal sense, what is the meaning of, "And there is no hurt in them" (Dan. 3:25) [Since they had been castrated]?

G. It is that the fire did them no injury.

H. But has it not been written, "Nor the smell of fire had passed on them" (Dan. 3:27)?

I. There was neither injury nor the smell of fire.

J. In the view of him who has said that idolatry was made a eunuch in their time, that is in line with the following verse: "For thus says the Lord to the eunuchs who keep my Sabbaths" (Is. 56:4).

K. But in the view of him who says that eunuch is in its literal sense, would Scripture dwell on what is embarrassing to the righteous?

L.   Among the group were both sorts [actual eunuchs, as well as those in whose day were idols sterilized].

M.   Now there is no difficulty for the view of him who says that they were literally eunuchs in the following verse: "Even to them will I give in my house and within my walls a place and a name better than of sons and of daughters" (Is. 56:5).

N.   But in the view of the one who says that the sense is that in their day idolatry was made a eunuch, what is the sense of the statement, "Better than of sons and of daughters"?

O.   Said R. Nahman bar Isaac, "Better than the sons whom they had already had and who had died."

P.   What is the meaning of the statement, "I shall give them an everlasting name, that shall not be cut off" (Is. 56:5)?

Q.   Said R. Tanhum, "Bar Qappara interpreted the matter in Sepphoris: 'This refers to the book of Daniel, which is called by his name."

L.

A.   Now since whatever concerns Ezra was stated by Nehemiah b. Hachlia, what is the reason that the book was not called by his name?

B.   Said R. Jeremiah bar Abba, "It is because he took pride in himself, as it is written, 'Think up on me for good, my God' (Neh. 5:19)."

C.   David also made such a statement, "Remember me, Lord, with the favor that you bear for your people, visit me with your salvation" (Ps. 106:4).

D.   It was supplication that David sought.

E.   R. Joseph said, "It was because [Nehemiah] had spoken disparagingly about his predecessors, as it is said, 'But the former governors who had been before me were chargeable unto the people and had taken of them bread and wine, beside forty shekels of silver' (Neh. 5:15).

F.   "Furthermore, he spoke in this way even of Daniel, who was greater than he was."

G.   And how do we know that Daniel was greater than he was?

H.   As it is written, "And I Daniel alone saw the vision, for the men that were with me did not see the vision, but a great quaking fell upon them, so that they fled to hide themselves" (Dan. 10:7).

I.   "For the men that were with me did not see the vision" (Dan. 10:7):

J.   Who were they?

K.   R. Jeremiah (some say, R. Hiyya b. Abba) said, "They were Haggai, Zechariah, and Malachi [94A]."

L.   They were greater than he, and he was greater than they.

M.   They were greater than he, for they were prophets, and he was not a prophet.

N.   And he was greater than they, for he saw a vision and they did not see a vision.

O.   And since they did not see it, what is the reason that they were frightened?

P.   Even though they did not see it, their star saw it.

Q.   Said Rabina, "That yields the conclusion that one who is afraid even though he saw nothing is so because his star saw something.

R. "What is his remedy?

S. "Let him jump four cubits from where he is standing.

T. "Or let him recite the Shema.

U. "But if he is standing in an unclean place, let him say, 'The butcher's goat is fatter than I am.'"

LI.

A. "Of the increase of his government and peace there shall be no end" (Is. 9:6):

B. R. Tanhum said, "In Sepphoris, Bar Qappara expounded this verse as follows:

C. "'On what account is every M in the middle of a word open, but the one in the word "increase" is closed?

D. "'The Holy One, blessed be he, proposed to make Hezekiah Messiah, and Sennacherib into Gog and Magog.

E. "'The attribute of justice said before the Holy One, blessed be he, "Lord of the world, Now if David, king of Israel, who recited how many songs and praises before you, you did not make Messiah, Hezekiah, for whom you have done all these miracles, and who did not recite a song before you, surely should not be made Messiah."

F. "On what account the M was closed.

G. "'Forthwith, the earth went and said before him, "Lord of the world, I shall say a song before you in the place of this righteous man, so you make him Messiah."

H. "'The earth went and said a song before him, as it is said, "From the uttermost part of the earth we have heard songs, even glory to the righteous" (Is. 24:16).

I. "'Said the prince of the world before him, "Lord of the world, [The earth] has carried out your wish in behalf of this righteous man."

J. "'An echo went forth and said, "It is my secret, it is my secret" (Ps. 24:16).

K. "'Said the prophet, "Woe is me, woe is me" (Is. 24:16). How long?'

L. How dealt treacherously, yes, the treacherous dealers have dealt very treacherously" (Is. 24:16).'"

M. And said Raba, and some say, R. Isaac, "Until spoilers come, and those who spoil spoilers."

LII.

A. "The burden of Dumah. He calls to me out of Seir, Watchman, what of the night? Watchman, what of the night?" (Is. 21:11):

B. Said R. Yohanan, "That angel who is appointed over the souls is named Dumah. All the souls gathered to Dumah, and said to him, "'Watchman, what of the night? Watchman, what of the night?' (Is. 21:11).

C. "Said the watchman, 'The morning comes and also the night, if you will inquire, inquire, return, come' (Is. 21:11)."

LIII.

A. A Tannaite authority in the name of R. Pappias [said], "It was a shame for Hezekiah and his associates that they did not recite a song, until the earth opened and said a song, as it is said, 'From the uttermost part of the earth have we hard songs, even glory to the righteous' (Is. 24:16)."

B. Along these same lines you may say, "And Jethro said, Blessed be the Lord who has delivered you" (Ex. 18:10).

C. A Tannaite authority in the name of R. Pappias said, "It was a shame for Moses and the six hundred thousand, that they did not say, 'Blessed ...,' until Jethro came and said, 'Blessed is the Lord.'"

LIV.

A. And Jethro rejoiced" (Ex. 18:9):

B. Rab and Samuel --

C. Rab said, "It was that he passed a sharp knife across his flesh [circumcizing himself]."

D. And Samuel said, "All his flesh became goose-pimples [because of the destruction of the Egyptians]."

E. Said Rab, "That is in line with what people say, 'As to a proselyte, up to the tenth generation do not insult an Aramaean [since he retains his former loyalty, as Jethro did to the Egyptians]."

LV.

A. "Therefore shall the Lord, the Lord of hosts, send among his fat ones leanness" (Is. 10:16):

B. What is "among his fat ones leanness"?

C. Said the Holy One, blessed be he, "Let Hezekiah come, who has eight names, and exact punishment from Sennacherib, who has eight names."

D. As to Hezekiah, it is written, "For unto us a child is born, unto us a son is given, and the government shall be upon his shoulder, and his name shall be called wonderful, counsellor, mighty, judge, everlasting, father, prince, and peace" (Is. 9:5).

E. And there is yet the name "Hezekiah" too?

F. [Hezekiah] means "Whom God has strengthened."

G. Another matter: it is Hezekiah, for he strengthened Israel for their father in heaven.

H. As to Senacherib, it is written, "Tiglath-pileser" (2 Kgs. 15:29), "Pilneser" (1 Chr. 5:26), "Shalmeneser" (2 Kgs. 17:3), "Pul" (2 Kgs. 15:29), "Sargon" (Is. 20:1), "Asnapper" (Ezra 4:10), "Rabba" (Ezra 4:10), and "Yaqqira" (Ezra 4:10).

I. And there is yet the name "Sennacherib" too.

J. It bears the sense that his conversation is contentious.

K. Another matter: He talked and babbled against the Most High.

L. [Referring to Ezra 4:10] said R. Yohanan, "On what account did that wicked man have the merit of being called 'the great and noble Asnapper' (Ezra 4:10)?

M. "Because he did not speak critically of the land of Israel, as it is said, 'Until I come and take you away to a land like your own land' (2 Kgs. 18:32)."

N. Rab and Samuel: One said he was a shrewd king, and the other said he was a foolish king.

O. In the view of him who said that he was a shrewd king, if he had said, "A land that is better than yours," they would have said to him, "You are lying to us."

P. In the view of him who said that he was a foolish king, If [the land to which they would be exiled was no better than their own], then what value was there [in their agreeing to go].

Q. Where did he exile them?

R. Mar Zutra said, "To Africa."

S. R. Hanina said, "To the mountains of Salug."

T. But [for its part], the Israelites spoke critically about the land of Israel. When they came to Shush, they said, "This is the same as our land."

U. When they got to Elmin, they said, "It is like the house of eternities [Jerusalem]."

V. When they go to Shush Tere, they said, "This is twice as good."

LVI.

A. "And beneath his glory shall he kindle a burning like the burning of a fire" (Is. 10:16):

B. Said R. Yohanan, "Under his glory, but not actually his glory."

C. That is in line with how R. Yohanan called his clothing "Those who do me honor."

D. R. Eleazar said, "'Under his glory' literally, just as is the burning of the sons of Aaron.

E. "Just as in that case it was a burning of the soul while the body endured, so here there is a burning of the soul while the body remained intact."

LVII.

A. A Tannaite authority in the name of R. Joshua b. Qorhah taught, "Since Pharaoh blasphemed personally, the Holy One, blessed be he, exacted punishment from him personally.

B. "Since Sennacherib blasphemed [94B] through a messenger, the Holy One, blessed be he, exacted punishment from him through a messenger.

C. "In the case of Pharaoh, it is written, "Who is the Lord, that I should obey his voice' (Ex. 5:2).

D. "The Holy One, blessed be he, exacted punishment from him personally, as it is written, 'And the Lord overthrew the Egyptians in the midst of the sea' (Ex. 14:27), and it also is written, 'You did walk through the sea with your horses' (Hab. 3:15).

E. "In the case of Sennacherib, it is written, 'By your messengers you have reproached the Lord' (2 Kgs. 19:23), so the Holy One, blessed be he, exacted punishment from him through a messenger, as it is written, 'And the angel of the Lord went out and smote in the camp of the Assyrians a hundred fourscore and five thousand' (2 Kgs. 19:23)."

LVIII.

A. R. Hanina b. Pappa contrasted two verses: "It is written, 'I will enter the height of his border' (Is. 37:24), and it is further written, 'I will enter into the lodgings of his borders' (2 Kgs. 19:23).

B. "Said that wicked man, 'First I shall destroy the lower dwelling, and afterward I shall destroy the upper dwelling."

LIX.

A.   Said R. Joshua b. Levi, "What is the meaning of the verse of Scripture, 'Am I now come up without the Lord against this place to destroy it? The Lord said to me, Go up against this land and destroy it' (2 Kgs. 18:25).

B.   "What is the sense of the passage?

C.   "He had heard the prophet, who had said, 'Since this people refuses the waters of Shiloah that go softly and rejoice in Rezina and Ramaliah's son, [now therefore behold the Lord brings up upon them the waters of the river, strong and many, even the king of Assyria and all his glory, and he shall come up over all his channels and go over all his banks]' (Is. 8:6). [Freedman, p. 635, n. 3: This was understood by Sennacherib as an order to possess Jerusalem.]"

D.   Said R. Joseph, "Were it not for the following rendering of this verse of Scripture, I should not have understood what it meant: 'Because this people is tired of the rule of the house of David, which rules them mildly, like the waters of Shiloah, which flow gently, and have preferred Razin and the son of Ramaliah.'"

LX.

A.   Said R. Yohanan, "What is the meaning of this verse: 'The curse of the Lord is in the house of the wicked, but he blesses the habitation of the just' (Prov. 3:33)?

B.   "'The curse of the Lord is in the house of the wicked' refers to Pekah, son of Ramaliah, who would eat forty seahs of pigeons for desert.

C.   "'But he blesses the habitation of the just' refers to Hezekiah, king of Judea, who would eat a litra of vegetables for a whole meal."

LXI.

A.   "Now therefore behold, the Lord brings up upon them the waters of the river, strong and many, even the king of Assyria and all his glory" (Is. 8:7).

B.   And it is written, "And he shall pass through Judea, he shall overflow and go over, he shall reach even to the neck" (Is. 8:8).

C.   Then why was [Sennacherib] punished?

D.   The prophet prophesied about the ten tribes, but [Sennacherib] gave mind to the whole of Jerusalem.

E.   The prophet came to him and said to him, "'For the wearied is not for the oppressor' (Is. 8:23)."

F.   Said R. Eleazar b. R. Berekhiah, "The people that is weary because of its devotion to Torah-study will not be given into the power of the one that oppresses it."

LXII.

A.   What is the meaning of this verse: "When aforetime the land of Zebulun and the land of Naphtali lightened its burden, but in later times it was made heavy by the way of the sea, beyond Jordan, in Galilee of the nations" (Is. 8:23)?

B.   It was not like the early generations, who made the yoke of the Torah light for themselves, but the later generations, who made the yoke of the Torah heavy for themselves.

C.   And these were worthy that a miracle should be done for them, just as was done for those who passed through the sea and trampled over the Jordan.

D.   If Sennacherib should repent, well and good, but if not, I shall make him into dung among the nations [a play on the latters GLL, the word for Galilee and dung].

LXIII.

A.   "After these things, and the truth thereof, Sennacherib, king of Assyria, came and entered Judea and encamped against the fortified cities and thought to win them for himself" (2 Chr. 32:1):

B.   Such a recompense [to Hezekiah] for such a gift? [Freedman, p. 636, n. 9: The previous verse relates that Hezekiah turned earnestly to the service of God. Was then Sennacherib's invasion his just reward?]

C.   What is the sense of, "After these things and the truth thereof" (2 Chr. 32:1)?

D.   Said Rabina, "After the Holy One, blessed be he, went and took an oath, saying 'If I say to Hezekiah that I am going to bring Sennacherib and hand him over to you, he will say to me, "I don't want him and I don't want his terror either."'"

E.   "So the Holy One, blessed be he, went ahead and took an oath ahead of time that he would bring him, as it is said, 'The Lord of hosts has sworn, saying, Surely as I have thought, so shall it come to pass, and as I have purposed, so shall it stand, that I will break the Assyrian in my land and upon my mountains tread him under foot; then shall his yoke depart from off them, and his burden depart from off their shoulders' (Is. 14:24-25)."

F.   Said R. Yohanan, "Said the Holy One, blessed be he, 'Let Sennacherib and his company come and serve as a crib for Hezekiah and his company.'"

LXIV.

A.   "And it shall come to pass in that day that his burden shall be taken away from off your shoulders and his yoke from off your neck, and the yoke shall be destroyed because of the oil" (Is. 10:27):

B.   Said R. Isaac Nappaha, "The yoke of Sennacherib will be destroyed because of the oil of Hezekiah, which he would kindle in the synagogues and school houses.

C.   "What did [Hezekiah] do? He affixed a sword at the door of the school house and said, 'Whoever does not take up study of the Torah will be pierced by this sword.'

D.   "They searched from Dan to Beer Sheba and found no ignoramus, from Gabbath to Antipatris and found no boy or girl, no man or woman, not expert in the laws of uncleanness and cleanness.

E.   "Concerning that generation Scripture says, 'And it shall come to pass in that day that a man shall nourish a young cow and two sheep' (Is. 7:21), and it says, 'And it shall come to pass on that day that every place shall be, where there were a thousand vines at a thousand silverlings, it shall even be for briers and thorns' (Is. 7:23).

F.   "Even though 'a thousand vines are worth a thousand pieces of silver,' yet it shall be 'for briers and thorns.'"

LXV.

A.   "And your spoil shall be gathered like the gathering of a caterpillar" (Is. 33:4):

B.   Said the prophet to Israel, "Gather your spoil."

C.   They said to him, "Is it for individual spoil or for sharing?"

D.   He said to them, "'Like the gathering of a caterpillar' (Is. 33:4): Just as in the gathering of a caterpillar it is each one for himself, so in your spoil it is each one for himself."

E.   They said to him, "And is not the money of the ten tribes mixed up with it?"

F.   He said to them, "'As the watering of pools does he water it' (Is. 33:4): Just as pools of water serve to raise up a human being from a state of uncleanness to a state of cleanness, so the money that has belonged to Israelites, once it has fallen into the hands of idolators, forthwith imparts cleanness. [Freedman, p. 638, n. 5: When the Israelites have abandoned all hope of the return thereof other Jews may take it.]"

LXVI.

A.   Said R. Huna, "That wicked man [Sennacherib] made ten marches that day,

B.   "as it is said, 'He is come to Aiath, he is passed at Migron, at Michmash he has laid up his carriages, they are gone over the passage, they have taken up their lodgings at Geba, Ramah is afraid, Gibeah of Saul is fled, Lift up your voice, O daughter of Gallim, cause it to be heard to Laish, O poor Anathoth, Madmenah is removed, the inhabitants of Gebim gather themselves to flee' (Is. 10:28-31)."

C.   But they are more than [ten]?

D.   [Huna responded,] "Life up your voice, O daughter of Gallim," was said by the prophet to the congregation of Israel [as follows]:

E.   "'Life up your voice, O daughter of Gallim' -- daughter of Abraham, Isaac, and Jacob, who carried out religious duties like the waves of the ocean [in number].

F.   "'Cause it to be heard to Laish" -- from this one do not fear, but fear the wicked Nebuchadnezzar, who is compared to a lion.

G.   "For it is written, 'The lion is come up from his thicket' (Jer. 4:7)."

H.   What is [95A] the sense of "O poor Anathoth" (Is. 10:31)?

I.   Jeremiah b. Hilkiah is destined to come up from Anathoth and to prophesy, as it is written, "The words of Jeremiah, son of Hilkiah, of the priests who were in Anathoth in the land of Benjamin" (Jer. 1:1).

J.   But is there any parallel? There [Nebuchadnezzar] is called a lion, but what is written here is laish [another word for lion].

K.   Said R. Yohanan, "A lion is called six things: ari (Jer. 4:7), kefir (Gen. 49:9), labi (Gen. 39:9), laish (Judges 14:5), shahal (Ps. 91:13), and shahaz (Job 28:8)."

L.   If so, they are fewer [than ten]?

M.   "They are gone over" [and] "the passage" add up to two [more].

LXVII.

A.   What is the meaning of the statement, "As yet shall be halt at Nob that day" (Is. 10:32)?

B.   Said R. Huna, "That day alone remained [for the punishment of] the sin committed at Nob [Sam. 22:17-19]. [Freedman, p. 639, n. 9: When the priests of Nob were massacred. God set a term for punishment, of which that day was the last.]

C.   "The Chaldean [soothsayers] said to him, 'If you go now, you will overpower it, and if not, you will not overpower it.'

D. "A journey that should require ten days required only one day.

E. "When they got to Jerusalem, they piled up mattresses so that, when he climbed up and took up his position on the top one, he could see Jerusalem. When he saw it, it looked tiny in his eyes. He said, 'Is this really the city of Jerusalem, on account of which I moved all my troops and came up and conquered the entire province? Is it not smaller and weaker than all of the cities of the peoples that by my power I have already conquered?!'

F. "He went and got up and shook his head and waved his hand backward and forward, with contempt, toward the mountain of the house of the sanctuary in Zion and toward the courts of Jerusalem.'

G. "They said, 'Let us raise a hand against it right now.'

H. "He said to them, 'You are tired. Tomorrow each one of your bring me a stone and we shall stone it [Freedman, following Jastrow].'

I. "Forthwith: 'And it came to pass that night that the angel of the Lord went out and smote in the camp of the Assyrians a hundred fourscore and five thousand, and when they arose early in the morning, behold they were all dead corpses' (2 Kgs. 19:35)."

J. Said R. Pappa, "That is in line with what people say: 'Justice delayed is justice denied.'"

LXVIII.

A. "And Ishbi-benob, who was of the sons of the giant, the weight of whose spear weighed three hundred shekels of brass in weight, being girded with a new sword, thought to have slain David" (2 Sam. 21:16):

B. What is the sense of "Ishbi-be-nob"?

C. Said R. Judah said Rab, "It was a man [ish] who came on account of the matter of [the sin committed at] Nob.

D. "Said the Holy One, blessed be he, to David, 'How long will the sin committed [against Nob] be concealed in your hand. On your account, Nob was put to death, the city of priests, on your account, Doeg the Edomite was sent into exile; on your account, Saul and his three sons were killed.

E. "'Do you want you descendents to be wiped out, or do you want to be handed over into the power of an enemy?'

F. "He said to him, 'Lord of the world, It is better that I be handed over to an enemy but that my descendents not be wiped out.'"

G. One day, when he went out to Sekhor Bizzae [Freedman, p. 640, n. 7: literally: "your seed to cease"], Satan appeared to him in the form of a deer. He shot an arrow at it, and the arrow did not reach [the deer]. It drew him until he came to the land of the Philistines. When Ishbi-benob saw him, he said, 'This is the one who killed Goliath, my brother."

H. He bound him, doubled him up, and threw him under an olive press. A miracle was done for [David], in that the earth underneath him became soft. This is in line with the following verse of Scripture: "You have enlarged my steps under me, that my feet did not slip" (Ps. 18:37).

I.   That day was the eve of the Sabbath [Friday]. Abishai ben Zeruiah [David's nephew] was washing his head in four casks of water. He saw stains of blood [in the water].

J.   Some say a dove came and slapped its wings before him.

K.   He said, "The congregation of Israel is compared to a dove, for it is said, 'You are as the wings of a dove covered with silver' (Ps. 68:14). This then bears the inference that David, king of Israel, is in trouble."

L.   He came to his house and did not find him. He said, "We have learned in the Mishnah: People are not to ride on his horse or sit on his throne or hand his sceptre [M. San. 2:5].

M.   "What is the rule about a time of crisis?"

N.   He came and asked at the school house. They said to him, "In a time of crisis it is all right."

O.   He mounted his mule and rode off and the earth crumbled up [to make the journey quick]. While he was riding along, he saw Orpah, mother of [Ishbi-benob] who was spinning. When she saw him, she broke off the spindle." He threw it at her head and killed her.

P.   When Ishbi-benob saw him, he said, "Now there are two against me, and they will kill me."

Q.   He threw David up and stuck his spear [into the ground], saying, "Let him fall on it and be killed."

R.   [Abishai] shouted the Name [of God], so David was suspended between heaven and earth.

S.   But why should David himself not have said it?

T.   Because one who is bound cannot free himself from his chains.

U.   He said to him, "What do you want here?"

V.   He said to him, "This is what the Holy One, blessed be he, has said to me, and this is what I said to him."

W.   He said to him, "Take back your prayer. May your son's son sell wax, but may you not suffer."

X.   He said to him, "If so, help me."

Y.   That is in accord with what is written, "But Abishai, son of Zeruiah, helped him" (2 Sam. 21:17).

Z.   Said R. Judah said Rab, "He helped him in prayer."

AA.   Abishai pronounced the Name and brought [David] down.

BB.   He pursued the two of them. When they came to Kubi, they said, "Let us stand against him."

CC.   When they came to Bethre, they said, "Will two whelps kill a lion?"

DD.   They said to him, "Go find Orpah, your mother, in the grave."

EE.   When they mentioned the name of his mother to him, he grew weak, and they killed him.

FF.   So it is written, "Then the men of David swore to him, saying, You shall no more go out with us to battle, that you not put out the light of Israel" (2 Sam. 21:17).

LXIX.

A.   Our rabbis have taught on Tannaite authority:

B.   For three did the earth fold up [to make their journey quicker]: Eliezer, Abraham's servant, Jacob our father, and Abishai b. Zeruiah.

C.   As to Abishai, son of Zeruiah, it is as we have just said.

D.   As to Eliezer, Abraham's servant, it is written, "And I came this day to the well" (Gen. 24:42), meaning that that very day he had set out.

E.   As to Jacob, our father, [95B] as it is written, "And Jacob went out from Beer Sheba and went to Haran" (Gen. 28:10), and it is said, "And he lighted upon a certain place and tarried there all night, because the sun had set" (Gen. 28:11).

F.   When he got to Haran, he said, "Is it possible that I have passed through a place in which my ancestors have prayed, and I did not say a prayer there?"

G.   He wanted to go back. As soon as the thought of going back had entered his mind, the earth folded up for him. Forthwith: "He lighted upon a place" (Gen. 28:11).

H.   Another matter: "Lighting upon..." refers only to praying, as it is written, "Therefore do not pray for this people or lift up a cry or prayer for them nor make intercession [using the same root] to me" (Jer. 7:16).

I.   "And he tarried there all night, because the sun had set" (Gen. 28:10):

J.   After he had prayed, he wanted to go back. Said the Holy One, blessed be he, "This righteous man has come to the house of my dwelling. Should he go forth without spending the night?"

K.   Forthwith the sun set. That is in line with what is written, "And as he passed over Penuel, the sun rose for him" (Gen. 32:32).

L.   And did it rise only for him? And did not it not rise for the entire world?

M.   "But," said R. Isaac, "Since the sun had set [too soon] on his account, it also rose on his account."

LXX.

A.   And how do we know that the seed of David ceased [cf. LXVIII E]?

B.   As it is written, "And when Athaliah, mother of Ahaziah, saw that her son was dead, she rose and destroyed all the royal seed" (2 Kgs. 11:1).

C.   And lo, Joash remained. Also Abiathar remained, for it is written, "And one of the sons of Ahimelech, son of Ahitub, named Abiathar, escaped" (1 Sam. 22:20).

D.   Said R. Judah said Rab, "If Abiathar were not left to Ahimelech, son of Ahitub, neither shred nor remnant of the seed of David would have survived."

LXXI.

A.   Said R. Judah said Rab, "The wicked Sennacherib came against them with forty-five thousand men, sons of kings seated on golden chariots, with their concubines and whores, and with eighty thousand mighty soldiers, garbed in coats of mail, and sixty thousand swordsmen running before him, and the rest cavalry.

B.   And so they came against Abraham, and in the age to come so they will come with Gog and Magog.

C.   On Tannaite authority it was taught: The length of his camp was four hundred parasangs, and the breadth of his horses, neck to neck, was forty parasangs, and the total of his army was two million six hundred thousand less one.

D.   Abayye asked, "Does this mean less one myriad or one thousand?"

E.   The question stands.

LXXII.

A.   It was taught on Tannaite authority:

B.   The first ones crossed by swimming, as it is said, "He shall overflow and go over" (Is. 8:8).

C.   The middle ones crossed standing up, as it is said, "He shall reach even to the neck" (Is. 8:8).

D.   The last group brought up the dirt [of the river] with their feet and so found no water in the river to drink, so that they had to bring them water from some other place, which they drank, as it is said, "I have digged and drunk water" (Is. 37:25).

E.   [How could the army have been so large,] for is it not written, "Then the angel of the Lord went forth and smote in the camp of the Assyrians a hundred and fourscore and five thousand, and when they arose early in the morning, behold, they were all dead corpses" (Is. 37:36)?

F.   Said R. Abbahu, "Those were the heads of the troops."

G.   Said R. Ashi, "Read the text closely with the same result, for it is written, '[therefore shall the Lord... send] among his fat ones leanness [i.e. the cream of the crop].

H.   Said Rabina, "Read the text closely with the same result; for it is written, 'And the Lord sent an angel, which cut off all the men of valor, and the leaders and the princes in the camp of the king of Assyria. So he returned with shamefacedness to his own land, and when he entered into the house of his god, they that came forth of his own bowels slew him there with the sword" (2 Chr. 32:21).

I.   This proves [that the reference is only to the leaders (Freedman, p. 644, n. 6)].

LXXIII.

A.   How did [the angel] smite [the army]?

B.   R. Eliezer says, "He hit them with his hand, as it is said, 'And Israel saw the great hand' (Ex. 14:31), that was destined to exact punishment of Sennacherib."

C.   R. Joshua says, "He hit them with a finger, as it is said, 'Then the magicians said to Pharaoh, This is the finger of God' (Ex. 8:14), that finger that was destined to exact punishment of Sennacherib."

D.   R. Eleazar, son of R. Yose the Galilean, says, "Said the Holy One, blessed be he, to Gabriel, 'Is your sickle sharpened?'

E.   "He said before him, 'Lord of the world, it has been ready and sharpened since the six days of creation, as it is said, 'For they fled from the swords, from the sharpened sword' (Is. 21:15)."

F.   R. Simeon b. Yohai says, "That season was the time for the ripening of the produce. Said the Holy One, blessed be he, to Gabriel, When you go forth to ripen the produce, attack them, as it is said, 'As he passes, he shall take you, for morning by morning shall he pass by, by day and by night, and it shall be a sheer terror to understand the report' (Is. 28:19)."

G.   Said R. Pappa, "This is in line with what people say: 'As you pass by, reveal yourself to your enemy' [and so take revenge whenever you have the chance]."

H.   Others say, "He blew into their noses and they died, as it is said, 'And he shall also blow upon them, and they shall wither' (Is. 40:24)."

I.   R. Jeremiah b. Abba said, "He clapped his hands at them and they died, as it is written, 'I will also smite my hands together and I will cause my fury to rest' (Ez. 21:22)."

J.   R. Isaac Nappaha said, "He opened their eyes for them and they heard a song of the living creatures [of the heaven] and they died, as it is written, 'At your exaltation the people were scattered' (Is. 33:3)."

LXXIV.

A.   How many [of Sennacherib's army] remained?

B.   Rab said, "Ten, as it is said, 'And the rest of the trees of his forest shall be few, that a child may write them' (Is. 10:19).

C.   "What is the letter representing a number that a child can write? The one that stands for ten."

D.   Samuel said, "Nine, as it is written, 'Yet gleaning grapes shall be left in it, as the shaking of an olive tree, two and three berries in the top of the uppermost bough, four and five in the utmost fruitful branches thereof' (Is. 17:6). [Freedman, p. 645, n. 12: This is rendered: "just as after the shaking of an olive tree there may remain two olives here and three there, so shall there be left of the arm army _four_ here and _five_ there -- nine in all."]

E.   R. Joshua b. Levi said, "Fourteen, as it is written, 'Two, three..., four, five' (Is. 17:6)."

F.   R. Yohanan said, "Five: Sennacherib, his two sons, Nebuchadnezzar, and Nebuzaradan.

G.   "Nebuzaradan['s survival is] a tradition.

H.   "Nebuchadnezzar, as it is written, 'And the form of the fourth is like an angel of God' (Dan. 3:25).

I.   "If he had not seen [an angel], how would he have known?

J.   "Sennacherib and his two sons, as it is written, 'And it came to pass, as he was worshipping in the house of Nisroch his god, that Adrammelech and Sharezer, his sons, smote him with the sword' (2 Kgs. 19:37)."

LXXV.

A.   Said R. Abbahu, "Were it not that a verse of Scripture is explicitly spelled out, it would not have been possible to say it:

B.   "For it is written, 'In the same day shall the Lord shave with a razor that is hired, namely, by the riverside, by the king of Assyria, the head and the hair of the feet, and it shall consume the beard' (Is. 7:20.

C. "The Holy One, blessed be he, came and appeared before [Sennacherib] as an old man. He said to him, 'When you go against the kings of east and west, whose sons you brought and saw killed, what will you say to them?'

D. "He said to him, 'This man [I] was also fearful on that account.'

E. "He said to him, 'What should we do?'

F. "He said to him, 'Go [96A] and change your appearance.'

G. "'How shall I change?'

H. "He said to him, 'Go and bring me a razor, and I shall shave you.'

I. "'Where shall I get it?'

J. "He said to him, 'Go to that house and bring it from there.'

K. "He went and found it. Ministering angels came and appeared to him in the form of men, grinding palm-nuts.'

L. "He said to them, 'Give me the razor.'

M. "They said to him, 'Grind a cask of palm-nuts, and we shall give it to you.'

N. "He ground a cask of palm-nuts, and they gave the razor to him.

O. "It got dark before he came back. [God] said to [Sennacherib], 'Go and bring fire.'

P. "He went and brought fire. While he was blowing on it, the fire caught his beard, so [God] shaved his head as well as his beard. [Freedman, p. 646, n. 8: Thus he was shaved with a razor hired by his own work, a work which is done 'by the riverside,' 'grinding,' the water providing power for the mill.]"

Q. They said, "This is in line with what is written: 'And it shall also consume the beard' (Is. 7:20)."

R. Said R. Pappa, "This is in line with what people say: 'If you are singeing an Aramaean's hair and it suits him, light a fire to his beard, so you will not suffer his mockery.'"

S. [Reverting to the tale of Abbahu:] "He went and found a plank from Noah's ark. He said, 'This must be the great god who saved Noah from the flood.'

T. "He said, 'If that man [I] goes and is victorious, he will offer his two sons before you.'

U. "His sons heard and killed him. That is in line with the verse of Scripture, 'And it came to pass, as he was worshipping in the house of Nisroch his god, that Adrammelech and Sharezer his sons smote him with the sword' (2 Kgs. 19:37)."

LXXVI.

A. "And he fought against them, he and his servants, by night, and smote them" (Gen. 14:15):

B. Said R. Yohanan, "That angel who was assigned to Abraham was named 'Night,' as it is said, '[Let the day perish wherein I was born] and the Night which said, There is a man-child conceived' (Job 3:3). [Freedman, p. 647, n. 4: The verse, Gen. 14:15, is translated, and Night fought on their behalf, he and his....]'"

C. R. Isaac Nappaha ["the smith"] said, "It did for him the deeds that are done by night, as it is said, 'They fought from heaven, the stars in their courses fought against Sisera' (Judges 5:20)."

D. R. Simeon b. Laqish said, "What the smith [Yohanan] has said is better than what the son of the smith [Isaac] has said."

E. "And he pursued them to Dan" (Gen. 14:14):

F. Said R. Yohanan, "When that righteous man came to Dan, he grew weak. He foresaw that the children of his children were destined to commit acts of idolatry in Dan, as it is said, 'And he set the one in Beth El, and the other he put in Dan' (1 Kgs. 12:29).

G. "And also that wicked man [Nebuchadnezzar] did not grow strong until he reached Dan, as it is said, 'From Dan the snorting of his horses was heard' (Jer. 8:16)."

LXXVII.

A. Said R. Zira, "Even though R. Judah b. Beterah sent word from Nisibis, 'Pay heed to an elder who has forgotten his learning through not fault of his own and to cut the jugular veins [in slaughtering a beast], in accord with the view of R. Judah,

B. "'and take heed of the sons of the ordinary folk, for from them [too] will Torah go forth,'

C. "for such a matter as the following we may convey matters to them [and not refrain from teaching this lesson:]

D. """You are righteous, Lord, when I please with you, yet let met talk to thee of your judgments, wherefore does the way of the wicked prosper? Wherefore are all they happy who deal very treacherously? You have planted them, yes, they have taken root, they grow, yes, they bring forth fruit" (Jer. 12:1-2).

E. "'What did he answer him? "If you have run with the footmen and they have tired you, then how can you contend with the horses? And if in a land of peace, in which you trust, they have wearied you, how will you do in the prideful swelling of the Jordan" (Jer. 12:5).

F. "'The matter may be compared to the case of a man who said "I can run in a marsh three parasangs before horses." He happened upon a man on foot and ran before him for only three mils on dry land, and he got tired.

G. "'He said to him, "Now if matters are this way when you run before a man on foot, all the more so [will you be unable to run] before horses! And if matters are this way for three mils, how much the more so in three parasangs! And if matters are this way in dry land, how much the more so in a marsh!"

H. """So it is with you. If on account of the reward for taking four steps [explained later, J-Y] that I paid that wicked man, which he took in running on account of my honor, you are amazed, when I pay the reward owing to Abraham, Isaac, and Jacob, who ran before me like horses, how much the more so [will you be amazed]!"

I. "'This is in line with the following verse of Scripture: "My heart within me is broken because of the prophets, all my bones shake, I am like a drunken man, and like a man whose wine has overcome, because of the Lord and because of the words of his holiness" (Jer. 23:9).'"

J. As to the reference to the four steps [taken by the wicked man in honor of God], what is its meaning?

K. It is in accord with that which is written: "At that time Merodach-baladan, son of Baladan, king of Babylonia, sent letters and a present to Hezekiah [for he had heard that he had been sick and recovered]" (Is. 39:1).

L. And merely because Hezekiah was sick and got better, did he sent him letters and a present?!

M. Yes, so as "to inquire of the wonder that was done in the land" (2 Chr. 32:31).

N. For R. Yohanan said, "That day on which Ahaz died was only two hours long, and on the day on which Hezekiah got sick and got better, the Holy One, blessed be he, gave back the other ten hours.

O. "For it is written, 'Behold I will bring again the shadow of the degrees which is gone down in the sun dial of Ahaz, ten degrees backward. So the sun returned ten degrees, by which degrees it was gone down' (Is. 38:8). [Freedman, p. 649, ns. 5-6: The sun had set ten hours too soon, to allow no time for funeral eulogies. This was in order to make atonement for his sins, for the disgrace of being deprived of the usual funeral honors expiates one's misdeeds. The return of the ten degrees to which Isaiah refers is assumed to mean a prolongation of the day by ten hours, light having healing powers.]

P. "Merodach-baladan] said to [his staff], 'What is going on?'

Q. "They said to him, 'Hezekiah got sick and got better.'

R. "He said, 'Is there such a great man in the world, and should I know want to greet him?'

S. "He wrote him, 'Peace to King Hezekiah, peace to the city of Jerusalem, peace to the Great God!'

T. "Nebuchadnezzar was the scribe of Baladan. At that time he was not there. When he came, he said to him, 'What did you write?'

U. "They said to him, 'This is what we wrote.'

V. "He said to him, 'You called him "the great God" and yet you mentioned him last?'

W. "He said, 'Rather, this is how you should write: "Peace to the great God, peace to the city of Jerusalem, peace to King Hezekiah."'

X. "They said to him, 'Let the one who has read the letter serve as the messenger.'

Y. "He ran after [the messenger] [thus in honor of God]. But when he had run four steps, Gabriel came and froze him in place."

Z. Said R. Yohanan, "Had Gabriel not come and kept him standing in place, there would have been no remedy for (the enemies of) Israel." [Freedman, p. 650, n. 3: The learned children of the ordinary folk should thus be informed that the honor paid to them is due to the slight merit of their fathers, as in this case.]

LXXVIII.

A. What is the meaning of the fact that [Merodach-] Baladan is called "the son of Baladan"?

B. They say: Baladan was king, and his appearance changed into that of a dog, so his son sat on the throne.

C. When he would sign a document, he would write his name and the name of his father, "King Baladan."

D. This is the sense of that which is written: "A son honors his father, and a servant his master" (Mal. 1:6).

E. "A son honors his father" (Mal. 1:6) refers to what we have just said.

F. As to "A servant his master" (Mal. 1:6)?

G. It is in line with that which is written: "Now in the fifth month, on the tenth day of the month, the nineteenth year of Nebuchadnezzar, king of Babylonia, came Nebuzaradan, captain of the guard, and stood before the king of Babylonia in Jerusalem. And he burned the house of the Lord and the house of the king" (Jer. 52:12-13).

H. [96B] But did Nebuchadnezzar go up to Jerusalem? Has it not been written, "They carried him up to the King of Babylonia, to Riblah" (Jer. 52:9)? And, said R. Abbahu, "That town is the same as Antioch."

I. R. Hisda and R. Isaac b. Abudimi: One said, "His picture was engraved on [Nebuzaradan's] chariot."

J. "The other said, "He was so much in awe of him that it was as though he were standing before him."

LXXIX.

A. Said Raba, "It was bearing three hundred mules loaded with iron axes that could break iron that Nebuchadnezzar sent Nebuzaradan. All of them broke on one gate of Jerusalem, as it is said, 'And now they attack its gate together; with axes and hammers they hit it' (Ps. 74:6).

B. "He wanted to go back. He said, 'I am afraid that they might do to me as they did to Sennacherib.

C. "A voice came forth: 'Leaper son of a leaper, leap, Nebuzaradan! The time has come for the sanctuary to be destroyed and the palace burned.'

D. "Left to him was only a single axe. He went and hit it with its head, ad the gate opened, as it is said, 'A man was famous according as he had lifted up axes upon thick trees' (Ps. 74:5).

E. "He continued with the killing until he reached the Temple. He set fire to it. The Temple sought to rise up [to heaven], but from heaven it was pushed down, as it is said, 'The Lord has trodden down the virgin daughter of Judah as in a winepress' (Lam. 1:15).

F. "He was elated, but an echo came and said, 'You have killed a dead people, you have burned a burned Temple, you have crushed already ground corn, as it is said, 'Take the millstones and grind meal, uncover your locks, make the leg bare, uncover the thigh, pass over the rivers' (Is. 47:2).

G. "What is said is not 'wheat' but 'ground meal.'"

H. [Nebuzaradan] saw the blood of Zechariah boiling. He said to them, "What is this?"

I. They said to him, "It is the blood of the sacrifices, that has been poured out."

J. He said to them, "Come and let us bring [animal blood to make a comparison to see whether they are alike or not alike]." He slaughtered an animal and the blood was not like [that which was boiling].

K.   He said to them, "Explain it to me, and if not, I shall comb your flesh with iron combs."

L.   They said to him, "This one was a priest and a prophet, and he prophesied to Israel concerning the destruction of Jerusalem, so they killed him."

M.   He said to them, "I shall be the one to appease him." He brought rabbis and killed them over him, but [the blood] did not come to rest. He brought school children and killed them over him, but still the blood did not come to rest. He brought the blossoms of the priesthood and killed them over him, and still the blood did not come to rest, until he had killed over him ninety-four myriads, and still his blood did not rest.

N.   He drew near [the blood] and said, "Zechariah, Zechariah, I have destroyed the best of them. Do you want me to kill them all?"

O.   Forthwith the blood came to rest.

P.   He gave thought to repentance, saying, "Now if they, who killed only a single person, were treated in such a way, that man [I] -- what will come of him?"

Q.   He fled, sent his instructions to his household [giving over his property to his family], and then converted [to Judaism].

LXXX.

A.   Our rabbis have taught on Tannaite authority:

B.   Naaman was a resident proselyte.

C.   Nebuzaradan was a righteous proselyte.

D.   Grandsons of Sisera studied Torah in Jerusalem.

E.   Grandsons of Sennacherib taught Torah in public.

F.   And who were they? Shemaiah and Abtalion.

G.   Grandsons of Haman studied Torah in Bene Beraq.

H.   And so too grandsons of that wicked man [Nebuchadnezzar] did the Holy One, blessed be he, want to bring under the wings of the Presence of God.

I.   Said the ministering angels before the Holy One, blessed be he, "Lord of the world, will you bring under the wings of your Presence him who destroyed your house and burned your Temple?"

J.   For it is written, "We should have healed Babylonia, but she is not healed" (Jer. 21:9).

K.   Said Ulla, "This speaks of Nebuchadnezzar."

L.   Said R. Samuel b. Nahmani, "This refers to the 'canals of Babylonia' (Ps. 137:1), which flow among the palm trees of Babylonia."

LXXXI.

A.   Said Ulla, "Ammon and Moab were bad neighbors of Jerusalem.

B.   "When they heard the prophets prophesying the destruction of Jerusalem, they sent word to Nebuchadnezzar, 'Go out and come here.'

C.   "He said, 'I am afraid that they will do to me what they did to those who came before me.'

D.   "They sent to him, '"For the man is not at home" (Prov. 7:19), and "man" can refer only to the Holy One, blessed be he, as it is said, "The Lord is a man of war" (Ex. 15:3).'

E. "He replied, 'He is nearby and he will come.'

F. "They sent to him, '"He has gone on a far journey" (Prov. 7:19).'

G. "He sent to them, 'There are righteous men there, who will pray for mercy and bring him back.'

H. "They sent to him, '"He has taken a bag of money with him" (Prov. 7:20), and "money" refers only to the righteous, as it is said, "So I bought her to me for fifteen pieces of silver and for a <u>homer</u> of barley and a half-<u>homer</u> of barley" (Hos. 3:2).'

I. "He sent word to them, 'The wicked may repent and pray for mercy and bring him back.'

J. "They sent to him, '"He has already set a time for them, as it is said, "And he will come home at the day appointed" (Prov. 7:20), and "day appointed" can refer only to time, as it is said, "In the time appointed on our solemn feast day" (Ps. 81:1,3).'

K. "He sent word to them, 'It is winter, and I cannot make the trip because of the snow and rain.'

L. "They sent to him, 'Come through the mountains [if need be]. For it is said, "Send you a messenger to the ruler of the earth [that he may come] by way of the rocks to the wilderness to the mountain of the daughter of Zion" (Is. 16:1).'

M. "He sent to them, 'If I come, I shall not have a place in which to make camp.'

N. "They sent word to him, 'Their cemeteries are superior to your palaces, as it is written, "At that time, says the Lord, they shall bring out the bones of the king of Judea and the bones of his princes and the bones of the priests and the bones of the prophets and the bones of the inhabitants of Jerusalem, out of their graves. And they shall spread them before the sun and the moon and all the host of heaven, whom they have loved and whom they have served and after whom they have walked" (Jer. 8:1-2).' [Freedman, p. 654, n. 1: The great burial vaults will be cleared out to give shelter to Nebuchadnezzar's army.]'

LXXXII.

A. Said R. Nahman to R. Isaac, "have you heard when the son of 'the fallen one' will come?"

B. He said to him, "Who is the son of 'the fallen one'?"

C. He said to him, "It is the Messiah."

D. "Do you call the Messiah 'the son of the fallen one'?"

E. He said to him, "Yes, for it is written, 'On that day I will raise up [97A] the tabernacle of David, the fallen one' (Amos 9:11)."

F. He said to him, "This is what R. Yohanan said, 'The generation to which the son of David will come will be one in which disciples of sages grow fewer,

G. "'and, as to the others, their eyes will wear out through suffering and sighing,

H. "'and troubles will be many, and laws harsh, forever renewing themselves so that the new one will hasten onward before the old one has come to an end.'"

LXXXIII.

A. Our rabbis have taught on Tannaite authority:

B. The seven year cycle in which the son of David will come:

C.   As to the first one, the following verse of Scripture will be fulfilled: "And I will cause it to rain upon one city and not upon another" (Amos 4:7).

D.   As to the second year, the arrows of famine will be sent forth.

E.   As to the third, there will be a great famine, in which men, women, and children will die, pious men and wonder-workers alike, and the Torah will be forgotten by those that study it.

F.   As to the fourth year, there will be plenty which is no plenty.

G.   As to the fifth year, there will be great prosperity, and people will eat, drink, and rejoice, and the Torah will be restored to those that study it.

H.   As to the sixth year, there will be rumors.

I.   As to the seventh year, there will be wars.

J.   As to the end of the seventh year [the eighth year], the son of David will come.

K.   Said R. Joseph, "Lo, how many septennates have passed like that one, and yet he has not come."

L.   Said Abayye, "Were there rumors in the sixth year and wars in the seventh year?

M.   "And furthermore, did they come in the right order?"

LXXXIV.

A.   It has been taught on Tannaite authority:

B.   R. Judah says, "In the generation in which the son of David will come, the gathering place will be for prostitution, Galilee will be laid waste, Gablan will be made desolate, and the men of the frontier will go about from town to town, and none will take pity on them; and the wisdom of scribes will putrefy; and those who fear sin will be rejected; and the truth will be herded away [M. Sot. 9:15AA-GG].

C.   "For it is said, 'And the truth will be herded away' (Is. 59:15)."

D.   What is the meaning of the statement, "The truth will be herded away" (Is. 59:15)?

E.   Said members of the house of Rab, "This teaches that it will be divided into herds and herds, each going its way."

F.   What is the meaning [of the concluding passage of the same verse], "And he who departs from evil makes himself a prey" (Is. 59:15)?

G.   Said members of the house of R. Shila, "Whoever departs from evil will be treated as a fool [using the same letters as those for prey] by other people."

LXXXV.

A.   Said Raba, "To begin with I had supposed that there is no truth in the world. One of the rabbis, R. Tabut by name (and some say, R. Tabyomi by name), who would not go back on his word even though people gave him all the treasures of the world, said to me that one time he happened to come to a place called Truth.

B.   "It was a place in which people would not go back on their word, and in which no person died before his day.

C.   "He took a woman of theirs as wife and had two sons from her.

D.   "One day his wife was sitting and shampooing her hair. Her neighbor came and knocked on the door. Thinking that it would be improper [to say what his wife was doing], he said to her, 'She is not here.'

E. "His two sons died.

F. "The people of the place came to him and said to him, 'What is going on?'

G. "He said to them, 'This is what happened.'

H. "They said to him, 'By your leave, please go away from our place, so as not to encite Satan against these men [us]'"

LXXXVI.

A. It has been taught on Tannaite authority:

B. R. Nehorai says, "In the generation in which the son of David will come, <u>children will shame elders, and elders will stand up before children.</u> 'The daughter rises up against the mother, and the daughter-in-law against her mother-in-law' (Mic. 7:6). <u>The face of the generation is the face of a dog, and a son is not ashamed before his father</u>" [M. Sot. 9:15HH-KK].

LXXXVII.

A. It has been taught on Tannaite authority:

B. R. Nehemiah says, "In the generation in which the son of David will come, <u>presumption increases, and dearth increases, and the vine gives its fruit and wine at great cost. The government turns to heresy, and there is no reproof</u>" [M. Sot. 9:15W-Z].

C. That statement supports the view of R. Isaac.

D. For R. Isaac said, "The son of David will come only when the entire kingdom has turned to heresy."

E. Said Raba, "What is the text of Scripture that makes that point?

F. "'It is all turned white, he is clean' (Lev. 13:13). [Freedman, p. 656, n. 5: When all are heretics, it is a sign that the world is about to be purified by the advent of the Messiah.]'"

LXXXVIII.

A. Our rabbis have taught on Tannaite authority:

B. "For the Lord shall judge his people and repent himself of his servants, when he sees that their power has gone, and there is none shut up or left" (Deut. 32:36).

C. The son of David will come only when traitors are many.

D. Another matter: Only when disciples are few.

E. Another matter: Only when a penny will not be found in anyone's pocket.

F. Another matter: Only when people will have given up hope of redemption, as it is said, "There is none shut up or left" (Deut. 32:36), as it were, when there is none [God being absent] who supports and helps Israel.

G. That accords with the statement of R. Zira, who, when he would find rabbis involved in [figuring out when the Messiah would come], would say to them, 'By your leave, I ask you not to put it off.

H. "'For we have learned on Tannaite authority: "Three things come on the spur of the moment, and these are they: the Messiah, a lost object, and a scorpion."'"

LXXXIX.

A. Said R. Qattina, "The world will exist for six thousand years and be destroyed for one thousand,

B.   "as it is said, 'And the Lord alone shall be exalted in that day' (Is. 2:11)."

C.   Abayye said, "It will be desolate for two thousand years, as it is said, 'After two days will he revive us, in the third day, he will raise us up and we shall live in his sight' (Hos. 6:2)."

D.   It has been taught on Tannaite authority in accord with the view of R. Qattina:

E.   Just as at the advent of the Sabbatical Year the world will lie fallow for one out of seven years,

F.   so it is with the world. A thousand years will the world lie fallow out of seven thousand years,

G.   as it is said, "And the Lord alone shall be exalted in that day" (Is. 2:11), and Scripture says, "A Psalm and song for the Sabbath Day" (Ps. 92:1) -- a day that is wholly the Sabbath.

H.   And Scripture says, "For a thousand years in your sight are but as yesterday when they are past" (Ps. 90:4). [A day stands for a thousand years.]

XC.

A.   A Tannaite authority of the house of Elijah [said], "For six thousand years the world will exist.

B.   "For two thousand it will be desolate, two thousand years [will be the time of] Torah, and two thousand years will be the days of the Messiah.

C.   [97B] but on account of our numerous sins what has been lost [of those years, in which the Messiah should have come but has not come] has been lost.

XCI.

A.   Said Elijah to R. Sala the Pious, "The world will last for no fewer than eighty-five Jubilees [of fifty years each], and the son of David will come in the last one."

B.   He said to him, "Will it be in the first or the last year of the last Jubilee?"

C.   He said to him, "I do not know."

D.   "Will it come at the end or not come at the end of the fiftieth year?"

E.   He said to him, "I do not know."

F.   R. Ashi said, "This is what he said to him: 'Up to that time, do not look for his coming, but from that time onward, do look for his coming.'"

XCII.

A.   R. Hanan, son of Tahalipa, sent to R. Joseph, "I came across a man who had in hand a scroll, written in Assyrian [block] letters in the holy language.

B.   "I said to him, 'Where did you get this?'

C.   "He said to me, 'I was employed in the Roman armies, and I found it in the Roman archives.'

D.   "In the scroll it is written that after four thousand two hundred ninety-two years from the creation of the world, the world will be an orphan.

E.   "[As to the years to follow] in some there will be wars of the great dragons, and in some, wars of Gog and Magog, and the rest will be the days of the Messiah.

F.   "And the Holy One, blessed be he, will renew his world only after seven thousand years."

G.   R. Aha, son of Raba, said, "'After five thousand years' is what is to be repeated."

XCIII.

A. It has been taught on Tannaite authority:

B. R. Nathan says, "This verse of Scripture pierces to the depth:

C. "'For the vision is yet for an appointed time, but at the end it shall speak and not lie; though he tarry, wait for him; because it will surely come, it will not tarry' (Hab. 2:3)."

D. This is not in accord with our rabbis, who interpreted, "Until a time and times and the dividing of time" (Dan. 7:25).

E. Nor does it accord with R. Simlai, who would interpret, "You feed them with the bread of tears and given them tears to drink a third time" (Ps. 80:6).

F. Nor does it accord with R. Aqiba, who would interpret the verse, "Yet once, it is a little while, and I will shake the heavens and the earth" (Hag. 2:6).

G. Rather, the first kingdom will last for seventy years, the second kingdom for fifty-two years, and the kingdom of Ben Koziba will be for two and a half years.

XCIV.

A. What is the meaning of the verse, "But at the end it shall speak and not lie" (Hab. 2:3)?

B. Said R. Samuel bar Nahmani said R. Jonathan, "[Freedman, p. 659, n. 5: Reading the verse as, 'He will blast him who calculates the end,'] blasted be the bones of those who calculate the end [when the Messiah will come].

C. "For they might say, 'Since the end has come and he has not come, he will not come.'

D. "Rather, wait for him, as it is said, 'Though he tarry, wait for him' (Hab. 2:3).

E. "Should you say that we shall wait, but he may not wait, Scripture responds, 'And therefore will the Lord wait, that he may be gracious to you, and therefore will he be exalted, that he may have mercy upon you' (Is. 30:18).

F. "Then, since we are waiting and he is waiting, what is holding things up?

G. "It is the attribute of justice that is holding things up.

H. "But if the attribute of justice is holding things up, why should we wait?

I. "It is so as to receive the reward for our patience, as it is written, 'Blessed are all those who wait for him' (Is. 30:9)."

XCV.

A. Said Abayye, "There are in the world never fewer than thirty-six righteous men, who look upon the face of the Presence of God every day, for it is said, 'Happy are those who wait for him' (Is. 30:18), and the numerical value of the letters in the word 'for him' is thirty-six."

B. Is this so? And did not Raba say, "The row of the righteous before the Holy One, blessed be he, is made up of eighteen thousand, as it is said, 'There shall be eighteen thousand round about' (Ez. 48:35)"?

C. There is no contradiction between the two views. The former number refers to those few who see him through a bright mirror, the latter number refers to those many who see him only through a dirty mirror.

D. And are they so numerous?

E.   And did not Hezekiah said R. Jeremiah said in the name of R. Simeon b. Yohai, "I have myself seen the inhabitants of the upper world, and they are only a few. If they are a thousand, my son and I are among their number. If they are only a hundred, my son and I are among their number. If they are only two, they are only my son and I."

F.   There is still no contradiction. The larger number speaks of those who go inside only with permission, the smaller number those who go inside even without permission.

XCVI.

A.   Said Rab, "All of the ends have passed, and the matter now depends only on repentance and good deeds."

B.   And Samuel said, "It is sufficient for a mourner to remain firm in his mourning."

C.   This accords with the following dispute among Tannaite authorities:

D.   R. Eliezer says, "If the Israelites repent, they will be redeemed, and if not, they will not be redeemed."

E.   Said R. Joshua to him, "If they do not repent, will they not be redeemed?!

F.   "Rather, the Holy One, blessed be he, will raise up for them a king whose decrees will be as harsh as those of Haman, and the Israelites will repent, and [God] will restore them to a good path]."

G.   A further Tannaite version:

H.   R. Eliezer says, "If the Israelites repent, they will be redeemed, as it is said, 'Return, backsliding children, and I will heal your backslidings' (Jer. 3:22)."

I.   Said to him R. Joshua, "And is it not written, 'You have sold yourselves for nought, and you shall be redeemed without money' (Is. 52:3)?

J.   "'You have sold yourselves for nought' -- for idolatry.

K.   "'But you shall be redeemed without money' -- with neither repentance nor do good deeds."

L.   Said to him R. Eliezer, "But is it not written, 'Return to me and I shall return to you' (Mal. 3:7)?"

M.   Said to him R. Joshua, "But is it not written, 'For I am master over you, and I will take you, one from a city and two from a family and I will bring you to Zion' (Jer. 3:14)?"

N.   Said to him R. Eliezer, "But it is written, 'In returning and rest you shall be saved' (Is. 30:5)."

O.   Said R. Joshua to R. Eliezer, "But is it not written, 'Thus says the Lord, the redeemer of Israel, and his holy one, to whom man despises, to him whom the nations abhor, to a servant of rulers, [98A] kings shall see and arise, princes also shall worship' (Is. 49:7)?"

P.   Said to him R. Eliezer, "But is it not written, 'If you will return, O Israel, says the Lord, return to me' (Jer. 4:1)?"

Q.   Said to him R. Joshua, "But it is written elsewhere, 'And I heard the man clothed in linen, which was upon the waters of the river, when he held up his right hand and his left hand to heaven and swore by him who lives forever that it shall be for a year,

two years, and half a year and when he shall have accomplished scattering the power
of the holy people, all these things shall be finished' (Dan. 12:7)."

R.   And R. Eliezer shut up.

XCVII.

A.   And said R. Abba, "You have no indication of the end more openly stated than the
following, as it is said: 'But you, O Mountains of Israel, shall shoot forth your
branches and yield your fruit to my people, Israel, for they are at hand to come' (Ez.
36:8)."

B.   R. Eliezer says, "Also the following, as it is said: 'For before these days there was
no hire for man, nor any hire for beast neither was there any peace to him that went
out or came in because of the affliction' (Zech. 8:10)."

C.   What is the meaning of the phrase, "Neither was there any peace to him that went
out or came in because of the affliction"?

D.   Rab said, "Even to disciples of sages, concerning whom peace is written in Scripture,
as it is written, 'Great peace shall they have who love your Torah' (Ps. 119:165)."

E.   "Neither was there any peace... because of the affliction" (Zech. 8:10):

F.   And Samuel said, "Until all prices will be equal."

XCVIII.

A.   Said R. Hanina, "The son of David will come only when a fish will be sought for a
sick person and not be found, as it is said, 'Then I will make their waters deep and
cause their rivers to run like oil' (Ez. 32:14), and it is written, 'In that day I will
cause the horn of the house of Israel to sprout forth' (Ez. 29:21)."

B.   Said R. Hama bar Hanina, "The son of David will come only when the rule over Israel
by the least of the kingdoms will come to an end, as it is said, 'He shall both cut off
the springs with pruning hooks and take away and cut down the branches' (Is. 18:5),
and further: 'In that time shall the present be brought to the Lord of hosts of a
people that is scattered and peeled' (Is. 18:7)."

C.   Said Zeiri said R. Hanina, "The son of David will come only when arrogant people
will no longer be [found] in Israel, as it is said, 'For then I will take away out of the
midst of you those who rejoice in your pride' (Zeph. 8:11), followed by: 'I will also
leave in the midst of you an afflicted and poor people, and they shall take refuge in
the name of the Lord' (Zeph. 3:12)."

D.   Said R. Simlai in the name of R. Eliezer b. R. Simeon, "The son of David will come
only when all judges and rulers come to an end in Israel, as it is said, 'And I will turn
my hand upon you and purely purge away your dross and take away all your tin, and I
will restore your judges as at the first' (Is. 1:25-26)."

XCIX.

A.   Said Ulla, "Jerusalem will be redeemed only through righteousness, as it is written,
'Zion shall be redeemed with judgment and her converts with righteousness' (Is.
1:27)."

B.   Said R. Pappa, "If the arrogant end [in Israel], the Magi will end [in Iran], if the
judges end [in Israel], the rulers of thousands will come to an end [in Iran].

C.   "If the arrogant end [in Israel], the magi will end [in Iran], as it is written, 'And I will purely purge away your haughty ones and take away all your tin' (Is. 1:25).

D.   "If judges end [in Israel], the rulers of thousands will come to an end [in Iran], as it is written, 'The Lord has taken away your judgments, he has cast out your enemy' (Zeph. 3:15)."

C.

A.   Said R. Yohanan, "If you see a generation growing less and less, hope for him, as it is said, 'And the afflicted people will you save' (2 Sam. 22:28)."

B.   Said R. Yohanan, "If you see a generation over which many troubles flow like a river, hope for him, as it is written, 'When the enemy shall come in like a flood, the spirit of the Lord shall lift up a standard against him' (Is. 59:19), followed by: 'And the redeemer shall come to Zion' (Is. 59:20)."

C.   And said R. Yohanan, "The son of David will come to a generation that is either entirely righteous or entirely wicked.

D.   "A generation that is entirely righteous, as it is written, 'Your people also shall be all righteous, they shall inherit the land for ever' (Is. 60:21),

E.   "or a generation that is entirely wicked, as it is written, 'And he saw that there was no man and wondered that there was no intercessor' (Is. 59:16), and it is written, 'For my own sake, even for my own sake I will do it' (Is. 60:22)."

CI.

A.   Said R. Alexandri, "R. Joshua b. Levi contrasted verses as follows:

B.   It is written; "in its time [will the Messiah come]," and it is also written; "I [the Lord] will hasten it."

C.   [What is the meaning of the contrast?]

D.   "If [the Israelites] have merit, I will hasten it, if they do not, [the messiah] will come in due course.

E.   "'It is written, "And behold, one like the son of man came with the clouds of heaven" (Dan. 7:13, and it is written, "Behold your king comes to you... lowly and riding upon an ass" (Zech. 9:7). [What is the meaning of the contrast?]

F.   "'If [the Israelites] have merit, it will be "with the clouds of heaven" (Dan. 7:13), and if they do not have merit, it will be "lowly and riding upon an ass" (Zech. 9:7).'"

CII.

A.   Said King Shapur to Samuel, "You say that the Messiah will come on an ass [which is a humble way]. Come and I shall send him a white horse that I have."

B.   He said to him, "Do you have one of many colors?"

CIII.

A.   R. Joshua b. Levi found Elijah standing at the door of the burial vault of R. Simeon b. Yohai. He said to him, "Am I going to come to the world to come?"

B.   He said to him, "If this master wants."

C.   Said R. Joshua b. Levi, "Two did I see, but a third voice did I hear."

D.   He said to him, "When is the Messiah coming?"

E.   He said to him, "Go and ask him."

F.   "And where is he sitting?"

G.   "At the gate of the city."

H.   "And what are the marks that indicate who he is?"

I.   "He is sitting among the poor who suffer illness, and all of them untie and tie their bandages all together, but he unties them and ties them one by one. He is thinking, 'Perhaps I may be wanted, and I do not want to be held up.'"

J.   He went to him, saying to him, "Peace be unto you, my master and teacher."

K.   He said to him, "Peace be unto you, son of Levi."

L.   He said to him, "When is the master coming?"

M.   He said to him, "Today."

N.   He went back to Elijah, who said to him, "What did he tell you?"

O.   He said to him, "'Peace be unto you, son of Levi.'"

P.   He said to him, "He [thereby] promised you and your father the world to come."

Q.   He said to him, "But he lied to me. For he said to me, 'I am coming today,' but he did not come."

R.   He said to him, "This is what he said to you, '"Today, if you will obey his voice" (Ps. 95:7).'"

CIV.

A.   His disciples asked R. Yose b. Qisma, "When is the son of David coming?"

B.   He said to them, "I am afraid [to answer], lest you ask an omen from me [that my answer is right]."

C.   They said to him, "We shall not ask for an omen from you." He said to them, "When this gate falls and is rebuilt, falls and is rebuilt, and falls a third time. They will not suffice to rebuild it before the son of David will come."

D.   They said to him, "Our master, give us an omen."

E.   He said to them, "But did you not say to me that you would not ask for an omen from me?"

F.   They said to him, "Even so."

G.   He said to them, "Then let the waters of the grotto of Banias turn to blood," and they turned to blood.

H.   When he died, he said to them, "Dig my bier deep into the ground, [98B] for there is not a palm tree in Babylonia on which a Persian horse has not been tied, nor is there a bier in the land of Israel from which a Median horse will not eat straw."

CV.

A.   Said Rab, "The son of David will come only when the monarchy [of Rome] will spread over Israel for nine months,

B.   "as it is said, 'Therefore will he give them up, until the time that she who travails has brought forth; then the remnant of his brethren shall return to the children of Israel' (Mic. 5:2)."

CVI.

A.   Said Ulla, "Let him come, but may I not see him."

B.   Said Rabba, "Let him come, but may I not see him."

C.   R. Joseph said, "May he come, and may I have the merit of sitting in the shade of the dung of his ass."

D.   Said Abayye to Rabbah, "What is the reason [that some do not wish to see the coming of the messiah]? Is it because of the turmoil of the Messiah?

E.   "And has it not been taught on Tannaite authority:

F.   "His disciples asked R. Eliezar, 'What should someone do to save himself from the turmoil of the Messiah?'

G.   "[He replied to them], 'Let him engage in study of the Torah and acts of loving kindness.'

H.   "And lo, the master [at hand] practices Torah-study and acts of loving kindness. [So why not want to see him?]"

I.   He said to him, "Perhaps he fears sin will cause [him to suffer], in line with what R. Jacob bar Idi said."

J.   For R. Jacob bar Idi contrasted two verses of Scripture, as follows: "It is written, 'And behold, I am with you and will keep you wherever you go' (Gen. 28:15), and another verse states, 'Then Jacob was greatly afraid' (Gen. 32:8).

K.   "[Why the contrast between God's promise and Jacob's fear?] Jacob feared [and thought to himself,] 'Sin which I have done may cause [punishment for me instead].'"

L.   That accords with what has been taught on Tannaite authority:

M.   "Till your people pass over, O Lord, till your people pass over, that you have acquired" (Ex. 15:16).

N.   "Till your people pass over" refers to the first entry into the land [in Joshua's time].

O.   "Till your people pass over, that you have acquired" refers to the second entry into the land [in the time of Ezra and Nehemiah. Thus a miracle was promised not only on the first occasion, but also on the second. But it did not happen the second time around. Why not?]

P.   On the basis of this statement, sages have said, "The Israelites were worthy of having a miracle performed for them in the time of Ezra also, just as it had been performed for them in the time of Joshua b. Nun, but sin caused the miracle to be withheld."

CVII.

A.   So said R. Yohanan, "Let him come, but let me not see him."

B.   Said R. Simeon b. Laqish to him, "What is the scriptural basis for that view? Shall we say that it is because it is written, 'As if a man fled from a lion and a bear met him, or went into the house and leaned his hand on the wall and a serpent bit him' (Amos 5:19)?

C.   "Come and I shall show you an example of such a case in this world.

D.   "When a man goes out to the field and bailiff meets him, it is like one whom a lion meets. He goes into town and a tax-collector meets him, it is like one whom a bear meets.

E.   "He goes into his house and finds his sons and daughters suffering from hunger, it is like one whom a snake bit.

F.   "Rather, it is because it is written, 'Ask you now and see whether a man travails with child? Why do I see every man with his hands on his loins, as women in travail, and all faces are turned into paleness' (Jer. 30:6)."

G.   What is the sense of, "Why do I see every man..."?

H.   Said Raba bar Isaac said Rab, "It speaks of him to whom all [manly] power belongs [God]."

I.   And what is the sense of "all faces are turned into paleness"?

J.   Said R. Yohanan, "[It speaks of God's] heavenly family and his earthly family, at the moment at which God says, 'These are the creation of my hands, and those are the creation of my hands. How shall I destroy these [gentiles] on account of [what they have done to] those [Israelites]? [Freedman, p. 667, n. 2: to avenge the wrongs suffered by the Jews. Because the suffering would be so great that even the Almighty would lament it, Yohanan desired to be spared the Messiah's coming.]"

K.   Said R. Pappa, "This is in line with what people say: 'The ox runs and falls, so the horse is put in its stall.' [Freedman, p. 667, n. 3: Then it is hard to get the horse out. So the Israelites, having fallen, were replaced in power by the gentiles, but on their recovery, it will be difficult to remove the gentiles from their position without inflicting much suffering.]"

CVIII.

A.   Said R. Giddal said Rab, "The Israelites are going to eat [and not starve] in the years of the Messiah."

B.   Said R. Joseph, "That is self-evident. If not, then who will eat? Joe and Mo?! [Text: Hiliq and Bileq?]"

C.   [The statement at hand] serves to exclude the view of R. Hillel, who has said, "There will be no further Messiah for Israel, for they already consumed him in the time of Hezekiah."

CIX.

A.   Said Rab, "The world was created only for David."

B.   And Samuel said, "For Moses."

C.   And R. Yohanan said, "For the Messiah."

D.   What is his name?

E.   The house of R. Shila said, "His name is Shiloh, as it is said, 'Until Shiloh come' (Gen. 49:10)."

F.   Members of the house of R. Yannai say, "His name is Yinnon, for it is written, 'His name shall endure forever, before the sun was, his name is Yinnon' (Ps. 72:17)."

G.   Members of the house of R. Haninah said, "It is Haninah, as it is said, 'Where I will not give you Haninah' (Jer. 16:13)."

H.   Others say, "His name is Menahem, son of Hezekiah, for it is written, 'Because Menahem that would relieve my soul, is far' (Lam. 1:16)."

I.   Rabbis said, "His name is 'the leper of the school house,' as it is written, 'Surely he has borne our griefs and carried our sorrows, yet we did esteem him a leper, smitten of God and afflicted' (Is. 53:4)."

CX.

A.   Said R. Nahman, "If he is among the living, he is such as I, as it is said, 'And their nobles shall be of themselves and their governors shall proceed from the midst of them' (Jer. 30:21)."

B.   Said Rab, "If he is among the living, he is such as our Holy Rabbi [Judah the Patriarch], and if he is among the dead, he is such as Daniel, the most desirable man."

C.   Said R. Judah said Rab, "The Holy One, blessed be he, is destined to raise up for [Israel] another David, as it is said, 'But they shall serve the Lord their God and David their king, whom I will raise up for them' (Jer. 30:9).

D.   "'Raised up' is not what is said, but rather, 'will raise up.'"

E.   Said R. Pappa to Abayye, "But lo, it is written, 'And my servant David shall be their prince forever' (Ez. 37:25) [with the title for prince standing for less than the title for king]."

F.   [He said to him,] "It is like a king and a viceroy [the second David being king]."

CXI.

A.   R. Simlai interpreted the following verse: "What is the meaning of that which is written, 'Woe to you who desire the day of the Lord! to what end is it for you? the day of the Lord is darkness and not light' (Amos 5:18)?

B.   "The matter may be compared to the case of the cock and the bat who were waiting for light.

C.   "The cock said to the bat, 'I am waiting for the light, for the light belongs to me, but what do you need light for [99A]?'"

D.   That is in line with what a min said to R. Abbahu, "When is the Messiah coming?"

E.   He said to him, "When darkness covers those men."

F.   He said to him, "You are cursing me."

G.   He said to him, "I am merely citing a verse of Scripture: 'For behold, the darkness shall cover the earth, and great darkness the people, but the Lord shall shine upon you, and his glory shall be seen upon you' (Is. 60:2)."

CXII.

A.   It has been taught on Tannaite authority:

B.   R. Eliezer says, "The days of the Messiah will last forty years, as it is said, 'Forty years long shall I take hold of the generation' (Ps. 95:10)."

C.   R. Eliezer b. Azariah says, "Seventy years, as it is said, 'And it shall come to pass in that day that Tyre shall be forgotten seventy years, according to the days of one king' (Is. 23:15).

D.   "Now what would be a one [and singular] king? We must say that it is the Messiah."

E.   Rabbi says, "Three generations, as it is said, 'They shall fear you with the sun and before the moon, a generation and generations' (Ps. 72:5)."

CXIII.

A.   R. Hillel says, "Israel will have no Messiah, for they consumed him in the time of Hezekiah."

B. Said R. Joseph, "May R. Hillel's master forgive him. When did Hezekiah live? It
    was in the time of the first Temple. But Zechariah prophesied in the second
    Temple's time and said, 'Rejoice greatly, O daughter of Zion, shout, O daughter of
    Jerusalem, behold your king comes to you; he is just and has salvation; lowly and
    riding upon an ass and upon a colt the foal of an ass' (Zech. 9:9)."

CXIV.

A. A further teaching on Tannaite authority:

B. R. Eliezer says, "The days of the Messiah will last for forty years. Here it is
    written, 'And he afflicted you and made you hunger and fed you with manna' (Deut.
    8:3), and elsewhere: 'Make us glad according to the days [forty years in the
    wilderness] in which you have afflicted us' (Ps. 90:15)."

C. R. Dosa says, "Four hundred years. Here it is written, 'And they shall serve them
    and they shall afflict them four hundred years' (Gen. 15:13), and elsewhere: 'Make
    us glad according to the days wherein you have afflicted us' (Ps. 90:15)."

D. Rabbi says, "Three hundred and sixty-five years, according to the number of days in
    the solar year, as it is said, 'For the day of vengeance is in my heart and the year of
    my redemption has come' (Is. 63:4)."

E. What is the meaning of "the day of vengeance is in my heart" (Is. 63:4)?

F. Said R. Yohanan, "I have revealed it to my heart, but I have not revealed it to my
    limbs."

G. R. Simeon b. Laqish said, "To my heart I have revealed it, to the ministering angels I
    have not revealed it."

H. Abimi, son of R. Abbahu, stated on Tannaite authority, "The days of the Messiah for
    Israel will be seven thousand years, as it is said, 'And as the bridegroom rejoices
    over the bride [a week], so shall your God rejoice over you' (Is. 62:5)."

I. Said R. Judah said Samuel, "The days of the Messiah are the same as the days that
    have passed from the day of the creation of the world even to now, as it is said, 'As
    the days of heaven upon earth' (Deut. 11:21)."

J. R. Nahman bar Isaac said, "As the days from Noah to now, as it is said, 'For this is
    as the waters of Noah, which are mine, so I have sworn it' (Is. 54:9)."

CXV.

A. Said R. Hiyya bar Abba said R. Yohanan, "All of the prophets prophesied only
    concerning the days of the Messiah.

B. "But as to the world to come [thereafter]: 'Eye has not seen, O Lord, beside you,
    what he has prepared for him who waits for him' (Is. 64:3)."

C. That statement differs from the view of Samuel.

D. For said Samuel, "There is no difference between this world and the days of the
    Messiah except for [Israel's] subjugation to the rule of the empires alone."

E. And said R. Hiyya bar Abba said R. Yohanan, "All of the prophets prophesied only
    concerning those who repent, but as to the perfectly righteous people [who have
    never sinned to begin with]: 'Eye has not seen, O God, beside you, what he has
    prepared for him who waits for him' (Is. 54:3)."

F.   That statement differs from the view of R. Abbahu.

G.   For, said R. Abbahu, "In the place in which those who repent stand, the righteous cannot stand, for it is said, 'Peace, peace to him who is far off and to him that is near' (Is. 57:19).

H.   "'To begin with, he was 'far off,' and then he repented and so became 'near.'

I.   "What is the sense of 'far off'? Originally far off [a sinner] and what is the sense of 'near'? Originally near and still near. [Freedman, p. 671, n. 3: Thus he assigns a higher rank to the repentant sinner than to the completely righteous.]'

J.   R. Yohanan said, "'To the one who was distant' because he was far from sin, and 'near' in that he was near sin but distanced himself from it."

K.   And said R. Hiyya bar Abba said R. Yohanan, "All of the prophets prophesied only concerning him who marries his daughter off to a disciple of sages, conducts business to the advantage of a disciple of a sage, and benefits a disciple of a sage from his wealth.

L.   "But as to disciples of sages themselves: 'Eye has not seen, O God beside you' (Is. 64:3)."

M.   What is the meaning of the phrase, "Eye has not seen"?

N.   Said R. Joshua b. Levi, "This refers to wine that has been kept in the grapes from the six days of creation."

O.   R. Simeon b. Laqish said, "This refers to Eden, which no eye has ever seen.

P.   "And if you should say, 'Then we where did Adam dwell?' the answer is, in the garden.

Q.   "And if you should say, 'But it was the Garden that was Eden,' Scripture says, 'And a river issued from Eden to water the garden' (Gen. 2:10)."

CXVI.

A.   And he who says, "The Torah does not come from heaven" [M. 11:1D]:

B.   Our rabbis have taught on Tannaite authority:

C.   "Because he has despised the word of the Lord and broken his commandment, that soul shall utterly be cut off" (Num. 15:31):

D.   This refers to one who says, "The Torah does not come from heaven."

E.   Another matter:

F.   "Because he has despised the word of the Lord": This refers to an Epicurean.

G.   Another matter:

H.   "Because he has despised the word of the Lord": This refers to one who is without shame in interpreting the Torah.

I.   "And broken his commandment": This refers to one who removes the mark fleshly arks of the covenant.

J.   "That soul shatter utterly be cut off": "Be cut off" -- in this world. "Utterly" in the world to come.

K.   On the basis of this exegesis, said R. Eliezer the Modite, "He who treats Holy Things as secular, he who despises the appointed times, he who humiliates his companion in public, he who removes the signs of the covenant of Abraham, our father, and he who exposes aspects of the Torah not in accord with the law, even though he has in hand learning in Torah and good deeds, will have no share in the world to come" [M. Abot 3:11].

L. A further teaching on Tannaite authority:

M. "Because he has despised the word of the Lord" (Num. 14:31): This refers to one who says, "The Torah does not come from heaven."

N. And even if he had said, "The entire Torah comes from heaven, except for this one verse, which the Holy One, blessed be he, did not say, but which Moses said on his own," such a one falls under the verse, "Because he has despised the word of the Lord" (Num. 15:31).

O. And even if he had said, "The entire Torah comes from heaven, except for one minor point, an argument a fortiori, an argument based on analogy," such a one falls under the verse, "Because he has despised the way of the Lord" (Num. 15:31).

CXVII.

A. It has been taught on Tannaite authority"

B. R. Meir would say, "He who studies the Torah but does not teach it falls under the verse, "Because he has despised the word of the Lord" (Num. 15:31)."

C. R. Nathan says, "Whoever does not pay close attention to the Mishnah."

D. R. Nehorai says, "Whoever has the possibility of taking up the study of the Torah and does not do so."

E. R. Ishmael says, "This refers to one who worships an idol."

F. What provides the implication that such a one is subject to discussion here?

G. It accords with what the Tannaite authority of the house of R. Ishmael [said], "'Because he has despised the word of the Lord' (Num. 15:31) refers to one who despises the statement that was made to Moses at Sinai: 'I am the Lord your God. You shall have no other gods before me' (Ex. 20:2-3)."

CXVIII.

A. R. Joshua b. Qorhah says, "Whoever studies the Torah and does not review it is like a man who sows seed but does not harvest it."

B. R. Joshua says, "Whoever learns the Torah and forgets it is like a woman who bears and buries."

C. R. Aqiba says, "[99B] A song is in me, a song always" [T. Ah. 16:8H-I].

D. Said R. Isaac b. Abudimi, "What is the pertinent proof-text? As it is said, 'He who labors labors for himself, for his mouth craves it of him' (Prov. 16:26).

E. "He labors in one place, and the Torah labors for him in a different place."

CXIX.

A. Said R. Eleazar, "Every man was born to work, as it is said, 'For man is born to work' (Job 5:7).

B. "I do knot know whether it is for work done with the mouth that he is created, or whether it is for labor done through physical work that he was created.

C. "When Scripture says, 'For his mouth craves it of him' (Prov. 16:26), one has to conclude that it is for work done with the mouth that he was created.

D.   "Yet I still do not know whether it was to labor in the Torah or to labor in some sort of other conversation.

E.   "When Scripture says, 'This book of the Torah shall not depart out of your mouth' (Josh. 1:8), one must conclude that it is for labor in the Torah that he is created."

F.   That is in line with what Raba said, "All bodies serve to bear burdens. Happy are those who have the merit of bearing the burden of the Torah."

CXX.

A.   "Whoever commits adultery with a woman lacks understanding" (Prov. 6:32).:

B.   Said R. Simeon b. Laqish, "This refers to one who studies the Torah at occasional intervals.

C.   "For it is said, 'For it is a pleasant thing if you keep them within you, they shall withal be fitted in your lips' (Prov. 22:18). [Freedman, p. 673, n. 11: One can keep the Torah only if its words are fitted always on his lips, not at rare intervals only.]"

CXXI.

A.   Our rabbis have taught on Tannaite authority:

B.   "But the soul that does anything presumptuously" (Num. 15:30):

C.   This refers to Manasseh, son of Hezekiah, who would go into session and interpret tales seeking flaws in them, saying, "Did Moses have nothing better to do than to write such verses as 'And Lotan's sister was Timna' (Gen. 36:22). 'And Timna was concubine to Eliphaz' (Gen. 36:12). 'And Reuben went in the days of the wheat harvest and found mandrakes in the field' (Gen. 30:14)?"

D.   An echo came forth and said to him, "'You sit and speak against your brother; you slander your own mother's son. These things you have done, and I kept silence, you thought that I was altogether such a one as yourself, but I will reprove you and set them in order before your eyes' (Ps. 50:20-21)."

E.   Concerning him it is spelled out in tradition: "Woe to them who draw iniquity with cords of vanity and sin as it were with a cart rope" (Is. 5:18).

F.   What is the sense of "and sin as it were with a cart rope"?

G.   Said R. Assi, "The inclination to do evil to begin with is like a spider's thread and ends up like a cart do rope."

H.   In any event, what is the meaning of, "And Lotan's sister was Timna" (Gen. 36:22)?

I.   She was a princess, as it is written, "Duke Lotan, Duke Timna," and "duke" refers to a kid who has not yet got his crown.

J.   She had wanted to convert to Judaism. She came to Abraham, Isaac, and Jacob, and they did not accept her. She went and became the concubine to Eliphaz, son of Esau, saying, "It is better to he a handmaiden to this nation and not a noble woman to any other nation."

K.   From her descended Amalak, who distressed Israel.

L.   What is the reason? It was because they should not have put her off [but should have accepted her].

M.   "And Reuben went in the days of the wheat harvest [and found mandrakes in the field]" (Gen. 36:12)"

N.   Said Raba, son of R. Isaac, said Rab, "On the basis of this verse, we learn that righteous folk do not lay hands on what is stolen."

O.   "And found mandrakes in the field" (Gen. 36:12):

P.   What are these?

Q.   Said Rab, "Mandrakes."

R.   Said Levi, "Violets."

S.   Said R. Jonathan, "Mandrake flowers."

CXXII.

A.   Said R. Alexandri, "Whoever is occupied in study of the Torah for the sake of heaven brings peace to the family above and to the family below,

B.   "as it is said, 'Or let him take hold of my strength that he may make peace with me, and he shall may make peace with me' (Is. 27:5)."

C.   Rab said, "It is as if he built the palace above and the one below, as it is said, 'And I have put my words in your mouth and I have covered you in the shadow of my hand, that I may plant the heavens and lay the foundations of the earth, and say to Zion, You are my people' (Is. 51:16)."

D.   R. Yohanan said, "Also he shields the world, as it is said, 'And I have covered you in the shadow of my hand' (Is. 51:16)."

E.   Levi said, "Also he draws the redemption nearer, as it is said, 'And say to Zion, you are my people' (Is. 51:16)."

CXXIII.

A.   Said R. Simeon b. Laqish, "Whoever teaches Torah to the son of his neighbor is credited by Scripture as if he had made him,

B.   "as it is said, 'And the souls which they had made in Haran' I (Gen. 12:5)."

C.   R. Eleazar said, "It is as though he had made the words of Torah, as it is said, 'Therefore keep the words of this covenant and make them' (Deut. 29:9)."

D.   Raba said, "It is as though he had made himself, as it is said - 'And make them' (Deut. 29:9).

E.   "Do not read 'them' but 'yourselves.'"

CXXIV.

A.   Said R. Abbahu, "Whoever makes his neighbor carry out a religious duty is credited by Scripture as if he himself had done it, as it is said, 'The Lord said to Moses, Take...your rod, with which you hit the river' (Ex. 17:5).

B.   "But did Moses hit the river? It was Aaron who hit the river.

C.   "Rather, this shows, whoever makes his neighbor carry out a religious duty is credited by Scripture as if he himself had done it."

CXXV.

A.   An Epicurean [M. 11:1D]:

B.   Both Rab and R. Hanina say, "This refers to one who humiliates disciples of sages."

C.   Both R. Yohanan and R. Joshua b. Levi say, "It is one who humiliates his fellow before a disciple of a sage."

D.   Now from the viewpoint of him who says it is one who humiliates his fellow before a sage, it would also encompass a disciple of a sage himself, who exposes aspects of the Torah not in accord with the law [M. Abot 3:11] [acts impudently against the Torah (Freedman)].

E.   But in the view of him who says that an Epicurean is one who humiliates a disciple of a sage himself, then at sort of person would fall into the category of one who exposes aspects of the Torah not in accord with the law [M. Abot 3:11]?

F.   It would be someone of the sort of Manasseh b. Hezekiah.

G.   There are those who repeat on Tannaite authority the dispute at hand in conjunction with the latter, rather than the former category, as follows:

H.   One who exposes aspects of the Torah [not in accord with the law] [M. Abot 3:11]:

I.   Rab and R. Hanina say, "It is one who humiliates a disciple of sages."

J.   R. Yohanan and R. Joshua b. Levi say, "It is one who humiliates his fellow before a disciple of a sage."

K.   Now from the viewpoint of him who says it is one who humiliates a disciple of a sage himself, then one who reveals aspects of the Torah, one who humiliates his fellow before a disciple of a sage, would be an Epicurean.

L.   But from the viewpoint of him who says that it is one who humiliates his fellow before a disciple of a sage, with one who reveals aspects of the Torah [in an improper way] as an Epicurean, then who would fall into that latter category?

M.   Said R. Joseph, "It would, for example, be those who say, 'What good are the rabbis for us? It is for their own benefit that they study Scripture. It is for their own benefit that they repeat Mishnah-teachings.'"

N.   Said Abayye to him, "That too falls into the category of one who reveals aspects of the Torah in an improper way, for it is written, 'Thus says the Lord, But for my covenant [studied] day and night, I had not appointed the ordinances of heaven and earth' (Jer. 33:25). [Freedman, p. 676, n. 3: The world endures only because the Torah -- 'my covenant' -- is studied. To deny the utility of scholars therefore is to express disbelief of what is asserted in the Torah.]"

O.   Said R. Nahman bar Isaac, "The proof derives as well from the following, as it is said, 'Then I will spare all the place for their sakes' (Gen. 18:26)."

P.   Rather, it is one who for example was sitting before his master, and the topic of discussion moved to another subject, and he said, "This is what we said on the subject," rather than, "Master, you have said [on that topic]."

Q.   Raba said, "It would, for example, be like the members of the house of Benjamin, the physician, who say, 'What good are rabbis to us. They have never [100A] permitted us to eat a raven or forbidden us to eat a dove [but are limited to what the Torah itself states]."

R.   When people of the house of Benjamin brought Raba a problem involving the validity of a beast that had been slaughtered and that may or may not have been able to survive, if he found a reason to permit the matter, he would say to them, "See, I do permit the raven to you."

S. When he found a reason to prohibit it, he would say to them, "See, I do forbid the dove to you."

T. R. Pappa said, "It would be such as one who said, 'O, these rabbis!'"

U. R. Pappa forgot himself and said, "O these rabbis!" He sat and fasted.

CXXVI.

A. Levi bar Samuel and R. Huna bar Hiyya were fixing the mantles of the Torah scrolls of the house of R. Judah. When they got to the scroll of Esther, they said, "Lo, this scroll of Esther does not have to have a mantle at all."

B. He said to them, "This sort of talk also appears to be Epicureanism."

CXXVII.

A. R. Nahman said, "It is one who refers to his master by his name.

B. For R. Yohanan said, "On what account was Gehazi punished because he called his master by name.

C. "as it is said, 'My lord, O King, this is the woman, and this is her son whom Elisha restored to life' (2 Kgs. 8:5)."

CXXVIII.

A. R. Jeremiah was in session before R. Zira and said, "The Holy One, blessed be he, by which there will be many kinds of delicious produce, as it is said, 'And by the river upon that bank thereof, on this side and on that side, shall grow all trees for meat, whose leaf shall not fade, neither shall the fruit thereof be consumed; it shall bring forth new fruit, according to his months, because their waters they issued out of the sanctuary, and the fruit therefore shall be for meat, and the leaf thereof for medicine' (Ez. 47:12)."

B. "Said to him a certain old man, 'Well said, and so did R. Yohanan say.'"

C. Said R. Jeremiah to R. Zira, "Behavior of this sort [condescension to the master] likewise appears to be Epicureanism."

D. He said to him, "But this represented a mere support for your position.

E. "But if you have heard any tradition, this is the tradition that you heard:

F. "R. Yohanan was in session and interpreting Scripture as follows: 'The Holy One, blessed be he, is destined to bring forth precious stones and jewels which are thirty cubits long and thirty cubits high, and engrave on them an engraving ten by twenty cubits, and he will set them up as the gates of Jerusalem, for it is written, "And I will make your windows of agates and your gates of carbuncles" (Is. 54:12).'

G. "'A disciple ridiculed him, saying "Now if we do not find jewels the size of a dove's egg, are we going to find any that big?"'

H. "'After some time he took a sea voyage, and he saw ministering angels cutting precious stones and jewels. He said to them, "As to these, what are they for?"

I. "'They said to him, "The Holy One, blessed be he, is destined to set them up as the gates of Jerusalem."

J. "'When he came back, he found R. Yohanan in session and expounding Scripture. He said to him, "Rabbi, indeed give your exposition, for it is appropriate that you should expound Scripture. Exactly as you said, so I myself saw."

K.   "'He said to him, "Empty head! Had you not seen, would you not have believed me!
      You are one who ridicules teachings of sages." He set his eye on him and turned him
      into a hill o bones.'"

L.   An objection was raised [to the teaching of Yohanan]'

M.   "And I will make you go upright (Lev. 26:13).

N.   R. Meir says, "It is the height of two hundred cubits, twice the height of Adam."

O.   R. Judah says, "A hundred cubits, the length of the Temple and its walls, as it is
      written, 'That our sons may be as plants grown up in their youth, that our daughters
      may be as corner stones, fashioned after the similitude of the Temple' (Ps. 144:12)."

P.   What R. Yohanan meant was [Freedman]: the ventilation - windows. [These would
      be ten by twenty, but the gates themselves would be much taller (Freedman, p. 678,
      n. 7)].

Q.   What is the meaning of the phrase, "And the leaf thereof is for medicine" (Ez. 47:12)"

R.   R. Isaac bar. Abodimi and R. Hisda: one said, "It is to open up the upper mouth [and
      help the dumb to speak]."

S.   One said, "It is to open the lower mouth [and heal the barrenness of a barren
      woman]."

T.   It has been taught on Tannaite authority"

U.   Hezekiah said, "It is to open the mouth of the dumb."

V.   Bar Qappara said, "It is to open the mouth of the barren women."

W.   R. Yohanan said, "It serves as medicine, literally."

X.   What is the meaning of the statement, "Medicine"?

Y.   R. Ramual bar Nahmani said, "It is to improve the appearance of masters of mouths
      [disciples]."

CXXIX.

A.   R. Judah b. R. Simon interpreted, "Whoever blackens his face [in fasting] on account
      of teachings of Torah in this world will find that the Holy One, blessed be he,
      polishes his luster in the world to come.

B.   "For it is said, 'His countenance shall be as the Lebanon, excellent as the cedars'
      (Song 5:15)."

C.   R. Ranhum bar Hanilai said, "Whoever starves himself for words of Torah in his
      world will the Holy One, blessed be he, feed to satisfaction in the world to come,

D.   "as it is said, 'They shall be abundantly satisfied with the fatness of your house, and
      you shall make them drink of the river of your pleasures' (Ps. 36:9)."

E.   When R. Dimi came, he said, "The Holy One, blessed be he, is destined to give to
      every righteous person his full pack-load, as it is said, 'Blessed be the Lord, day by
      day, who loads us with benefits, even the God of our salvation, Selah' (Ps. 68:20)."

F.   Said Abayye to him, "And is it possible to say so? Is it not said, 'Who has measured
      the waters in the hollow of his hand and measured out heaven with the span' (Is.
      40:12)?"

G. He said to him, "What is the reason that you are not at home in matters of lore. They say in the West in the name of Raba bar Mari, 'The Holy One, blessed be he, is destined to give each righteous person three hundred and ten worlds, as it is said, "That I may cause those who love me to inherit substance and I will fill their treasures," (Prov. 8:21), and the numerical value of the word for substance is three hundred ten.'"

CXXX.

A. It has been taught on Tannaite authority"

B. R. Meir says, "By the same measure by which a mate metes out, do they mete out to him [M. Sot. 1:7A],

C. "For it is written, By measure in sending her away thou dost contend with her' (Is. 27:8).

D. Said R. Judah, "And can one say so? If a person gives a handful [to charity] to a poor man in this world, will the Holy One, blessed be he, give him a handful [of his, so much larger hand], in the world to come?

E. "And has it not been written, 'And meted out heaven with a span' (Is. 40:12)?"

F. [Meir replied] "But do you not say so? Which measure is greater? That of goodness or that of punishment? [100B]

G. "With regard to the measure of goodness it is written, 'And he commanded the clouds from above, and opened the doors of heaven and rained down manna upon them to eat' (Ps. 78:23-24).

H. "With regard to the measure of punishment it is written, 'And the windows of heaven were opened' (Gen. 7:11) [Freedman, p. 680, n. 5: 'Doors' implies a greater opening than windows; God metes out reward more fully than punishment.]

I. "In respect to the measure even of punishment it is written, 'And they shall go forth and look upon the carcasses of the men who have transgressed against me, for their worm shall not die, neither shall their fire be quenched, and they shall be a horror to all flesh' (Is. 66:24).

J. "But is it not so that if a person put his finger into a fire in this world, he will be burned right away.

K. "But just as the Holy One, blessed be he, gives the wicked the power to receive their punishment, so the Holy One, blessed be he, gives the righteous the power to receive the goodness that is coming to them."

CXXXI.

A. R. Aqiba says, "Also: He who reads in heretical books..." [M. 11:1E]:

B. It was taught on Tannaite authority: That is the books of the minim.

CXXXII.

A. R. Joseph said, "It is also forbidden to read in the book of Ben Sira."

B. Said to him Abayye, "What is the reason for that view?

C. Should I say that it is because it is written in it, 'Do not skin the fish, even from the ear, so that you will not go and bruise it, but roast it in the fire and eat two loaves with it'?

D. "In point of fact in the explicit view of Scripture it is also said, 'You shall not destroy the trees thereof' (Deut. 20:19). [Freedman, p. 681, ns. 1-2: A fish is fit for consumption even if baked or roasted with its skin and therefore it is wasteful to remove it. Likewise, one must not wantonly destroy what is fit for use].

E. "And if it is a matter of exegesis [and not the literal sense], then the saying teaches us proper conduct, namely, that one should not have sexual relations in an unnatural way.

F. "Rather, might it be because it is written in it, 'A daughter is a worthless treasure for her father. For concern for her, he cannot sleep by night. In her childhood, it is lest she be seduced; in her girlhood, it is lest she play the whore; in her maturity, it is lest she not wed; once she is wed, it is lest she not have sons. In her old age it is lest she practice witchcraft'?

G. "But rabbis have also made the same statement: 'The world cannot exist without males and without females. Happy is he whose children are males, and woe is him whose children are females.'

H. "Rather, might it be because it is written in [Ben Sira]: 'Do not admit despair into your heart, for despair has killed many men'?

I. "Lo, Solomon made the same statement; 'Anxiety in the heart of man makes him stoop' (Prov. 12:25)."

J. R. Ammi and R. Assi: One said, "Let him banish it from his mind."

K. "The other said, "Let him tell it to others."

L. [Reverting to Abayye's inquiry:] "Rather, might it be because it is written in [Ben Sira]: 'Keep large numbers of people away from your house, and do not let just anyone into your house'?

M. "Lo, Rabbi also made that statement.

N. "For it has been taught on Tannaite authority:

O. "Rabbi says, 'A person should never admit a great many friends into his house, as it is said, "A man who has many friends brings evil upon himself" (Prov. 18:24).'

P. "Rather, it is because it is written in it: 'A man with a thin beard is wise, a man with a thick beard is a fool; one who blows forth his beard is not thirsty. One who says, "What is there to eat with my bread" -- take the bread away from him. [He too is not hungry.] He who parts his beard will overpower the world [being very clever.]' [This foolish statement, in point of fact, forms the basis for Joseph's judgment.]"

Q. Said R. Joseph, "But the excellent statements in the book [of Ben Sira] we do expound.

R. "[For example:] 'A good woman is a good gift, who will be put into the bosom of a God-fearing man. A bad woman is a plague for her husband. What is his remedy? Let him drive her from his house and be healed from what is plaguing him.

S. "A lovely wife -- happy is her husband. The number of his days is doubled.

T. "Keep your eyes from a woman of charm, lest you be taken in her trap. Do not turn to her husband to drink wine with him, or strong drink, for through the looks of a beautiful woman many have been slain, and numerous are those who have been slain by her.

U. "Many are the blows with which a peddler is smitten [for dealing with women]. Those who make it a habit of committing fornication are like a spark that lights the ember. As a cage is full of birds, so are their houses full of deceit" (Jer. 5:27).

V. "'Keep large numbers of people away from your house, and do not let just anybody into your house.

W. "'Let many people ask how you are, but reveal your secret to one out of a thousand. From her who lies in your house keep protected the opening of your mouth.

X. "'Do not worry about tomorrow's sorrow,' "For you do not know what a day may bring forth" (Prov. 27:1). Perhaps tomorrow you will no longer exist and it will turn out that you will worry about a world that is not yours.

Y. "'All the days of the poor are evil" (Prov. 15:15). Ben Sira said, "So too his nights. His roof is the lowest in town, his vineyard on the topmost mountain. Rain flows from other roofs onto his and from his vineyard onto other vineyards."

CXXXIII.

A. Said R. Zira said Rab, "What is the meaning of the verse of Scripture, 'All the days of the afflicted are evil' (Prov. 15:15)?

B. "This refers to masters of Talmud.

C. "'But he that is of a good heart has a continuous banquet' (Prov. 15:15)? This refers to masters of the Mishnah."

D. Raba said, "Matters are just the opposite."

E. And that is in line with what R. Mesharshia said in the name of Raba, "What is the meaning of the verse of Scripture: 'Whoever removes stones shall be hurt with them' (Qoh. 10:9)?

F. "This refers to masters of the Mishnah.

G. "'But he who cleaves wood shall be warmed by it' (Qoh. 10:9)?

H. "This refers to masters of Talmud."

I. R. Hanina says, "'All of the days of the afflicted are evil' (Prov. 15:15) refers to a man who has a bad wife.

J. "'But he that is of a good heart has a continuous banquet' (Prov. 15:15) refers to a man who has a good wife.

K. R. Yannai says, "'All the days of the afflicted are evil' (Prov. 15:15) refers to one who is fastidious.

L. "'But he that is of a good heart has a continuous banquet (Prov. 15:15) refers to one who is easy to please."

M. R. Yohanan said, "'All the days of the afflicted are evil' (Prov. 15:15) refers to a merciful person.

N. "'But he that is of a good heart has a continuous banquet' (Prov. 15:15) refers to someone who is cruel by nature [so nothing bothers him]."

O. R. Joshua b. Levi said, "'All the days of the afflicted are evil' (Prov. 15:15) refers to [101A] someone who is worrisome.

P.   "'But he that is of a good heart has a continuous banquet' (Prov. 154:15) refers to one who is serene."

Q.   R. Joshua b. Levi said, "'All the days of the afflicted are evil' (Prov. 15:1) -- but [not] there are Sabbaths and festival days [on which the afflicted gets some pleasure]?"

R.   The matter accords with what Samuel said. For Samuel said, "The change in diet [for festival meals] is the beginning of stomach ache."

CXXXIV.

A.   Our rabbis have taught on Tannaite authority:

B.   **He who recites a verse of the Song of Songs and turns it into a kind of love-song, and he who recites a verse in a banquet hall not at the proper time [but in a time of carousal] bring evil into the world [cf. T. San. 12:10A].**

C.   For the Torah puts on sack cloth and stands before the Holy One, blessed be he, and says before him, "Lord of the world, your children have treated me like a harp which scoffers play.

D.   He then says to her, "My daughter, when they eat and drink, what should keep them busy?"

E.   She will say to him, "Lord of the world, if they are masters of Scripture, let them keep busy with the Torah, prophets, and writings; if they are masters of the Mishnah, let them keep busy with the Mishnah, law and lore; and if they are masters of the Talmud, let them keep busy on Passover with the laws of the Passover, with the laws of Pentecost on Pentecost, and with the laws of the Festival [of Tabernacles] on the Festival."

F.   R. Simeon b. Eleazar gave testimony in the name of R. Simeon b. Hanania, "Whoever recites a verse of Scripture at the proper time brings good to the world,

G.   "as it is said, 'And a word spoken in season, how good is it' (Prov. 15:23)."

CXXXV.

A.   And he who whispers over a wound [M. 1:1F]:

B.   Said R. Yohanan, "That is the rule if one spits over the wound, for people may not make mention of the Name of heaven over spit."

CXXXVI.

A.   It has been stated on Amoraic authority:

B.   Rab said, "Even 'When the plague of leprosy' (Lev. 1:1) [may not be recited]."

CXXXVII.

A.   Our rabbis have taught on Tannaite authority:

B.   People may anoint and massage the intestines on the Sabbath, and whisper to snakes and scorpions on the Sabbath, and place utensils on the eyes on the Sabbath.

C.   Said Rabban Simeon b. Gamaliel, "Under what circumstances? In the case of a utensil that may be carried [on the Sabbath], but in the case of a utensil that may not be carried, it is forbidden."

D.   And a question may not be addressed on a matter having to do with demons on the Sabbath.

E.   R. Yose says, "Even on a weekday it is forbidden to do so.

F.   Said R. Huna, "The decided law accords with the view of R. Yose.

G.   And R. Yose made that statement only on account of the danger involving in doing so.

H.   This is illustrated by the case of R. Isaac bar Joseph, who got stuck in a cedar tree, and a miracle was done for him, so that the cedar tree split open and spit him out [Freedman, p. 685, n. 5: He consulted a demon, which turned itself into a tree and swallowed him; it was only through a miracle that he escaped.]

CXXXVIII.

A.   Our rabbis have taught on Tannaite authority:

B.   People may anoint and massage the intestines on the Sabbath, so long as one not do so as he does on a weekday.

C.   How then should one do it?

D.   R. Hama, son of R. Hanini, said, "One puts on some oil and then massages."

E.   R. Yohanan said, "One puts on oil and massages simultaneously."

CXXXIX.

A.   Our rabbis have taught on Tannaite authority:

B.   As to the spirits of oil or eggs, it is permitted to address questions to them, except that they prove unreliable.

C.   People whisper over oil that is in a utensil but not over oil that is held in the hand.

D.   Therefore people apply oil by hand and not out of a utensil.

CXL.

A.   R. Isaac bar Samuel bar Marta happened to stay at a certain inn. They brought him oil in a utensil, and he anointed himself.

B.   He broke out in blisters all over his face.

C.   He went to a market place, and a certain woman saw him and said to him, "The blast of Hamath do I see here."

D.   She did something for him, and he was healed.

CXLI.

A.   Said R. Abba to Rabba bar Mari, "It is written, 'I will put none of these diseases upon you, which I have brought upon the Egyptians, for I am the Lord who heals you' (Ex. 15:26).

B.   "But if he does not place those diseases, what need is there for healing anyhow?"

C.   He said to him, "This is what R. Yohanan said, 'This verse of Scripture provides its own interpretation, since it is said, "And he said, If you will diligently obey the voice of the Lord your God" (Ex. 15:16). "If you obey, I shall not place those diseases upon you, and if you will not obey, I will do so."

D.   "'Yet even so: "I am the Lord who heals you"(Ex. 15:26).'"

CXLII.

A.   Said Rabbah bar bar Hanah, "When R. Eliezer fell ill, his disciples came in to call on him.

B.   "He said to them, 'There is great anger in the world [to account for my sickness].'

C.   "They began to cry, but R. Aqiba began to laugh. They said to him, 'Why are you laughing?'

D.   "He said to them, 'Why are you crying?'

E.   "They said to him, 'Is it possible that, when a scroll of the Torah [such as Eliezer] is afflicted with disease, we should not cry?'

F.   "He said to them, 'For that reason I am laughing. So long as I observed that, as to my master, his wine did not turn to vinegar, his flux was not smitten, his oil did not putrefy, and his honey did not become rancid,

G.   "I though to myself, "Perhaps, God forbid, my master has received his reward in this world." But now that I see my master in distress, I rejoice [knowing that he will receive his full reward in the world to come.]'

H.   "[Eliezer] said to him, 'Aqiba, have I left out anything at all from the whole of the Torah?'

I.   "He said to him, '[Indeed so, for] you have taught us, our master, "For there is not a just man upon earth, who does good and does not sin" (Qoh. 7:20).'"

CXLIII.

A.   Our rabbis have taught on Tannaite authority:

B.   When R. Eliezer fell ill, four elders came to call on him: R. Tarfon, R. Joshua, R. Eleazar b. Azariah, and R. Aqiba.

C.   R. Tarfon responded first and said, "You are better for Israel than a drop of rain, for a drop of rain is good for this world, but my master is good for this world and the world to come."

D.   R. Joshua responded and said, "You are better for Israel than the orb of the sun, for the orb of the sun serves for this world, but my master serves for this world and the world to come."

E.   R. Eleazar b. Azariah responded and said, "You are better for Israel than a father and a mother, for a father and a mother are for this world, but my master is for this world and the world to come."

F.   R. Aqiba responded and said, "Suffering is precious."

G.   He said to them, "Prop me up so that I may hear the statement of Aqiba, my disciple, who has said, 'Suffering is precious.'"

H.   He said to him, "Aqiba, how do you know?"

I.   He said to him, "I interpret a verse of Scripture: "Manasseh was twelve years old when he began to reign, and he reigned fifty five years in Jerusalem...and he did what was evil in the sight of the Lord' (2 Kgs. 21:1-2).

J.   "And it is written [101B], 'These are the proverbs of Solomon, which the men of Hezekiah, king of Judan, copied out' (Prov. 25:1).

K.   "Now is it possible that Hezekiah, king of Judah, taught the Torah to the entire world, but to his son, Manasseh, he did not teach the Torah? [Obviously not!]

L.   "But out of all the trouble that [his father] took with him, and with all the labor that he poured into him, nothing brought him back to the good way except for suffering.

M. "For it is said, 'And the Lord spoke to Manasseh and to his people, but they would not hearken to him. Therefore the Lord brought upon them the captains of the host of the king of Assyria, who took Manasseh among the thorns and bound him with chains and carried him to Babylonia' (2 Chr. 33:10-11).

N. "And it is written, 'And when he was in affliction, he sought the Lord his God and humbled himself greatly before the God of his fathers. And he prayed to him and he was entreated of him and heard his supplication and brought him again to Jerusalem to his kingdom, and Manasseh knew that the Lord is God' (2 Chr. 33:12-13).

O. "So you learn that suffering is precious."

CXLIV.

A. Our rabbis have taught on Tannaite authority:

B. Three came with a self-serving plea, and these are they: Cain, Esau, and Manasseh.

C. Cain, as it is written, "Is my sin too great to be forgiven?" (Gen. 4:13).

D. He said before him, "Lord of the world, Is my sin any greater than that of the six hundred thousand who are destined to sin before you? And yet you will forgive them!"

E. Esau, as it is written, "Have you but one blessing, my father" (Gen. 27:38).

F. Manasseh: To begin with he called upon many gods and in the end he called upon the God of his fathers.

CXLV.

A. Abba Saul says, "Also: he who pronounces the divine Name as it is spelled out" [M. 11:1G].:

B. On Tannaite authority [it was stated]:

C. That is the rule in the provinces, and [when it is] in blasphemous language.

CXLVI.

A. Three kings and four ordinary folk [have no portion in the world to come. Three kings: Jeroboam, Ahab, and Manasseh] [M. 11:2A-B]:

B. Our rabbis have taught on Tannaite authority:

C. "Jerobam": for he treated the people as his sexual object.

D. Another matter: "Jeroboam: "for he made strife in the people.

E. Another matter: "Jeroboam: "for he brought strife between the people of Israel and their father in heaven.

F. Son of Nebat, a son who saw [a vision] but did not see [its meaning].

CXLVII.

A. On Tannaite [authority it was stated]:

B. Nebat is the same as Micah and Sheba son of Bichri.

C. Nebat: Because he saw a vision but did not see [its meaning].

D. Micah: because he was [Freedman]: crushed in the building. [Freedman, pp. 688-689, n. 11: According to legend, when the Israelites in Egypt did not complete their tale of bricks, their children were built into the walls instead. On Moses' complaining thereof to God, He answered him that He was thus weeding out the destined wicked. As proof, he was empowered to save Micah, who had already been built it, but only to become an idolator on his reaching manhood. Rashi also gives an alternative rendering: he became impoverished through building -- presumably his idolatrous shrine.]

E.   But what was his real name? It was Sheba, son of Bichri.

CXLVIII.

A.   Our rabbis have taught on Tannaite authority:

B.   There were three who saw [a vision] but did not see [its meaning], and these are they: Nabat, Ahitophel, and Pharaoh's astrologers.

C.   Nabat saw fire coming forth from his penis. He thought that [it meant that] he would rule, but that was not the case. It was that Jeroboam would come forth from him [who would rule].

D.   Ahitophel saw saraat spread over him and over his penis. He thought that it meant that he would be king, and that was not the case. It was Sheba, his daughter, from whom Solomon would come forth.

E.   The astrologers of Pharaoh: In line with what R. Hama, son of R. Hanina, said, "What is the meaning of the verse of Scripture, 'These are the waters of rebellion, because they strove' (Num. 20:13)?

F.   "These are the waters which the astrologers of Pharaoh foresaw, and about which they erred.

G.   "They saw that the savior of Israel would be smitten because of water. So [Pharaoh] decreed, 'Every son that is born you shall cast into the river' (Ex. 1:22).

H.   "But they did not know that it was on account of the water of rebellion that he would be smitten:

CXLIX.

A.   And how do we know that [Jeroboam] will not come into the world to come?

B.   As it is written, "And this thing became sin to the house of Jeroboam, even to cut if off and to destroy it from off the face of the earth" (1 Kgs. 13:34).

C.   "To cut it off" in this world.

D.   "And to destroy it" in the world to come.

CL.

A.   Said R. Yohanan, "On what account did Jeroboam have the merit to rule?

B.   Because he reproved Solomon.

C.   "And on what account was he punished?

D.   "Because he reproved him publicly.

E.   "So it is said, 'And this was the cause that the lifted up his hand against the king: Solomon built Millo and repaired the breaches of the city of David his father' (1 Kgs. 11:27).

F.   "He said to him, 'David your father made breaches in the wall so that the Israelites might come up for the pilgrim-festivals, but you have filled them in so as to collect a tax for the daughter of Pharaoh.'"

G.   And what is the meaning of the phrase, "That he lifted up his hand against the king" (1 Kgs. 11:27)?

H.   Said R. Nahman, "Because he took off his phylacteries in his presence."

CLI.

A.   Said R. Nahman, "The arrogance that characterized Jeroboam is what drove him out of the world.

B.   "For it is said, 'Now Jeroboam said in his heart, Now shall the kingdom return to the house of David. If this people go up to sacrifice in the house of the Lord at Jerusalem, then shall the heart of this people turn to their Lord, even to Rehoboam, king of Judah, and they shall kill me and go again to Rehoboan, king of Judah' (1 Kgs. 12:27-26).

C.   "He said, 'We have a tradition that no one may sit down in the Temple courtyard except kings of the house of Judah alone. When the people see that Rehoboam is sitting down and I am standing, they will think that he is king, and I am merely a servant.

D.   "'But if I sit down, I shall be in the position of rebelling against the monarchy, and they will kill me and follow.'

E.   "Forthwith: 'Wherefore the king took counsel and made two calves of gold and said to them, It is too much for you to go up to Jerusalem. Behold your gods O Israel, who brought you up out of the land of Egypt, and he put one in Beth El and the other he put in Dan' (1 Kgs. 12:28)."

F.   What is the meaning of the phrase, "The king took counsel"?

G.   Said R. Judah, "That he sat a wicked person next to a righteous person. He said to them, 'Will you sign everything that I do.'

H.   "They said to him, 'Yes.'

I.   "He said to them, 'I want to be king.'

J.   "They said to him, 'Yes.'

K.   "He said to them, 'Will you do whatever I say?'

L.   "They said to him, 'Yes.'"

M.   "'Even to worship an idol.'

N.   "The righteous one said to him, 'God forbid.'

O.   "The wicked one said to the righteous one, 'Do you think that a person such as Jeroboam would really worship an idol? Rather, what he wants to do is to test us to see whether or not we shall accept his word [102A].'"

P.   "Even Ahijah the Shilonite made a mistake and signed, for Jehu was a very righteous man, as it is said, And the Lord said to Jehu, Because you have done well in executing what is right in my eyes and have done to the house of Ahab according to all that was in my heart, your children of the fourth generation shall sit upon the throne of Israel' (2 Kgs. 10:30).

Q.   "But it is written, 'But Jehu took no heed to walk in the law of the Lord God of Israel with all his heart, for he did not depart from the sins of Jeroboam, which he had made Israel to sin' (2 Kgs. 10:31)."

R.   What caused it?

S.   Said Abayye, "A covenant made orally, as it is said, 'And Jehu gathered all the people together and said to them, Ahab served Baal a little, but Jehu shall serve him much' (2 Kgs. 10:18). [Freedman, p. 691, n. 5: These words, though spoken guilefully, had to be fulfilled.]"

T.   Raba said, "He saw the signature of Ahijah the Shilonite, and he erred on that account."

CLII.

A.   It is written, "And the revolters are profound to make slaughter, though I have been a rebuke of all of them" (Hos. 5:2):

B.   Said R. Yohanan, "Said the Holy One, blessed be he, 'They have gone deeper than I did. I said, "Whoever does not go up to Jerusalem for the Festival transgresses an affirmative requirement," but they have said, "Whoever does go up to Jerusalem for the festival will be stabbed with a sword."'"

CLIII.

A.   "And it came to pass at that time, when Jeroboam went out of Jerusalem, that the prophet Ahijah the Shilonite found him in the way, and he had clad himself with a new garment" (1 Kgs. 11:20):

B.   It was taught on Tannaite authority in the name of R. Yose, "It was a time designated for punishment. [Freedman, p. 691, n. 9: On that occasion Ahijah prophesied the division of the kingdom as a punishment for Solomon's backsliding.]"

C.   "In the time of their visitation they shall perish" (Jer. 51:18):

D.   It was taught on Tannaite authority in the name of R. Yose, "A time designated for punishment."

E.   "In an acceptable time I have heard you" (Is. 49:8):

F.   It was taught on Tannaite authority in the name of R. Yose, "A time designated for good."

G.   "Nevertheless in the day when I visit, I will visit their sin upon them: (Ex. 32:34):

H.   It was taught on Tannaite authority in the name of R. Yose, "A time designated for punishment."

I.   "And it came to pass at that time, that Judah went down from his brethren" (Gen. 38:1):

J.   It was taught on Tannaite authority in the name of R. Yose, "A time designated for punishment."

K.   "And Rehoboam went to Shechem, for all Israel were come to Shechem to make him king" (1 Kgs. 12:1)"

L.   It was taught on Tannaite authority in the name of R. Yose, "A time designated for punishment. In Shechem men raped Dinah, in Shechem his brothers sold Joseph, in Shechem the kingdom of David was divided."

CLIV.

A.   "Now it came to pass at that time that Jeroboam went out of Jerusalem" (1 Kgs. 11:29)"

B.   Said R. Hanina bar Pappa, "He went out of the realm of Jerusalem."

CLV.

A.   "And the prophet Ahijah the Shilonite found him in the way, and he clad himself with a new garment, and the two were alone in the field" (1 Kgs. 11:29):

B.   What is this "new garment"?

C.   said R. Nahman, "It was as with a new garment: just as a new garment has no sort of blemish, so the Torah-learning of Jeroboam had no sort of flaw."

D.   Another matter: "A new garment:"

E.   It was that they said things so new that no ear had ever heard them.

F.   "And the two were alone in the field" (1 Kgs. 11:29): What is the meaning of this statement?

G.   Said R. Judah said Rab, "It is that all the disciples of sages were as grass of the field before them [and of no account]."

H.   And there is he who says, "It is that the reasons for the rulings of the Torah were revealed to them in the open as in a field."

CLVI.

A.   "Therefore shall you give parting gifts to Moresheth-gath, the houses of Achzib shall be a lie to the kings of Israel" (Mic. 1:14):

B.   Said R. Hanina bar Pappa, "An echo came forth and said to them, 'He who killed the Philistine and gave you possession of Gath -- to his sons you will give parting gifts.'"

C.   "Therefore the houses of Achzib shall be a lie to the kings of Israel" (Mich. 1:14) [Freedman, p. 693, n. 2: "Since you deal treacherously with the house of David, preferring the rule of the kings of Israel, therefore you shall be delivered into the hands of the heathen, whose religion is false."]

CLVII.

A.   Said R. Hinnena bar Pappa, "Whoever derives benefit from this world without reciting a blessing is as if he steals from the Holy One, blessed be he, and the community of Israel.

B.   "For it is said, 'Who robs from his father or his mother and says, It is no transgression, is the companion of a destroyer' (Prov. 28:24).

C.   "'His father' is only the Holy One, blessed be he, as it is said, 'Is not [God] your father, who has bought you' (Deut. 32:6), and 'his mother' can mean only the congregation of Israel, as it is said, 'My son, hear the instruction of your father and do not forsake the Torah of your mother' (Prov. 1:8)."

D.   "What is the sense of "He is the companion of a destroyer" (Prov. 28:24)?

E.   "He is companion of Jeroboam, son of Nebat, who destroyed Israel for their father in heaven."

CLVIII.

A.   "And Jeroboam drove Israel from following the Lord and made them sin a great sin" (2 Kgs. 17:21)"

B.   Said R. Hanin, "It was like two sticks that rebound from one another."

CLIX.

A.   "[These are the words which Moses spoke to all Israel in the wilderness] and Di Zahab" (Deut. 1:1):

B.   Said a member of the house of R. Yannai, "Moses said before the Holy One, blessed
      be he, 'Lord of the world, on account of the silver and gold which you showered on
      Israel until they said, "Enough," they were caused to make for themselves gods of
      gold.'

C.   "It is comparable to the case of a lion, who does not tear and roar on account of
      what is in a basket containing straw, but because of what is in a basket of meat."

D.   Said R. Oshaia, "Up to the time of Jeroboam, the Israelites would suck from a single
      calf [sinning on account of only one], but from that time on, it was from two or
      three calves."

E.   Said R. Isaac, "You do not have any sort of punishment that comes upon the world in
      which is contained at least one twenty-fourth of part of the overweight of a litra of
      the first calf.

F.   "For it is written, 'Nevertheless in the day when I visit, I will visit their sin upon
      them' (Ex. 32:34)."

G.   Said R. Hanina, "After twenty-four generations this verse of Scripture will be
      exacted: 'He cried also in my ears with a loud voice, saying, Cause the visitations
      of the city to draw near, even every man with his destroying weapon in his hand'
      (Ez. 9:1)." [Freedman, p. 694, n. 4: The use of "visitations" suggests that this was
      the fulfillment of the doom threatened in Ex. 32:34. There were twenty-four
      generations from that of the wilderness, when the calf was made, to that of
      Zedekiah, in whose reign the state was overthrown and Judah was deported to
      Babylonia.]"

CLX.

A.   "After this thing Jeroboam did not turn from his evil way" (1 Kgs. 13:33)"

B.   What is the sense of "after"?

C.   Said R. Abba, "After the Holy One, blessed be he, seized Jeroboam by his garment
      and said to him, 'Repent, and you and the son of Jesse and I shall walk about in the
      Garden of Eden.'

D.   "He said to him, 'He who will be at the head?'

E.   "'The son of Jesse will be at the head.'

F.   "If so, I don't want it.'"

CLXI.

A.   R. Abbahu would regularly give a public interpretation of the three kings [of M.
      11:2A]. He fell ill and undertook not to give such an address [since he thought the
      illness was punishment for speaking about the king's sins].

B.   When [102B] he got better, he reversed himself and gave an address. They said to
      him, "You undertook not to speak about them."

C.   He said to them, "Did they repent, that I should repent!"

CLXII.

A.   At the house of R. Ashi, [the group] arose [from studying] at the teaching of the
      three kings. He said, "Tomorrow we shall open discourse with the topic of 'our
      colleagues' [M. 11:2, that is, the three kings, all of whom were held to be disciples
      of sages.]"

B.   Manasseh came and appeared in a dream: "Do you call us 'your colleague' and 'your father's colleague'? [If you are as good as we are, then tell me] from what part of the bread do you take the piece for reciting the blessing, 'Who brings forth bread from the earth'?"

C.   He said to him, "I don't know."

D.   He said to him, "If you have not learned from what part of the bread do you take a piece for reciting the blessing, 'Who brings forth bread from the earth,' how can you call us 'your colleague'?"

E.   He said to him, "Teach me. Tomorrow I shall expound the matter in your name in the class-session."

F.   He said to him, "One takes the part that is baked into a crust [and not the dough on the inside]."

G.   He said to him, "If you are so wise, then what is the reason that you worshipped an idol?"

H.   He said to him, "If you had been there, you would have picked up the hem of your garment and run after me."

I.   The next day he said to the rabbis, "Let us begin with our teacher."

CLXIII.

A.   The name 'Ahab' signifies that he was a brother to heaven (ah) but father of idolatry (ab).

B.   "He was brother to heaven, as it is written, 'A brother is born for trouble' (Prov. 17:17).

C.   "He was father to idolatry, as it is written, 'As a father loves his children' (Ps. 103:13)."

CLXIV.

A.   "And it came to pass, that it was a light thing for him to walk in the sins of Jeroboam, the son of Nebat" (1 Kgs. 16:31):

B.   Said R. Yohanan, "The lightest [sins] committed by Ahab were as the most severe ones that were committed by Jeroboam.

C.   "And on what account did Scripture blame Jeroboam? It was because he was the beginning of the corruption."

CLXV.

A.   "Yes, their altars are as heaps in the furrows of the fields" (Hos. 12:12):

B.   Sad R. Yohanan, "You have no furrow in the whole of the land of Israel in which Ahab did not set up an idol and bow down to it."

CLXVI.

A.   And how do we know that [Ahab] will not enter the world to come?

B.   As it is written, "And I will cut off from Ahab him who pisses against the wall, him that is shut up and forsaken in Israel" (1 Kgs. 21:21).

C.   "Shut up" in this world.

D.   "Forsaken" in the world to come.

CLXVII.

A. Said R. Yohanan, "On what account did Omri merit the monarchy? Because he added a single town to the land of Israel, as it is written, 'And he bought the hill Samaria of Shemer for two talents of silver and built on the hill and called the name of the city which he built after the name of Shemer, owner of the hill, Samaria' (1 Kgs. 16:24)."

B. Said R. Yohanan, "On what account did Ahab merit ruling for twenty-two years? Because he honored the Torah, which was given with twenty-two letters [of the Hebrew alphabet], as it is said, 'And he sent messeges to Ahab, king of Israel, to the city, and said to him, Thus says Hen-hadad, Your silver and your gold is mine, your wives also and your children, even the goodliest are mine ... Yet will I send my servants to you tomorrow at this time and they shall search your house, and the houses of your servants, and it shall be, that whatsoever is pleasant in your eyes they shall put in their hand and take it away ... Therefore he said to the messengers of Ben-hadad, Tell my lord the king, all that you send for to your servants at the first I will do, but this thing I may not do' (1 Kgs. 20:3, 6, 9).

C. "What is the meaning of 'whatsoever is pleasant in your eyes'? Is it not a scroll of the Torah?"

D. But could it not be an idol?

E. "Let it not enter your mind, for it is written, 'And all the leader and all the people said to him, Do not listen to him or consent' (1 Kgs. 20:8) [the elders being sages]."

F. And perhaps they were elders [who were identified with] the shame [of the idol itself]?

G. Is it not written, "And the saying pleased Absalom well and all the elders of Israel" (2 Sam. 17:4)? On this passage, said R. Joseph, "They were elders [associated with] the shame."

H. "In that passage, it is not written, 'And all the people,' while here it is written, 'And all the people.' It is not possible that among them were no righteous men, for it is written, 'Yet have I left seven thousand in Israel, all the knees which have not bowed to Baal and every mouth which has not kissed him' (1 Kgs. 19:18)."

CLXVIII.

A. Said R. Nahman, "Ahab was right in the middle [between wickedness and righteousness], as it is said, 'And the Lord said, Who shall persuade Ahab, that he may go up and fall at Ramoth-gildean? And one said in this manner, and one said in that manner' (1 Kgs. 22:20). [Freedman, p. 697, n. 1: This shows that it was a difficult matter to lure him to his fate, and that must have been because his righteousness equalled his guilt.]"

B. To this proposition R. Joseph objected, "We speak of one concerning whom it is written, 'But there was none like Ahab, who sold himself to work wicknedness in the sight of the Lord, whom Jezebel his wife stirred up' (1 Kgs. 21:25),

C. on which passage it was repeated on Tannaite authority, 'Every day she would weigh out gold shekels for idolatry,' and can you say that he was right in the middle"

D.   "Rather, Ahab was generous with his money, and because he gave benefit to disciples of sages out of his property, half of his sins were forgiven."

CLXIX.

A.   "And there came forth the spirit and stood before the Lord and said, I will persuade him. And the Lord said to him, With what? And he said, I will go forth and I will be a lying spirit in the mouth of his prophets. And he said, You shall persuade him and also prevail. Go forth and do so" (1 Kgs. 22:21-23):

B.   What spirit was it?

C.   Said R. Yohanan, "It was the spirit of Naboth the Jezreelite."

D.   What is meant by "go forth"?

E.   Said Rabina, "Go forth from my precincts, as it is written, 'He who lies will not tarry in my sight' (Ps. 101:7)."

F.   Said R. Pappa, "This is in line with what people say, 'He who exacts vengeance destroys his house.'"

CLXX.

A.   "And Ahab made a grove, and Ahab did more to provoke the Lord God of Israel to anger than all of the kings of Israel that were before him" (1 Kgs. 16:33):

B.   Sad R. Yohanan, "It was that he wrote on the gates of Samaria, 'Ahab has denied the God of Israel.' Therefore he has no portion in the God of Israel."

CLXXI.

A.   "And he sought Ahaziah, and they caught him for he hid in Samaria" (2 Chr. 22:9):

B.   Said R. Levi, "He was blotting out the mentions of the divine name [in the Torah] and writing in their place the names of idols."

CLXXII.

A.   Manasseh -- [Based on the root for the word "forget"] for he forgot the Lord.

B.   Another explanation: Manasseh - for he made Israel forget their father in heaven.

C.   And how do we know that he will not come to the world to come?

D.   As it is written, "Manasseh was twelve years old when he began to reign, and he reigned fifty-five years in Jerusalem, ... and he mad a grove as did Ahab, king of Israel" (2 Kgs. 21:2-3).

E.   Just as Ahab has no share in the world to come, so Manasseh has no share in the world to come.

CLXXIII.

A.   R. Judah says, "Manasseh has a portion in the world to come, since it is said, 'And he prayed to him and he was entreated of him ...' (2 Chr. 33:13)" [M. 11:2C-D]:

B.   Said R. Yohanan, "Both authorities [who dispute the fate of Manasseh] interpret the same verse of Scripture, as it is said, 'And I will cause to be removed to all the kingdoms of the earth, because of Manasseh, son of Hezekiah, king of Judah' (Jer. 15:4).

C.   "One authority takes the view that it is 'on account of Manasseh,' who repented, while they did not repent.

D.   "The other authority takes the view [103A] that it is 'because of Manasseh,' who did not repent."

CLXXIV.

A.   Said R. Yohanan, "Whoever maintains that Manasseh has no share in the world to come weakens the hands of those who repent."

B.   For a Tannaite authority repeated before R. Yohanan, "Manasseh repented for thirty-three years, as it is written, 'Manasseh was twelve years old when he began to reign, and he reigned fifty-five years in Jerusalem and he made a grove as did Ahab, king of Israel' (2 Kgs. 21:2-3).

C.   "How long did Ahab rule? Twenty-two years. How long did Manasseh rule? Fifty-five years. Take away twenty-two years, and you are left with thirty-three."

CLXXV.

A.   Said R. Yohanan in the name of R. Simeon b. Yohai, "What is the meaning of the verse of Scripture, 'And he prayed to him and an opening was made for him' (2 Chr. 33:13)?

B.   "It should say, 'and he was entreated of him'!

C.   "It teaches that the Holy One, blessed be he, made a kind of cave for him in the firmament, so as to receive him in repentance, despite the [contrary will of] the attribute of justice."

D.   And said R. Yohanan in the name of R. Simeon b. Yohai, "What is the meaning of the verse of Scripture, 'In the beginning of the reign of Jehoiakim, son of Josiah, king of Judah' (Jer. 26:1)?

E.   "And it is written, 'In the beginning of the reign of Zedekiah, king of Judah' (Jer. 28:1).

F.   "And is it the case that, up to that time there were no kings?

G.   "Rather, the Holy One, blessed be he, planned to return the world to [its beginning condition of] chaos and formlessness on account of Jehoiakim. When, however, he took a close look at his generation, his anger subsided.

H.   "[Along these same lines], the Holy One, blessed be he, planned to return the world to chaos and formlessness on account of the generation of Zedekiah. But when he took a close look at Zedekiah, his anger subsided."

I.   But with regard to Zedekiah, also, it is written, "And he did that which was evil in the sight of God" (2 Kgs. 24:19)?

J.   He could have stopped others but did not do so.

K.   And said R. Yohanan in the name of R. Simeon b. Yohai, "What is the meaning of the verse of Scripture, 'If a wise man content with a foolish man, whether rage or laughter, there is no satisfaction' (Prov. 29:9)?

L.   "Said the Holy One, blessed be he, 'I was angry with Ahaz and I handed him over to the kinds of Damascus and he sacrificed and offered incense to their gods, as it is said, 'For he sacrificed to the gods of Damascus who smote him, and he said, Because the gods of the kinds of Syria help them, therefore will I sacrifice to them that they may help me. But they were the ruin of him and of all Israel' (2 Chr. 28:23).

M. "'I smiled upon Amaziah and delivered the kings of Edom into his power, so he brought their gods and bowed down to them, a it is said, 'Now it came to pass, after Amaziah was come from the slaughter of the Edomites, that he brought the gods of the children of Seir and set them up to be his gods and bowed down himself before them and burned incense to them' (2 Chr. 25:14)."

N. Said R. Pappa, "This is in line with what people say: 'Weep for the one who doe not know, laugh for the one who does not know. Woe to him who does not know the difference between good and bad.'"

O. "And all the princes of the king of Babylonia came in and sat in the middle gate" (Jer. 39:3):

P. Said R. Yohanan in the name of R. Simeon b. Yohai, "It was the place in which laws were mediated."

Q. Said R. Pappa, "That is in line with what people say: 'In the place in which the master hangs up his sword, the shepherd hangs up his pitcher.' [Freedman, p. 700, n. 3: Where the Jews decided upon their laws, there Nebuchadnezzer issued his decrees.]"

CLXXVI.

A. Said R. Hisda said R. Jeremiah bar Abba, "What is the meaning of the following verse: 'I went by the field of the slothful and by the vineyard of the man void of understanding. And lo, it was all grown over with thorns and nettles had covered the face thereof, and the stone wall thereof was broken down' (Prov. 24:30-31)?

B. "'I went by the field of the slothful' -- this speaks of Ahaz.

C. "'And by the vineyard of the man void of understanding' -- this speaks of Manasseh.

D. "'And lo, it was all grown over with thorns' -- this refers to Amon.

E. "'And nettles had covered the face thereof' -- this refers to Jehoiakim.

F. "'And the stone wall thereof was broken down' -- this refers to Zedekiah, in whose time the Temple was destroyed.

G. And said R. Hisda said R. Jeremiah bar Abba, "There are four categories who will not receive the face of the Presence of God:

H. "The categories of scoffers, flatterers, liars, and slanderers.

I. "The category of scoffers, as it is written, 'He has stretched out his hand against scorners' (Hos. 7:5).

J. "The category of flatterers, as it is written, 'He who speaks lies shall not be established in my sight' (Job. 13:16).

K. "The category of liars, as it is written, 'He who speaks lies shall not be established in my sight' (Ps. 101:7).

L. "The category of slanderers, as it is written, 'For you are not a God who has pleasure in wickedness; evil will not dwell with you' (Ps. 5:5). 'You are righteous, O Lord, and evil will not dwell in your house [Ps. 5 addresses slander.]"

M. And said R. Hisda said R. Jeremiah bar Abba, "What is the meaning of the verse, 'There shall nor evil befall you, neither shall any plague come near your dwelling' (Ps. 91:10)?

N.   "There shall not evil befall you' means that the evil impulse will not rule over you.

O.   "'Neither shall any plague come near your dwelling'means that, when you come home from a trip, you will never find that your wife is in doubt as to whether or not she is menstruating."

P.   "Another matter: 'There shall not evil befall you' means that bad dreams and fantasies will never frighten you.

Q.   "'Neither shall any plague come near your dwelling' means that you will not have a son or a disciple who in public burns his food [that is, teaches something heretical]'

R.   "Up to this point is the blessing that his father had given him.

S.   "From this point forward comes the blessing that his mother had given to him: 'For he shall give his angels charge over you, to keep you in all your ways. They shall bear you in their hands ... You shall tread upon the lion and the adder' (Ps. 91:10).

T.   "Up to this point is the blessing that his mother gave him.

U.   "From this point onward comes the blessing that heaven gave him:

V.   "'[103B] Because he has set his love upon me, therefore will I deliver him. I will set him on high, because he has known my name. He shall call upon me, and I will answer him. I will be with him in trouble. I will deliver him and honor him. With long life will I satisfy him and show him my salvation' (Ps. 91:14-16)."

CLXXVII.

A.   Said R. Simeon b. Laqish, "What is the meaning of the following verse of Scripture: 'And from the wicked their light is withheld, and the high arm shall be broken' (Job 38:15)?

B.   "Why is the letter ayin in the word for wicked suspended [in the text, being written above the level of the line, making it read 'poor,' rather than 'wicked' (Freedman, p. 701, n. 10)]?

C.   "When a person becomes poor below, he is made poor above [Freedman, p. 701, n. 11: Where one earns the disapproval of man, it is proof that he has earned the disapproval of God too.]"

D.   Then the letter should not be written at all?

E.   R. Yohanan and R. Eleazar: one said, "It is because of the honor owing to David."

F.   The other said, "It is because the honor owing to Nehemiah B. Hachaliah. [Freedman, p. 702, n. 1: Both had many enemies yet were truly righteous men.]"

CLXXVIII.

A.   Our rabbis have taught on Tannaite authority:

B.   Manasseh would teach the book of Leviticus from fifty-five viewpoints, corresponding to the years of his reign.

C.   Ahab did so in eighty-five ways.

D.   Jeroboam did so in a hundred and three ways.

CLXXIX.

A.   It has been taught on Tannaite authority:

B.   R. Meir would say, "Absalom has no share in the world to come,

C.   "as it is said, 'And they smote Absalom and slew him' (2 Sam. 18:15).

D.   "'They smote him' in this world.

E.   "And they slew him' in the world to come."

CLXXX.

A.   It has been taught on Tannaite authority"

B.   R. Simeon b. Eleazar says in the name of R. Meir, "Ahaz, Ahaziah, and all the kings of Israel concerning whom it is written, 'And he did what was evil in the sight of the Lord' will not live or be judged [in the world to come.]'"

CLXXXI.

A.   "Moreover Manasseh shed much innocent blood, until he had filled Jerusalem from one end to another, beside his sin wherewith he made Judah to sin, in doing that which was evil in the sight of the Lord" (2 Kgs. 21:16):

B.   Here [in Babylonia] it is explained that he killed Isaiah, [and that is the sin at hand].

C.   In the West they say that it was that he made an idol as heavy as a thousand men, and every day it killed them all.

D.   In accord with whose position is the following statement made by Rabbab b. b. Hana: "The soul of a righteous man is balanced against the whole world"?

E.   In accord with whom? With the position of him who has said that he had killed Isaiah.

CLXXXII.

A.   [It is written,] "And he set the graven image" (2 Chr. 33:7), and it is stated, "And the graves and the graven images which he had set up" (2 Chr. 33:19). [was there one image or were there many?]

B.   Said R. Yohanan, "In the beginning he made one face for it, and in the end he made four faces for it, so that the Presence of God should see it and become angry.

C.   "Ahaz set it up in the upper chamber, as it is written, 'And the altars that were on top of the upper chamber of Ahaz' (2 Kgs. 23:13).

D.   "Manasseh set it in the Temple, as it is written, 'And he set up a graven image of the grove that he had made in the house, of which the Lord said to David and to Solomon his son, In this house and in Jerusalem which I have chosen out of all tribes of Israel will I put my name for ever' (2 Kgs. 21:7).

E.   "Amon put it into the Holy of Holies, as it is said, 'For the bed is shorter than that a man can stretch himself on it, and the covering narrower than that he can wrap himself in it' (Is. 28:20)."

F.   What is the sense of, "For the bed is shorter than that one can stretch himself on it"?

G.   Said R. Samuel bar Nahmani said R. Jonathan, "This bed is too short for two neighhors to rule over it at one time."

H.   What is the sense of "And the covering is narrower"?

I.   Said R. Samuel bar Nahmani, "When R. Jonathan would reach this verse of Scripture, he would cry. 'He of whom it is written,"He gathers the waters of the sea together as a heap" (Ps. 33:7) -- should a molten statue rival him!'"

CLXXXIII.

A.   Ahaz annulled the sacrificial service and sealed the Torah, for it is said, "Bind up the testimony, seal the Torah among my disciples" (Is. 8:16).

B.   Manasseh blotted out the mentions of the divine Name and destroyed the altar.

C.   Amon burned the Torah and let spiderwebs cover the altar.

D.   Ahaz permitted consanguineous marriages.

E.   Manasseh had sexual relations with his sister.

F.   Amon had sexual relations with his mother, as it is said, "For Amon sinned very much" (2 Chr. 33:23).

G.   R. Yohanan and R. Eleazar: one said that he burned the torah.

H.   The other said that he had sexual relations with his mother.

I.   His mother said to him, "Do you have any pleasure from the place from which you came forth?"

J.   He said to her, "Am I doing anything except to spite my creator?"

K.   When Jehoiakim came, he said, "The ones who came before me really did not know how to anger him. Do we need him for anything more than his light? We have pure gold, which we use [for light] so let him take away his light."

L.   They said to him, "But do not silver and gold belong to him, as it is written, 'Mine is the silver, and mine is the gold, saith the Lord of hosts' (Hag. 2:8)."

M.   "He said to them, "He has already given them to us, as it is said, 'The heavens are the Lord's, and the earth he has given to the children of men' (Ps. 115:16)."

CLXXXIV.

A.   Said Raba to Rabbah bar Mari, "On what account did they not count Jehoiakim [among those who do not get the world to come]?

B.   "For it is written of him, 'And the remaining words of Jehoiakim and the abomination which he wrought and that which was found up upon him' (2 Chr. 36:8)."

C.   What is the sense of "that which was found upon him" (2 Chr. 36:8)?

D.   R. Yohanan and R. Eleazar: one said that he engraved the name of his idol on his penis.

E.   The other said that he engraved the name of heaven on his penis.

F.   [Rabbah b. Mari] said to him, "As to the matter of kings, I have not heard any answer. But a to ordinary people, I have heard an answer.

G.   "Why did they not count Micah? Because he made his bread available to travellers, for it is said, 'Every traveller turned to the Levites.'"

H.   "And he shall pad through the sea with affliction and shall smite the waves in the sea" (Zech. 10:11)."

I.   Said R. Yohanan, "This speaks f the idol of Micah."

J.   It has been taught on Tannaite authority:

K.   R. Nathan says, "From Hareb to Shiloah is three <u>mils</u>, and the smoke of the pile and the smoke of the image of Micah mixed together. The ministering angels wanted to drive [Micah] off. The Holy One, blessed be he, said to them, 'Leave him alone, for his bread is made available to travellers.'"

L.   And for the same matter those involved in the matter of the concubine at Gibeah [Judges 19] were punished.

M.   Said the Holy One, blessed be he, "On account of the honor owing to me you did not protest, and on account of the honor owing to a mortal you protested."

CLXXXV.

A.   Said R. Yohanan in the name of R. Yose b. Qisma, "Great is a mouthful of food, for it set a distance between two families and Israel,

B.   "as it is written, '[An Ammonite or Moabite shall not enter the congregation of the Lord] ... because they did not meet you with bread and water in the way when you came forth from Egypt' (Deut. 33:4-5)."

C.   And R. Yohanan on his own said, "It creates distance among those who are close; it draws near those who are afar; it blinds the eye [of God] from the wicked; it makes the Presence of God rest even on the prophets of Baal, and it makes an unwitting offense appear to be deliberate [if it is performed in connection with care of the wayfarer]."

D.   [Now to spell out the foregoing:] "It creates distance among those who are close:

E.   [Proof derives] from [104A] the case of Ammon and Moab.

F.   "It draws near those who are afar:"

G.   [Proof derives] from the case of Jethro.

H.   For said R. Yohanan, "As a reward for saying, 'Call him that he may eat bread' (Ex. 2:20), [Jethro]'s descendants had the merit of going taking seats [as authorities] in the chamber of the hewn stones, it is said, 'And the family of the scribes which dwell at Jabez, the Tirahites, the Shimeathites, and Suchathites. These are the Kenites that came of Hemath, the father of the house of Rechan' (1 Chr. 2:55).

I.   "And elsewhere it is written, 'And the children of the Kenite, Moses' father-in-law, went up out of the city of palm trees with the children of Judah into the wilderness of Judah, which lies in the south of Arab, and they went and dwelt among the people' (Judges 1:16). [Freedman, p. 705, n. 10: This shows that the Kenites were descended from Jethro and they sat in the hall of hewn stones as scribes and sanhedrin.]"

J.   "It blinds the eye [of God] from the wicked:"

K.   [Proof derives] from the case of Micah.

L.   "It makes the Presence of God rest even on the prophets of Baal:"

M.   [Proof derives] from the friend of Iddo, the prophet, for it is written, "And it came to pass, as they sat at the table, that the word of the Lord came to the prophet that brought him back" (1 Kgs. 13:20). [Freedman, p. 706, n. 2: He was a prophet of Baal, yet God's word came to him as a reward for his hospitality.]

N.   "And it makes an unwitting offense appear to be deliberate:"

O.   [Proof derives] from what R. Judah said Rab, said, "Had Jonathan only brought David two loaves of bread, Nob, the city of priests, would not have been put to death, Doeg the Edomite would not have been troubled, and Saul and his three sons would not have been killed. [Freedman, p. 706, n. 4: For had he provided him with food, he would not have taken any from Ahimelech. Thus all this happened, though Jonathan's initial offense was due to an oversight.]"

CLXXXVI.

A. Why did they not list Ahaz [at M. 11:2]?

B. Said R. Jeremiah bar Abba, "Because he was positioned between two righteous men, between Hotham and Hezekiah."

C. R. Joseph said, "Because he had the capacity to be ashamed on account of Isaiah, as it is said, 'Then said the Lord to Isaiah, Go forth now to meet Ahaz, you and Shear-jashub your son, at the end of the conduit of the upper pool in the highway of the field of the fuller's trough' (Is. 7:3)."

D. What is the source of "fuller's trough"?

E. Some say, "He hid his face [using the same consonants] and fled."

F. Some say, "He dragged a fuller's trough [the meaning of the word in general] on his head and fled."

CLXXXVII.

A. Why did they not list Amon [at M. 11:2]?

B. On account of the honor owing to Josiah.

C. In that case, they also should not have listed Manasseh, on account of the honor owing to Hezekiah.

D. The son imparts merit to the father, but the father does not give any merit to the son, for it is written, "Neither is there any one who can deliver out of my hand" (Deut. 32:39).

E. Abraham cannot save Ishmael. Isaac cannot save Esau.

F. If you go that far, then Ahaz also was omitted from the list on account of the honor owing to Hezekiah.

CLXXXVIII.

A. And on that account did they not list Jehoiakim?

B. It is on account of what R.Hiyya b. R. Abuyyah said.

C. For R. Hiyya b. R. Abuyyah said, "It was written on the skull of Jehoiakim, 'This and yet another.'"

D. The grandfather of R. Perida found a skull tossed at the gates of Jerusalem, on which was written, "This and yet another."

E. He buried it, but it did not stay buried, and he buried it again but it did not stay buried.

F. He said, "It must be the skull of Jehoiakim, for it is written in that connection, 'He shall be buried with the burial of an ass, drawn and cast forth beyond the gates of Jerusalem' (Jer. 22:19)."

G. He said, "Still, he was a king, and it is not proper to treat him lightly."

H. He wrapped the skull in silk and put it in a closet. His wife saw it. She thought, "This is [the bone of] his first wife, whom he has not forgotten."

I. She lit the oven and burned it up, and that is the meaning of what is written, "This and yet another." [Freedman, p. 707, n. 2: These indignities made sufficient atonement for him that he should share in the future world.]

CLXXXIX.

A. It has been taught on Tannaite authority:

B. R. Simeon b. Eleazar said, "On account of [Hezekiah's] statement, 'And I have done that which was good in your sight,' (2 Kgs. 20:3), [he had further to ask,] 'What shall be the sign [that the Lord will heal me] (2 Kgs. 20:9)."

C. "On account of the statement, 'What shall be the sign' (2 Kgs. 20:9), gentiles ate at his table.

D. "On account of gentiles' eating at his table, [2 Kgs. 20:17-18), he made his children go into exile."

E. That statement supports what Hezekiah said.

F. For Hezekiah said, "Whoever invites an idolator into his house and serves him [as host] causes his children to go into exile, as it is said, 'And of your sons who will issue from you, which you shall beget, shall they take away; and they shall be eunuchs in the palace of the king of Babylonia' (2 Kgs. 20:18)."

G. "And Hezekiah was happy about them and showed them the treasure house, the silver and gold, spices and precious ointment" (Is. 39:2):

H. Said Rab, "What is the sense of 'his treasure house'? It means, his wife, who served them drinks."

I. Samuel said, "His treasury is what he showed them"

J. R. Yohanan said, "His weapons, which had the capacity to consume other weapons, is what he showed them."

CXC.

A. "How does the city sit solitary" (Lam. 1:1):

B. Said Rabbah said R. Yohanan, "On what account were the Israelites smitten with the word 'how' [that begins the dirge]? [Since the numerical value of the letters of the word equals thirty-six], it is because they violated the thirty-six rules in the Torah that are penalized by extirpation."

C. Said R. Yohanan, "Why were they smitten [with a dirge that is] alphabetical?

D. "Because they violated the Torah, which is given through the alphabet. [Freedman, p. 708, n. 6: Its words are formed from the alphabet.]"

CXCI.

A. "Sit solitary" (Lam. 1:1)"

B. Said Rabbah said R. Yohanan, "Said the Holy One, blessed be he, 'I said, "Israel then shall dwell in safety alone, the foundation of Jacob shall be upon a land of corn and wine, also his heavens shall drop down dew" (Deut. 33:28) [so that sitting solitary was supposed to be a blessing (Freedman, p. 708, n. 8)], but now, where they dwell will be alone.'"

CXCII.

A. "The city that was full of people" (Lam. 1:1):

B. Said Rabbah said R. Yohanan, "For they used to marry off a minor girl to an adult male, or an adult woman to a minor boy, so that they should have many children. [But two minors would not marry.]"

CXCIII.

A.   "She is become as a widow" (Lam. 1:1):

B.   Said R. Judah said Rab, "Like a widow, but not actually a widow, but like a woman whose husband has gone overseas and plans to return to her."

CXCIV.

A.   "She was great among the nations and princess among the provinces" (Lam. 1:1):

B.   Said R. Rabbah said R. Yohanan, "Everywhere they go they become princes of their masters."

CXCV.

A.   Our rabbis have taught on Tannaite authority:

B.   There is the case of two men who were captured on Mount Carmel. The kidnapper was walking behind them. [104B] One of them said to his fellow, "The camel that is walking before us is blind in one eye, it is carrying two skins, one of wine and one of oil, and of the two men that are leading it, one is an Israelite and the other is a gentile."

C.   The kidnapper said to them, "Stiff-necked people, how do you know?"

D.   They said to him, "As to the camel, it is eating from the grass before it on the side on which it can see, but on the side on which it cannot see, it is not eating.

E.   "And it is carrying two skins, one of wine and one of oil. The one of wine drips and the drippings are absorbed in the ground, while the one of oil drips, and the drippings remain on the surface.

F.   "And as the two men who are leading it, one is a gentile and one is an Israelite. The gentile relieves himself right on the road, while the Israelite turns to the side [of the road]."

G.   The man ran after them and found that things were just as they had said. He came and kissed them on their head and brought them to his house. He made a great banquet for them and danced before them, saying, "Blessed is he who chose the seed of Abraham and gave part of his wisdom to them, and wherever they go they become the princess over their masters."

H.   He sent them away and they went home in peace.

CXCVI.

A.   "She weeps, yes, she weeps in the night" (Lam. 1:2):

B.   Why these two acts of weeping?

C.   Said Rabbah said R. Yohanan, "One is for the first Temple and the other is for the second Temple."

D.   "At night:"

E.   On account of things done in the night, as it is said, "And all the congregation lifted up their voice and cried, and the people wept that night [at the spies' false report]" (Num. 14:1).

F.   Said Rabbah said R. Yohanan, "That was the ninth of Ab. Said the Holy One, blessed be he, to Israel, 'You have wept tears for nothing. I now shall set up for you weeping for generations to come.'"

G.   Another interpretation of "At night:"

H.   Whoever cries at night will find that his voice is heard.

I.   Another interpretation of "At night:"

J.   Whoever cries at night finds that the stars and planets will cry with him.

K.   Another interpretation of "At night:"

L.   Whoever cries at night finds that whoever hears his voice will cry along with him.

M.   That was the case of a woman in the neighborhood of Rabban Gamaliel, whose child died. She was weeping by night on account of the child. Rabban Gamaliel heard her voice and cried with her, until his eyelashes fell out. The next day, his disciples recognized what had happened and removed the woman from his neighborhood.

CXCVII.

A.   "And her tears are on her cheeks" (Lam. 1:2):

B.   Said Rabbah said R. Yohanan, "It is like a woman who weeps for the husband of her youth, as it is said, 'Lamentation like a virgin girded with sackcloth for the husband of her youth' (Joel 1:8)."

CXCVIII.

A.   "Her adversaries are the chief" (Lam. 1:5):

B.   Said Rabbah said R. Yohanan, "Whoever persecutes Israel becomes head,

C.   "as it is said, 'Nevertheless, there shall be no weariness for her that oppressed her. In the former time he brought into contempt the land of Zebulun and the land of Naphtali, but in the latter time he has made it glorious, by way of the sea, beyond Jordan, the circuit of the nations' (Is. 8:23)."

D.   Said Rabbah said R. Yohanan, "Whoever oppresses Israel does not get tired."

CXCIX.

A.   "May it not happen to you, all passersby" (Lam. 1:12)."

B.   Said Rabbah said R. Yohanan, "On this basis we find in the Torah support for saying [when reciting woes], 'May it not happen to you.'"

CC.

A.   "All passersby" (Lam. 1:12):

B.   Said R. Amram said Rab, "They have turned me into one of those who transgress the law.

C.   "For in respect to Sodom, it is written, 'And the Lord rained upon Sodom [and upon Gomorrah brimstone and fire' (Gen. 19:24). But in respect to Jerusalem it is written, 'From above he has sent fire against my bones and it prevails against them' (Lam. 1:13). [Freedman, p. 711, n. 4: Thus Jerusalem was treated as Sodom and Gomorrah.]"

D.   "For the iniquity of the daughter of my people is greater than the sin of Sodom" (Lam. 4:6):

E.   And is any sort of favoritism shown in such a matter [since Jerusalem was left standing, Sodom was wiped out]?

F.   Said Rabbah said R. Yohanan, "[Not at all, in fact] there was a further measure [of punishment] directed against Jerusalem but not against Sodom.

G.   "For with respect to Sodom, it is written, 'Behold, this was the iniquity of your sister, Sodom, pride, fullness of bread, and abundance of idleness was in her and in her daughters, neither did she strengthen the hand of the poor and the needy' (Ez. 16:49).

H.   "With respect to Jerusalem, by contrast, it is written, 'The hands of merciful women have boiled their own children' (Lam. 4:10). [Freedman, p. 711, n. 8: Jerusalem suffered extreme hunger, which Sodom never did, and this fact counterbalanced her being spared total destruction.]"

CCI.

A.   "The Lord has trodden under foot all my mighty men in the midst of me" (Lam. 1:15):

B.   This is like a man who says to his fellow, "This coin has been invalidated."

C.   "All your enemies have opened their mouths against you" (Lam. 2:16):

D.   Said Rabbah said R. Yohanan, "On what account does the letter P come before the letter ayin [in the order of verses in the chapter of Lamentation, while in the alphabet, the ayin comes before the P]?

E.   "It is on account of the spies, who said with their mouths [and the word for mouth begins with a P] what their eyes had not seen [and the word for eye begins with an ayin.]"

CCII.

A.   "They eat my people as they eat bread and do not call upon the Lord" (Ps. 14:4):

B.   Said Rabbah said R. Yohanan, "Whoever eats the bread of Israelites tastes the flavor of bread, and who does not eat the bread of Israelites does not taste the flavor of bread."

CCIII.

A.   "They do not call upon the Lord" (Ps. 14:4):

B.   Rab said, "This refers to judges."

C.   And Samuel said, "This refers to those who teach children."

CCIV.

A.   Who counted [the kings and commoners of M. 11:2A]?

B.   Said R. Ashi, "The men of the great assembly counted them."

CCV.

A.   Said R. Judah said Rab, "They wanted to count yet another [namely, Solomon], but an apparition of his father's face came and prostrated himself before them. But they paid no attention to him. A fire came down from heaven and licked around their chairs, but they did not pay attention. An echo come forth and as said to them, 'Do you see a man diligent in his business? He shall stand before kings, he shall not stand before mean men' (Prov. 22:29).

B.   "'He who gave precedence to my house over his house, and not only so, but built my house over a span of seven years, while building his own house over a span of thirteen years "he shall stand before kings, he shall not stand before mean men."'

C.   "But they paid no attention to that either.

D.   "An echo came forth, saying, 'Should it be according to your mind? He will recompense it, whether you refuse or whether you choose, and not I' (Job 34:33)."

CCVI.

A. Those who interpret signs [symbolically] would say, "All of them [listed at M. 11:2] will enter the world to come, as it is said, 'Gilead is mine, Manasseh is mine, Ephraim also is the strength of my head, Judah is my lawgiver, Moab is my washpot, over Edom will I cast my shoe, Philistia, you triumph because of me' (Ps. 60:9-10):

B. "'Gideon is mine' speaks of Ahab, who fell at Ramoth-gilead.

C. "'Manasseh' -- literally.

D. "'Ephraim also is the strength of my head' speaks of Jeroboam, who comes from Ephraim.

E. "'Judah is my lawgiver' refers to Ahitophel, [105A] who comes from Judah.

F. "'Moab is my washpot' refers to Gehazi, who was smitten on account of matters having to with washing.

G. "'Over Edom will I cast my shoe' refers to Doeg the Edomite.

H. "'Philistia, you triumph because of me:' The Ministering angels said before the Holy One, blessed be he, 'Lord of the world, if David should come, who killed the Philistine, and who gave Gath to them as an inheritance, what are you going to do to him?'

I. "He said to them, 'It is my task to make them friends of one another.'"

CCVII.

A. "Why is this people of Jerusalem slidden back by a perpetual backsliding" (Jer. 8:5):

B. Said Rab, "The community of Israel answered the prophet with a lasting reply [a play on the words for backsliding and answer, using the same root].

C. "The prophet said to Israel, 'Return in repentence. Your fathers who sinned -- where are they now?'

D. "They said to him, 'And your prophets, who did not sin, where are they now? For it is said, "Your fathers, where are they? and the prophets, do they live forever" (Zech. 1:5)?'

E. "He said to them, 'They repented and confessed as it is said, "But my words and my statutes, which I commanded my servants the prophets, did they not take hold of your fathers? And they returned and said, Like as the Lord of hosts thought to do unto us, according to our ways and according to our doings, so has he dealt with us" (Zech. 1:6).'"

F. Samuel said, "Ten men came and sat before him. He said to them, 'Return in repentance.'

G. "They said to him, 'If a master has sold his slave, or a husband has divorced his wife, does one party have any further claim upon the other? [Surely not.] Freedman, p. 714, n. 3: Since God has sold us to Nebuchadnezzar, he has no further claim upon us, and we have no cause to repent. This in Samuel's view was the victorious answer.]

H. "Said the Holy One, blessed be he, to the prophet, 'Go and say to them, 'Thus says the Lord, where is the bill of your mother's divorcement, whom I have put away? Or which of my creditors is it to whom I have sold you? Behold for your iniquities you have sold yourselves, and for you transgressions is your mother put away' (Is. 50:1)."

I.   And this is in line with what R. Simeon b. Laqish said, "What is the meaning of what
      is written, 'David my servant [and] Nebuchadnezzar my servant' (Jer. 43:10)?

J.   "It is perfectly clear before him who spoke and brought the world into being that the
      Israelites were going to say this, and therefore the Holy One, blessed be he, went
      ahead and called him 'his servant.' [Why so?] If a slave acquires property, to whom
      does the slave belong, and to whom does the property belong?' [Freedman, p. 714, n.
      7: Even if God had sold them to Nebuchadnezzar, they still belong to God.]'"

CCVIII.

A.   "And that which comes into your mind shall not be at all, that you say, We will be as
      the heathen, as the families of the countries, to serve wood and stone. As I live,
      says the Lord God, surely with a mighty hand and with an outstretched arm, and
      with fury poured out, will I rule over you" (Ez 20:32-33):

B.   Said R. Nahman, "Even with such anger may the All-Merciful rage against us, so
      long as he redeems us."

CCIX.

A.   "For he chastizes him to discretion and his God teaches him" (Is. 28:26):

B.   Said Rabbah bar Hanah, "Said the prophet to Israel, 'Return in repentance.'

C.   "They said to him, 'We cannot do so. The impulse to do evil rules over us.'

D.   "He said to them, 'Reign in your desire.'

E.   "They said to him, 'Let his God teach us.'"

CCX.

A.   Four ordinary folk: Balaam, Doeg, Ahitophel, and Gehazi [M. 11:2F]:

B.   [The name] Balaam [means] not with [the rest of] the people [using the same
      consonants], [who will inherit the world to come].

C.   Another interpretation: Balaam, because he devoured the people.

D.   "Son of Beor" means that he had sexual relations with a cow [a play on the
      consonants of the word for Beor].

CCXI.

A.   It was taught on Tannaite authority:

B.   Beor, Cushan-rishathaim, and Laban, the Syrian, are one and the same person.

C.   Beor: because he had sexual relations with a cow.

D.   Cushan-rishathaim [two acts of wickedness], for he committed two acts of
      wickedness against Israel, one in the time of Jacob and one in the time of the Judges.

E.   But what was his real name? It was Laban the Aramaean.

CCXII

A.   It is written, "The son of Beor" (Num. 22:50), but it also is written, "His son was
      Beor" (Num. 24:3).

B.   Said R. Yohanan, "His father was his son as to prophecy."

CCXIII.

A.   Balaam is the one who will not come to the world to come. Lo, others will come.

B.   In accord with whose view is the Mishnah-passage at hand?

C.   It represents the view of R. Joshua.

D.   For it has been taught on Tannaite authority:

E.   [In Tosefta's version:] R. Eliezer says, "None of the gentiles has a portion in the world to come,

F.   "as it is said, 'The wicked shall return to sheol. All the gentiles who forget God' (Ps. (:17).

G.   "'The wicked shall return to Sheol' -- these are the wicked Israelites.

H.   "'And all the gentiles who forget God' -- these are the nations."

I.   Said to him R. Joshua, "If it had been written, 'The wicked shall return to Sheol -- all the gentiles' and then said nothing further, I should have maintained as you do.

J.   "Now that it is in fact written, 'All the gentiles who forget God,' it indicates that there also are righteous people among the nations of the world who have a portion in the world to come" [T. San. 13:2E-J].

K.   And that wicked man [Balaam] also gave a sign concerning his own fate, when he said, "Let me die the death of the righteous" (num. 23:10).

L.   [He said,] "If my soul dies the death of the righteous, may my future be like his, and if not, 'Then behold I go to my people' (Num. 24:14)."

CCXIV.

A.   "And the elders of Moab and the elders of Midian departed" (Num. 22:7):

B.   It was taught on Tannaite authority:

C.   There was never peace between Midian and Moab. The matter may be compared to two dogs who were in a kennel, barking at one another.

D.   A wolf came and attacked one. The other said, "If I do not help him today, he will kill him, and tomorrow he will come against me."

E.   So the two dogs went and killed the wolf.

F.   Said R. Pappa, "This is in line with what people say: 'The weasel and the cat can make a banquet on the fat of the unlucky.'"

CCXV.

A.   "And the princess of Moab abode with Balaam" (Num. 22:8):

B.   And as to the princess of Midian, where had they gone?

C.   When he said to them, "Lodge here this night and I will bring you word again [as the Lord shall speak to me]," (Num. 22:8), they said, "Does any father hate his son? [No chance!]"

CCXVI.

A.   Said R. Nahman, "Hutzbah, even against heaven, serves some good. To begin with, it is written, 'You shall not go with them' (Num. 22:12), and then it is said, 'Rise up and go with them' (Num. 22:20)."

B.   Said R. Sheshet, "Hutzbah is dominion without a crown.

C.   "For it is written, 'And I am this day weak, though anointed king, and these men, the sons of Zeruiah, be too hard for me' (2 Sam. 3:39). [Freedman, p. 717, n. 1: Thus their boldness and impudence outweighed sovereignty.]"

CCXVII.

A.   Said R. Yohanan, "Balaam had one crippled foot, for it is written, 'And he walked haltingly' (Num. 23:3).

B.   "Samson had two crippled feet, as it is said, 'An adder in the path that bites the horses' heels' (Gen. 49:17). [Freedman, p. 717, n. 3: This was a prophecy of Samson. "An adder in the path' is taken to mean that he would have to slither along like an adder, being lame in both feet.]

C.   "Balaam was blind in one eye, as it is said, 'Whose eye is open' (Num. 24:3).

D.   "He practiced enchantment with his penis.

E.   "Here it is written, 'Falling but having his eyes open' (Num. 24:3), and elsewhere: 'And Haman was fallen on the bed whereon Esther was' (Est. 7:8).."

F.   It has been stated on Amoraic authority:

G.   Mar Zutra said, "He practiced enchantment with his penis."

H.   Mar, son of Rabina, said, "He had sexual relations with his ass."

I.   As to the view that he practiced enchantment with his penis it is as we have just now stated.

J.   As to the view that he had sexual relations with his ass:

K.   Here it is written, "He bowed, he lay down as a lion and as a great lion" (Num. 24:9), and elsewhere it is written, "At her feet [105B] he bowed, he fell" (Jud. 5:27)."

CCXVIII.

A.   "He knows the mind of the most high" (Num. 24:16):

B.   Now if he did not know the mind of his own beast, how could he have known the mind of the most high?

C.   What is the case of the mind of his beast?

D.   People said to him, "What is the reason that you did not ride on your horse?"

E.   He said to them, "I put it out to graze in fresh pasture."

F.   [The ass] said to him, "Am I not your ass" (Num. 22:30). [That shows he rode an ass, not a horse.]

G.   "[You are] merely for carrying loads."

H.   "Upon whom you rode" (Num. 22:30).

I.   "It was a happenstance."

J.   "Ever since I was yours, until this day" (Num. 22:30).

K.   [The ass continued,] "And not only so, but I serve you for sexual relations by night."

L.   Here it is written, "Did I ever do so to you" (Num. 22:30) and elsewhere it is written, "Let her serve as his companion." [The same word is used, proving that sexual relations took place as with David and the maiden in his old age.]

M.   Then what is the meaning of the statement, "He knows the mind of the Most High" (Num. 24:16)?

N.   He knew how to tell the exact time at which the Holy One, blessed be he, was angry.

O.   That is in line with what the prophet said to Israel, "O my people, remember now what Balak, king of Moab, consulted, and what Balaam the son of Beor answered him from Shittim to Gilgal, that you may know the righteousness of the Lord" (Mic. 6:5).

P.   What is the meaning of the statement, "That you may know the righteousness of the Lord" (Mic. 6:5)?

Q.   Said the Holy One, blessed be he, to Israel, "Know that I have done many acts of charity with you, that I did not get angry with you in the time of the wicked Balaam.

R.   "For if I had become angry during all those days, there would not remain out of (the enemies of) Israel a shred or a remnant."

S.   That is in line with what Balaam said to Balak, "How shall I curse one whom God has not cursed? Or shall I rage, when the Lord has not raged?" (Num. 23:8).

T.   This teaches that for all those days the Lord had not been angry.

U.   But: "God is angry every day" (Ps. 7:12).

V.   And how long does his anger last? It is a moment, for it is said, "For his anger endures but a moment, but his favor is life" (Ps. 30:5).

W.   If you wish, I shall propose, "Come, my people, enter into your chambers and shut your doors about you, hide yourself as it were for a brief moment, until the indignation be past" (Is. 26:20).

X.   When is he angry? It is in the first three hours [of the day], when the comb of the cock is white.

Y.   But it is white all the time?

Z.   All the other time it has red streaks, but when God is angry, there are no red streaks in it.

CCXIX.

A.   There was a min living in the neighborhood of R. Joshua b. Levi, who bothered him a great deal. One day he took a chicken and tied it up at the foot of his bed and sat down. He said, "When that moment comes [at which God is angry], I shall curse him."

B.   When that moment came, he was dozing. He said, "What this teaches is that it is improper [to curse], for it is written, 'Also to punish is not good for the righteous' (Prov. 17:26) -- even in the case of a min."

CCXX.

A.   A Tannaite authority in the name of R. Meir [said], "When the sun shines and the kings put their crowns on their heads and bow down to the sun, forthwith he is angry."

CCXXI.

A.   "And Balaam rose up in the morning and saddled his ass" (Num. 22:21):

B.   A Tannaite authority taught in the name of R. Simeon b. Eleazar, "That love annuls the order of proprieties [we learn] from the case of Abraham.

C.   "For it is written, 'And Abraham rose up early in the morning and saddled his ass' (Gen. 22:3) [not waiting for the servant to do so].

D.   "And that hatred annuls the order of proprieties [we learn] from the case of Balaam.

E.   "For it is said, 'And Balaam rose up early in the morning and saddled his ass' (Num. 22.21)."

CCXXII.

A.   Said R. Judah said Rab, "Under all circumstances a person should engage in study of Torah and practice of religious duties, even if it is not for their own sake, for out of doing these things not for their own sake one will come to do them for their own sake."

B. For as a reward for the forty-two offerings that Balak offered, he had the merit that Ruth should come forth from him.

C. Said R. Yose bar Huna, "Ruth was the daughter of Egion, grandson of Balak, king of Moab."

CCXXIII.

A. Said Raba to Rabbah bar Mari, "It is written, '[And moreover the king's servants came to bless our lord king David, saying] God make the name of Solomon better than your name, and make his throne greater than your throne' (1 Kgs. 1:47).

B. "Now is this appropriate to speak in such a way to a king?"

C. He said to him, "What they meant is, 'as good as ....' [Freedman, p. 720, n. 2: 'God make the name of Solomon illustrious even as the nature of your own and make his throne great according to the character of your throne.']

D. "For if you do not say this, then [take account of the following:] 'Blessed above women shall be Jael, the wife of Heber the Kenite, be, blessed shall she be above women in the tent' (Jud. 5:24).

E. "Now who are the women in the tent? They are Sarah, Rebecca, Rachel, and Leah.

F. "Is it appropriate to speak in such a way? Rather, what is meant is 'as good as ...,' and here too the sense is, 'as good as ....'"

G. That statement differs from what R. Yose bar Honi said.

H. For R. Yose bar Honi said , "One may envy anybody except for his son and his disciple.

I. "One learns the fact about one's son from the case of Solomon.

J. "And as to the case of one's disciple, if you wish, I shall propose, 'Let a double quantity of your spirit be upon me.' (2 Kgs. 2:9)

K. "Or if you wish, I shall derive proof from the following: 'And he laid his hands upon him and gave him a charge' (Hum. 27:23)."

CCXXIV.

A. "And the Lord put a thing in the mouth of Balaam" (Num. 23:5):

B. R. Eleazar says, "It was an angel."

C. R. Jonathan said, "It was a hook."

CCXXV.

A. Said R. Yohanan, "From the blessing said by that wicked man, you learn what he had in his heart.

B. "He wanted to say that they should not have synagogues and school houses: 'How goodly are your tents, O Jacob' (Num. 24:5).

C. "[He wanted to say that] the Presence of God should not dwell on them: 'And your tabernacles, O Israel' (Num. 24:5).

D. "[He wanted to say] that their kingdom should not last [thus, to the contrary]: 'As the valleys are they spread forth' (Num. 24:6);

E. "... that they should have no olives and vineyards: 'As the trees of aloes which the Lord has planted' (Hum. 24:6);

G. "... that their kings should not be rall: 'And as cedar trees beside the waters' (Num. 24:6).

H.   "... that they should not have a king succeed his father as king: 'He shall pour the water out of his buckets' (Num. 24:6).

I.   "... that their kingdom should not rule over others: 'And his seed shall be in many waters' (Num. 24:6).

J.   "... that their kingdom should not be strong: 'And his king shall be higher than Agag' (Num. 24:6).

K.   "... that their kingdom not be fearful: 'And his kingdom shall be exalted' (Num. 24:6)."

L.   Said R. Abba b. Kahana, "All of them were [ultimately] turned into a curse, except for the one on the synagogues and school houses, as it is said, 'But the Lord your God turned the curse into a blessing for you, because the Lord your God loved you' (Deut. 23:6).

M.   "'The curse' -- not the [other] curses..."

CCXXVI.

A.   Said R. Samuel bar Nahmani said R. Jonathan, "What is the meaning of the verse of Scripture: 'Faithful are the wounds of a friend, but the kisses of an enemy are deceitful' (Prov. 27:6)?

B.   "Better was the curse with which Ahijah the Shilonite cursed the Israelites than the blessing with which the wicked Balaam blessed them.

C.   "Ahijah the Shilonite cursed the Israelites by reference to a reed, as it is said, 'For the Lord shall smite Israel as a reed is shaken in the water' (1 Kgs. 14:15).

D.   "Just as a reed stands in a place in which there is water, so its stem [106A] is renewed and its roots abundant, so that, even if all the winds in the world come and blow against it, they cannot move it from its place, but it goes on swaying with them. When the winds fall silent, the reed stands in its place. [So is Israel].

E.   "But the wicked Balaam blessed them by reference to a cedar tree [at 24:6].

F.   "Just as a cedar tree does not stand in a place in which there is water, so its roots are few, and its truck is not renewed, so that while, even if all the winds in the world come and blow against it, they will not move it from its place, when the south wind blows against it, it uproots it right away and turns it on its face, [so is Israel].

G.   "And not only so, but the reed has the merit that from it a quill is taken for the writing of scrolls of the Torah, prophets, and writings."

CCXXVII.

A.   "And he looked on the Kenite and took up his parable" (Num. 24:21):

B.   Said Balaam to Jethro the Kenite, "Were you not with us in that conspiracy [of Pharaoh, Ex. 1:22]? [Of course you were.] Then who gave you a seat among the mighty men of the earth [in the sanhedrin]?"

C.   This is in line with what R.Hiyya bar Abba said R. Simai said, "Three participated in that conspiracy [of Ex. 1:22, to destroy the Israelites in the river], Balaam, Job, and Jethro.

D.   "Balaam, who gave the advice, was slain. Job, who kept silent, was judged through suffering. Jethro, who fled, had the merit that some of his sons' sons would go into session [as judges] in the Hewn-Stone Chamber,

E.   "as it is said, 'And the families of scribes which dwelt at Jabez, the Tirahites, the Shemathites, the Sucathites. These are the Kenites that came of Hammath, the father of the house of Rehab' (2 Chr. 2:55). And it is written, 'And the children of the Kenite, Moses' father-in-law ...' (Jud. 1:16)."

CCXXVIII.

A.   "And he took up his parable and said, Alas, who shall live when God does this" (Num. 24:23):

B.   Said R. Yohanan, "Woe to the nation who is at hand when the Holy One, blessed be he, effects the redemption of his children!

C.   "Who would want to throw his garment between a lion and a lionness when they are having sexual relations?"

CCXXIX.

A.   "And ships shall come from the coast of Chittim" (Num. 24:24):

B.   Said Rab, "[Legions will come] from the coast of Chittim" [cf. Freedman, p. 722, n. 12].

C.   "And they shall afflict Assyria and they shall afflict Eber" (Num. 24:24):

D.   Up to Assyria they shall kill, from that point they shall enslave.

CCXXX.

A.   "And now, behold, I go to my people; come and I shall advise you what this people shall do to your people in the end of days" (Num. 24:24):

B.   Rather than saying, "This people to your people," it should say, "Your people to this people." [Freedman, p. 723, n. 4: He advised the Moabites to ensnare Israel through uncharity. Thus he was referring to an action by the former to the latter, while Scripture suggests otherwise.]

C.   Said R. Abba, "It is like a man who curses himself but assigns the curse to others. [Scripture alludes to Israel but refers to Moab.]

C.   "[Balaam] said to [Balak], 'The God of these people hates fornication, and they lust after linen [clothing, which rich people wear]. Come and I shall give you advice: Make tents and set whores in them, an old one outside and a girl inside. Let them sell linen garments to them.'

E.   "He made tents for them from the snowy mountain to Beth Hajeshimoth [north to south] and put whores in them, old women outside, young women inside.

F.   "When an Israelite was eating and drinking and carousing and going out for walks in the market, the old lady would say to him, 'Don't you want some linen clothes?'

G.   "The old lady would offer them at true value, and the girl would offer them at less.

H.   "This would happen two or three times, and then [the young one] would say to him, 'Lo, you are at home here. Sit down and make a choice for yourself.' Gourds of Ammonite wine would be set near her. (At this point the wine of gentiles had not yet been forbidden to Israelites.) She would say to him, 'Do you want to drink a cup of wine?'

I.   "When he had drunk a cup of wine, he would become inflamed. He said to her, 'Submit to me.' She would than take her god from her bosom and said to him, 'Worship this.'

J. "He would say to her, 'Am I not a Jew?'

K. "She would say to him, 'What difference does it make to you? Do they ask anything more from you than that you bare yourself?' But he did not know that that was how this idol was served.

L. "'And not only so, but I shall not let you do so until you deny the Torah of Moses, your master.'

M. "As it is said, 'They went in to Baal-peor and separated themselves unto that shame, and their abominations were according as they loved' (Hos. 9:10)."

CCXXXI.

A. "And Israel dwelt in Shittim" (Num. 25:1):

B. R. Eliezer says, "The name of the place actually was Shittim."

C. R. Joshua says, "It was so called because when there they did deeds of idiocy (STWT)."

D. "And they called the people to the sacrifices of their gods" (Num. 25:2):

E. R. Eliezer says, "They met them naked."

F. R. Joshua says, "They all had involuntary seminal emissions."

G. What is the meaning of Rephidim [Ex. 17:8: "Then came Amalek and fought with Israel in Rephidim"]?

H. R. Eliezer says, "It was actually called Rephidim."

I. R. Joshua says, "It was a place in which they weakened their [ties to] the teachings of the Torah, as it is written, 'The fathers shall not look back to their children for feebleness of hands' (Jer. 47:3)."

CCXXXII.

A. R. Yohanan said, "Any passage in which the word, 'And he abode' appears, it means suffering.

B. "So: 'And Israel abode in Shittim, and the people began to commit whoredom with the daughters of Moab' (Num. 23:1).

C. "'And Jacob dwelt in the land where his father was a stranger, in the land of Canaan' (Gen. 37:1). 'And Jospeh brought to his father their evil report' (Gen. 37:3).

D. "And Israel dwelt in the land of Egypt, in the country of Goshen' (Gen. 47:27), 'And the time drew near that Israel must die' (Gen. 47:29).

E. "'And Judah and Israel dwelt safely, every man under his vine and under his fig tree' (1 Kgs. 5:5). 'And the Lord stirred up an adversary to Solomon, Hadad the Edomite; he was the king's seed in Edom' (1 Kgs. 11:14).."

CCXXXIII.

A. "And they slew the kings of Midian, beside the rest of them that were slain ... Balaam also , the son of Beor, they slew with the sword" (Num. 31:8):

B. What was he doing there anyhow?

C. Said R. Yohanan, "He went to collect a salary on account of the twenty-four thousand Israelites whom he had brought down' [Cf. Num. 25:1-9]."

D. Mar Zutra b. Tobiah said Rab said, "That is in line with what people say: 'When the camel went to ask for horns, the ears that he had they cut off him.'"

CCXXXIV.

A.   "Balaam also, the son of Beor, the soothsayer, [did the children of Israel slay with the sword]" (Josh. 13:22):

B.   A soothsayer? He was a prophet!

C.   Said R. Yohanan, "At first he was a prophet, but in the end, a mere soothsayer."

D.   Said R. Pappa, "This is in line with what people say: 'She who came from princes and rulers played the whore with a carpenter.'"

CCXXXV.

A.   [106B] "Did the children of Israel slay with the sword, among thoses who were slain by them" (Josh. 13:22):

B.   Said Rab, "They inflicted upon him all four forms of execution: stoning, burning, decapitation, and strangulation."

CCXXXVI.

A.   A min said to R. Hanina, "Have you heard how old Balaam was?"

B.   He said to him, "It is not written out explicitly. But since it is written, 'Bloody and deceitful men shall not live out half their days' (Ps. 55:24), he would have been thirty-three or thirty-four years old."

C.   He said to him,"You have spoken well. I saw the notebook of Balaam, in which it is written, "Balaam, the lame, was thirty-three years old when Pineas, the brigand, killed him.'"

CCXXXVII.

A.   Said Mar, son of Rabina, to his son, "In regard to all of those [listed as not having a share in the world to come], you should take up the verses relating to them and expound them only in the case of the wicked Balaam.

B.   "In his case, in whatever way one can expound the relevant passages [to his detriment], you do so."

CCXXXVIII.

A.   It is written, "Doeg" (1 Sam. 21:8) [meaning, "anxious" (Freedman, p. 726, n. 1)] and it is written, "Doeeg" (1 Sam. 22:18) [with letters indicating "woe" being inserted (Freedman, ad loc.)].

B.   Said R. Yohanan, "To begin with, the Holy One, blessed be he, sits and worries lest such a son one go forth to bad ways. After he has gone forth to bad ways, he says, 'Woe that this one has gone forth!'"

CCXXXIX.

A.   Said R. Isaac, "What is the meaning of the verse of Scripture, 'Why do you boast yourself in mischief, O mighty man? The goodness of God endures forever' (Ps. 52:3)?

B.   "Said the Holy One, blessed be he, to Doeg, 'Are you not a hero in Torah-learning! 'Why do you boast in mischief?' Is not the love of God spread over you all day long?'"

C.   And said R. Isaac, "What is the meaning of the verse of Scripture, 'But to the wicked God says, What have you to do to declare my statutes?' (Ps. 50:16)?

D.   "So the Holy One, blessed be he, said to the wicked Doeg, '"What have you to do to declare my statutes? "When you come to the passages that deal with murderers and slanderers, what have you to say about them!"'

CCXL.

A.   "Or that you take my covenant in your mouth?" (Ps. 50:16):

B.   Said R. Ammi, "The Torah-knowledge of Doeg comes only from the lips and beyond [but not inside his heart]."

CCXLI.

A.   Said R. Isaac, "What is the meaning of the verse of Scripture, 'The righteous also shall see and fear and shall laugh at him' (Ps. 52:8)?

B.   "To begin with they shall fear [the wicked], but in the end they shall laugh at him."

C.   And said R. Isaac, "What is the meaning of the verse of Scripture: 'He has swallowed down riches and he shall vomit them up again, the God shall cast them out of his belly' (Job 20:15)?

D.   "Said David before the Holy One, blessed be he, 'Lord of the world, let Doeg die.'

E.   "He said to him, '"He has swallowed down riches, and he shall vomit them up again" (Job 20:15).'

F.   "He said to him, '"Let God cast them out of his belly" (Job 20:15).'"

G.   And said R. Isaac, "What is the meaning of the verse of Scripture: 'God shall likewise destroy you forever' (Ps. 52:7)?

H.   "Said the Holy One, blessed be he, to David, 'Should I bring Doeg to the world to come?'

I.   "He said to him, '"God shall likewise destroy you forever" (Ps. 52:7).'"

J.   "What is the meaning of the verse: 'He shall take you away and pluck you out of the tent and root you out of the land of the living, selah' (Ps. 52:7)?

K.   "Said the Holy One, blessed be he, 'Let a tradition in the school house be repeated in his name.'

L.   "He said to him, '"He shall take you away and pluck you out of the tent" (Ps. 52:7).'

M.   "'Then let his children be rabbis.'

N.   "'"And your root out of the land of the living, selah!"'"

O.   And said R. Isaac, "What is the meaning of the verse of Scripture: 'Where is he who counted, where is he who weighed? Where is he who counted the towers' (Is. 33:18)?

P.   "'Where is he who counted all the letters in the Torah? Where is he who weighed all of the arguments a fortiori in the Torah?'

Q.   "'Where is he who counted the towers' -- who counted the three hundred decided laws that concern the 'tower that flies in the air' [that is, the laws governing the status of the contents of a closed cabinet not standing on the ground]."

CCXLII.

A.   Said R. Ammi, "Four hundred questions did Doeg and Ahitophel raise concerning the 'tower flying in the air,' and they could not answer any one of them."

B.   Said Raba, "Is there any recognition of the achievement of raising questions? In the time of R. Judah, all of their repetition of Mishnah-teachings concerned the civil laws [of Baba Qamma, Baba Mesia, and Baba Batra], while, for our part, we repeat the Mishnah-traditions even dealing with tractate Uqsin [a rather peripheral topic].

C. "When for his part R. Judah came to the law, 'A woman who pickles vegetables in a pot' [M. Toh. 2:1], or some say, 'Olives which were pickled with their leaves are insusceptible to uncleanness' (M. Uqs. 2:1], he would say, 'I see here all the points of reflection of Rab and Samuel.

D. "But we repeat the tractate of Uqsin at thirteen sessions [having much more to say about it].

E. "When R. Judah merely removed his shoes [in preparation for a fast], it would rain.

F. "When we cry out [in supplication], no one pays any attention to us.

G. "But the Holy One, blessed be he, demands the heart, as it is written, 'But the Lord looks on the heart' (1 Sam. 16:7)."

CCXLIII.

A. Said R. Mesharsheya, "Doeg and Ahitophel did not know how to reason concerning traditions."

B. Objected Mar Zutra, "Can it be the case that one concerning whom it is written, 'Where is he who counted, where is he who weighed, where is he who counted the towers?' (Is. 33:18) should not be able to reason concerning traditions?

C. "But it never turned out that traditions [in their names] were stated in accord with the decided law, for it is written, 'The secret of the Lord is with those who fear him' (Ps. 25:14)."

CCXLIV.

A. Said R. Ammi, "Doeg did not die before he forgot his learning, as it is said, 'He shall die without instruction, and in the greatness of his folly he shall go astray' (Prov. 5:23)."

B. Rab said, "He was afflicted with saraat, for it is said, 'You have destroyed all them who go awhoring from you' (Ps. 73:27), and elsewhere it is written, 'And if it not be redeemed within the span of a full year, then the house shall be established finally [to him who bought it]' (Lev. 25:30).

C. "[The word indicated as 'finally' and the word for 'destroyed' use the same letters]. And we have learned in the Mishnah: The only difference between one who is definitely afflicted with saraat and one who is shut away for observation is in respect to letting the hair grow long and tearing the garment [M. Meg. 1:7], [Freedman, p. 729, n. 6: which shows that the term at hand is used to indicate someone is afflicted with saraat. Hence the first of the two verses is to be rendered, 'You have smitten with definite leprosy all those who go awhoring from you.']"

CCXLV.

A. Said R. Yohanan, "Three injurious angels were designated for Doeg: one to make him forget his learning, one to burn his soul, and one to scatter his dust among the synagogues and school houses."

B. And said R. Yohanan, "Doeg and Ahitophel never saw one another. Doeg lived in the time of Saul, and Ahitophel in the time of David.

C.   "And said R. Yohanan, "Doeg and Ahitophel did not live out half their days."

D.   It has been taught on Tannaite authority along these same lines:

E.   "Bloody and deceitful men shall not live out half their days" (Ps. 55:24):

F.   Doeg lived only for thirty-four years, Ahitophel for thirty three.

G.   And said R. Yohanan, "At the outset David called Ahitophel his master, at the end he called him his friend, and finally he called him his disciple.

H.   "At the beginning he called him his master: 'But it was you, a man my equal, my guide and my acquaintance' (Ps. 55:14).

I.   "Then his companion: 'We took sweet counsel together and walked into the house of God in company' (Ps. 55:15).

J.   "Finally, his disciple: 'Yea, my own familiar friend, in whom I trusted [107A], who ate my bread, has lifted his heel against me' (Ps. 56:10). [Freedman, p. 729, n. 10: This is understood to refer to Ahitophel, and eating bread is a metaphor for 'who learned of my teaching.']'

CCXLVI.

A.   Said R. Judah said Rab, "One should never put himself to the test, for lo, David, king of Israel, put himself to the test and he stumbled.

B.   "He said before him, 'Lord of the world, on what account do people say, "God of Abraham, God of Isaac, and God of Jacob, "but they do not say, "God of David"?'

C.   "He said to him, 'They endured a test for me, while you have not endured a test for me.'

D.   "He said before him, 'Lord of the world, here I am. Test me.'

E.   "For it is said, 'Examine me, O Lord, and try me' (Ps. 26:1).

F.   "He said to him, 'I shall test you, and I shall do for you something that I did not do for them. I did not inform them [what I was doing], while I shall tell you what I am going to do. I shall try you with a matter having to do with sexual relations.'

G.   "Forthwith: 'And it came to pass in an eventide that David arose from off his bed' (2 Sam. 11:2)."

H.   Said R. Judah, "He turned his habit of having sexual relations by night into one of having sexual relations by day.

I.   "He lost sight of the following law:

J.   "'There is in man a small organ, which makes him feel hungry when he is sated and makes him feel sated when he is hungry.'"

K.   "And he walked on the roof of the king's palace, and from the roof he saw a woman washing herself, and the woman was very beautiful to look upon" (2 Sam. 11:2):

L.   Bath Sheba was shampooing her hair behind a screen. Satan came to [David] and appeared to him in the form of a bird. He shot an arrow at [the screen] and broke it down, so that she stood out in the open, and he saw her.

M.   Forthwith: "And David sent and inquired after the woman. And one said, Is not this Bath Sheba, the daughter of Eliam, the wife of Uriah the Hittite? And David sent messengers and took her, and she came to him, and he lay with her; for she was purified from her uncleanness; and she returned to her house; (2 Sam. 11:203).

N.   That is in line with what is written: "You have tried my heart, you have visited me in the night, you have tried me and shall find nothing; I am purposed that my mouth shall not transgress" (Ps. 17:3).

O.   He said, "Would that a bridle had fallen into my mouth, that I had not said what I said!"

CCXLVII.

A.   Raba interpreted Scripture, asking, "What is the meaning of the following verse: 'To the chief musician, a Psalm of David. In the Lord I put my trust, how do you say to my soul, Flee as a bird to your mountain?' (Ps. 11:1)?

B.   "Said David before the Holy One, blessed be he, 'Lord of the world, Forgive me for that sin, so that people should not say, "The mountain that is among you [that is, your king] has been driven off by a bird.""

C.   Raba interpreted Scripture, asking, "What is the meaning of the following verse: 'Against you, you alone, have I sinned, and done this evil in your sight, that you might be justified when you speak and be clear when you judge' (Ps. 11:1)?

D.   "Said David before the Holy One, blessed be he, 'Lord of the world. It is perfectly clear to you that if I had wanted to overcome my impulse to do evil, I should have done so. But I had in mind that people not say, "The slave has conquered the Master [God, and should then be included as 'God of David'].""

E.   Raba interpreted Scripture, asking, "What is the meaning of the following verse: 'For I am ready to halt and my sorrow is continually before me' (Ps. 38:18)?

F.   "Bath Sheba, daughter of Eliam, was designated for David from the six days of creation, but she came to him through anguish."

G.   And so did a Tannaite authority of the house of R. Ishmael [teach], "Bath Sheba, daughter of Eliam, was designated for David, but he 'ate' her while she was yet unripe."

H.   Raba interpreted Scripture, asking, "What is the meaning of the following verse: 'But in my adversity they rejoiced and gathered themselves together, yes, the abjects gathered themselves together against me and I did not know it, they tore me and did not cease' (Ps. 35:15)?

I.   "Said David before the Holy One, blessed be he, 'Lord of the world, it is perfectly clear to you that if they had torn my flesh, my blood would not have flowed [because I was so embarassed].

J.   Not only so, but when they take up the four modes of execution inflicted by a court, they interrupt their Mishanh-study and say to me, "David, he who has sexual relations with a married woman -- how is he put to death?"

K.   "'I say to them, "He who has sexual relations with a married woman is put to death through strangulation, but he has a share in the world to come," while he who humiliates his fellow in public has no share in the world to come.""

CCXLVIII.

A.   Said R. Judah said Rab, "Even when David was sick, he carried out the eighteen acts of sexual relations that were owing to his [eighteen] wives, as it is written, 'I am weary with my groaning, all night I make my bed swim, I water my couch with my tears' (Ps. 6:7)."

B.   And said R. Judah said, Rab, "David wanted to worship idols, as it is said, 'And it happened that when David came to the head, where he worshipped God' (2 Sam. 15:32), and 'head' only means idols, as it is written, 'This image's head was of fine gold' (Dan. 2:32).

C.   "'Behold, Hushai, the Archite came to meet him with his coat rent and earth upon his head' (2 Sam. 15:32):

D.   "He said to David, 'Are people to say that a king such as you have worshipped idols?'

E.   "He said to him, 'Will the son of a king such as me kill him? It is better that such a king as me worship an idol and not profane the Name of heaven in public.'

F.   "He said, 'Why then did you marry a woman captured in battle? [Freedman, p. 732, n. 7: Absalom's mother, Maachah, the daughter of Talmai, king of Geshur, was a war captive.]'

G.   "He said to him, 'As to a woman captured in battle, the All-Merciful has permitted marrying her.'

H.   "He said to him, 'You did not correctly interpret the meaning of the proximity of two verses. For it is written, 'If a man has stubborn and rebellious son' (Deut. 21:18).

I.   "'[The proximity teaches that] whoever marries a woman captured in battle will have a stubborn and rebellious son.'"

CCXLIX.

A.   R. Dosetai of Biri interpreted Scripture, "To what may David be likened? To a gentile merchant.

B.   "Said David before the Holy One, blessed be he, 'Lord of the world, "Who can understand his errors?" (Ps. 19:13).'

C.   "He said to him, 'They are remitted for you.'

D.   """ Cleanse me of hidden faults" (Ps. 19:13).'

E.   "'They are remitted to you.'

F.   """Keep back your servant also from presumptuous sins" (Ps. 19:13).'

G.   "'They are remitted to you.'

H.   """Let them not have dominion over me, then I shall be upright" (Ps. 19:13), so that the rabbis will not hold me up as an example.'

I.   "'They are remitted to you.'

J.   """And I shall be innocent of great transgression" (Ps. 19:13), so that they will not write down my ruin.'

K.   "He said to him, 'That is not possible. Now if the Y that I took away from the name of Sarah [changing it from Sarah to Sarah] stood crying for so many years until Joshua came and I added the Y [removed from Sarah's name] to his name, as it is said, "And Moses called Oshea, the son of Nun, Jehoshua" (Num. 13:16), how much the more will a complete passage of Scripture [cry out if I remove that passage from its rightful place].'"

CCL.

A. "And I shall be innocent from great transgression: (Ps. 19:13):

B. He said before him, "Lord of the world, forgive me for the whole of that sin [as though I had never done it]."

C. He said to him, "Solomon, your son, even now is destined to say in his wisdom, 'Can a man take fire in his bosom, and his clothes not be burned? Can one go upon hot coals, and his feet not be burned? So he who goes in to his neighbor's wife, whoever touches her shall not be innocent' (Prov. 6:27-29)."

D. He said to him, "Will I be so deeply troubled?"

E. He said to him, "Accept suffering [as atonement]."

F. He accepted the suffering.

CCLI.

A. Said R. Judah said Rab, "For six months David was afflicted with saraat, and the Presence of God left him, and the sanhedrin abandoned him.

B. "He was afflicted with saraat, as it is written, 'Purge me with hyssop and I shall be clean, wash me and I shall be whiter than snow/ (Ps. 51:9).

C. "The Presence of God left him, as it is written, 'Restore to me the joy of your salvation and uphold me with your free spirit' (Ps. 51:14).

D. "The sanhedrin abandoned him, as it is written, 'Let those who fear you turn to me and those who have known your testimonies' (Ps. 119:79).

E. "How do we know that this lasted for six months? As it is written, 'And the days that David rules over Israel were forty years: [107B] Seven years he reigned in Hebron, and thirty-three years he reigned in Jerusalem' (1 Kgs. 2:11).

F. "Elsewhere it is written, 'In Hebron he reigned over Judah seven years and six months' (2 Sam. 5:5).

G. "So the six months were not taken into account. Accordingly, he was afflicted with saraat [for such a one is regarded as a corpse].

H. "He said before him, 'Lord of the world, forgive me for that sin.'

I. "'It is forgiven to you.'

J. "'"Then show me a token for good, that they who hate me may see it and be ashamed, because you, Lord, have helped me and comforted me" (Ps. 86:17).'

K. "He said to him, 'While you are alive, I shall not reveal [the fact that you are forgiven], but I shall reveal it in the lifetime of your son, Solomon.'

L. "When Solomon had built the house of the sanctuary, he tried to bring the ark into the house of the Holy of Holies. The gates cleaved to one another. He recited twenty-four prayers [Freedman, p. 734, n. 4: in 2 Chr. 6 words for prayer, supplication and hymn occur twenty-four times], but was not answered.

M. "He said, 'Lift up your head, O you gates, and be lifted up, you everlasting doors, and the King of glory shall come in. Who is this King of glory? The Lord strong and might, the Lord mighty in battle' (Ps. 24:7ff.).

N. "And it is further said, 'Lift up your heads, O you gates even lift them up, you everlasting doors/ (Ps. 24:7).

O.   "But he was not answered.

P.   "When he said, 'Lord God, turn not away the face of your anointed, remember the mercies of David, your servant'(2 Chr. 6:42), forthwith he was answered.

Q.   "At that moment the faces of David's enemies turned as black as the bottom of a pot, for all Israel knew that the Holy One, blessed be he, had forgiven him for that sin."

CCLII.

A.   Gehazi [M. 11:2F]:

B.   As it is written, "And Elisha came to Damascus" (2 Kgs. 8:7).

C.   Where was he traveling [when he came to Damascus]?

D.   Said R. Yohanan, "He went to bring Gehazi back in repentence, but he did not repent.

E.   "He said to him, 'Repent.'

F.   "He said to him, 'This is the tradition that I have received from you: "Whoever has both sinned and caused others to sin will never have sufficient means to do penitence."'"

G.   What had he done?

H.   Some say, "He hung a lodestone on the sin[ful statue built by] Jeroboam and suspended it between heaven and earth."

I.   Others say, "He carved on it the Name of God, so that it would say, 'I [am the Lord your God]...You shall not have [other gods...]' (Ex. 20:1-2)."

J.   Still others say, "He drove rabbis away from his presence, as it is said, 'And the sons of the prophets said to Elisha, "See now the place where we swell before you is too small for us"' (2 Kgs. 6:1). The sense then is that up to that time, it was not too small."

CCLIII.

A.   Our rabbis have taught on Tannaite authority:

B.   Under all circumstances the left hand should push away and the right hand should draw near,

C.   not in the manner of Elisha, who drove away Gehazi with both hands.

D.   What is the case with Gehazi?

E.   As it is written, "And Naaman said, 'Be pleased to accept two talents'" (2 Kgs. 5:23).

F.   And it is written, "But he said to him, 'Did I not go with you in spirit when the man turned from his chariot to meet you? Was it a time to accept money and garments, olive orchards and vineyards, sheep and oxen, menservants and maidservants'" (2 Kgs. 5:26).

G.   But did he receive all these things? He got only silver and garments.

H.   Said R. Isaac, "At that moment Elisha was occupied with the study of the list of eight dead creeping things (M. Shab. 14:1, Lev. 11:29FF.].

I.   Naaman, head of the army of the king of Syria, was afflicted with saraat. A young girl who had been taken captive from the land of Israel said to him, "If you go to Elisha, he will heal you."

J.   When he got there, he said to him, "Go, immerse in the Jordan."

K.   He said to him, "You are making fun of me!"

L.   Those who were with him said to him, "Go, try it, what difference does it make to you?"

M.   He went and immersed in the Jordan and was healed.

N.   He came and brought him everything that he had, but [Elisha] would not take it. Gehazi took leave of Elisha and went and took what he took and hid it.

O.   When he came back, Elisha saw the marks of saraat, as they blossomed all over his head.

P.   "He said to Gehazi, 'Wicked one! The time has come to receive the reward for the eight dead creeping things: "Therefore the leprosy of Naaman shall cleave to you and to your descendants forever" (2 Kgs. 8:27).'"

CCLIV.

A.   "Now there were four men who were lepers [at the entrance to the gate]" (2 Kgs. 7:3):

B.   R. Yohanan said, "This refers to Gehazi and his three sons."

C.   It has been taught on Tannaite authority:

D.   R. Simeon b. Eleazar says, "Also in one's natural impulse, as to a child or a woman, one should push away with the left hand and draw near with the right hand." [Freedman, p. 736, n. 2: The uncensored edition continues: What of R. Joshua b. Perahjah?--When King Jannai slew our Rabbis, R. Joshua b. Perahjah (and Jesus) fled to Alexandria of Egypt. On the resumption of peace, Simeon b. Shetach sent to him: 'From me, (Jerusalem) the holy city, to thee, Alexandria of Egypt (my sister). My husband dwelleth within thee and I am desolate.' He arose, went, and found himself in a certain inn, where great honour was shown him. 'How beautiful is this Acsania?' (The word denotes both inn and innkeeper. R. Joshua used it in the first sense; the answer assumes the second to be meant.) Thereupon (Jesus) observed, 'Rabbi, her eyes are narrow.' 'Wretch," he rebuked him, 'dost thou thus engage thyself.' He sounded four hundred trumpets and excommunicated him. He (Jesus) came before him many times pleading, 'Receive me!' But he would pay no heed to him. One day he (R. Joshua) was reciting the Shema', when Jesus came before him. He intended to receive him and made a sign to him. He (Jesus) thinking that it was to repel him, went, put up a brick, and worshipped it. 'Repent,' said he (R. Joshua) to him. He replied, 'I have thus learned from thee: He who sins and causes others to sin is not afforded the means of repentance.' And a Master has said, 'Jesus the Nazarene practiced magic and led Israel astray.']

CCLV.

A.   Our rabbis have taught on Tannaite authority:

B.   Elisha bore three illnesses,

C.   one because he brought the she-bears against the children, one because he pushed Gehazi away with both hands, and one on account of which he died.

D.   For it is said, "Now Elisha had fallen sick of the ailment of which he died" (2 Kgs. 13:14).

CCLVI.

A.   Until Abraham there was no such thing as [the sign of] old age. Whoever saw Abraham thought, "This is Isaac." Whoever saw Isaac thought, "This is Abraham."

B.   Abraham prayed for mercy so that he might have [signs of] old age, as it is said, "And Abraham was old, and well stricken in age" (Gen. 24:1).

C.   Until the time of Jacob there was no such thing as illness, so he prayed for mercy and illness came about, as it is written, "And someone told Joseph, behold, your father is sick: (Gen. 48:1).

D.   "Until the time of Elisha, no one who was sick ever got well. Elisha came along and prayed for mercy and got well, as it is written, "Now Elisha had fallen sick of the illness of which he died" (2 Kgs. 13:14) [Freedman: This shows that he had been sick on previous occasions too, but recovered.]

The important question at hand is self-evident: how has the compositor of this tractate of monstrous proportions arranged the materials at hand. The answer to the question is equally self-evident: he has laid out available materials, available in large blocks indeed, in accord with (1) the thematic program of the Mishnah, and (2) the further principles of agglutination and conglomeration dictated by the materials at hand. In each major unit (signified in what follows by a Roman numeral), he has taken up a fact -- a topic, and allegation -- of the Mishnah. Once he has dealt with that fact, he then drew upon materials that supplied a secondary expansion of it, and made use, further, of entire blocks of materials already arranged and joined together on the basis of principles of organization other than those deriving from Mishnah-exegesis. That, in a single statement, accounts for the arrangement of everything at hand. Let us proceed to test the thesis just now announced by reviewing an outline of the units of the immense construction at hand.

I.   The life of the world to come: when and why is it denied [M. 11:1A-D]

A.   Those who do not believe in it do not get it: I

B.   How on the basis of the Torah do we know that there will be resurrection of the dead: II-X

C.   Disputes with pagans on the resurrection of the dead: XI-XIV (Tradental construction based on Gebihah: XIV-XVII)

D.   Other disputes with pagan sages: XVIII-XXI

E.   Verses on the resurrection of the dead: XXII-XXV, XXVII-XXXV (Tradental construction based on Deut. 32:39: XXV-XXVI)

II. Examples in Scripture of the Resurrection of the Dead

A.   Daniel's case: Hananiah, Mishael, and Azariah: XXXVI-XLIV, XLVII-XLIX (Further materials on Nebuchadnezzer: XLV-XLVI) (Tradental continuation of XLIX:L)

III. Messianic Passages of Scripture. Sennacherib, Nebuchadnezzar

A.   Isaiah and Hezekiah: LI-LXVII, LXXI-LXXXI

B.   David: LXVIII-LXX

C.   When will the Messiah come: LXXXII-CXV

IV. He who says that the Torah does not come from heaven will not enter the world to come [M. 11:1D]:

A.   Those who do not believe in it do not get it: CXVI

B.   Importance of study of Torah: CXVII-CXXIV

V. An Epicurean [M. 11:1D]:

A.   Defined: CXXV-CXXX

VI. Aqiba: Also he who read heretical books [M. 11:1E]:

A.   Defined: CXXXIV

VII. He who whispers over a wound [M. 11:1F]:

A.   Defined: CXXXV-CXLIV

VIII. He who pronounces the divine name as it is spelled out [M. 11:1G]:

A.   Defined: CXLV

IX. Three kings and four ordinary folk [M. 11:2A-B]:

A.   Stories about Jeroboam: CXLVI-CLXI, CLXIV

B.   Stories about Manasseh: CLXII-CLXIII, CLXXII-CXXXV

C.   Stories about Ahah: CLXVI-CLXXI

D.   Those not listed who might have been: CXXXVI-CLXXXVIII (Excursus on the destruction of Jerusalem: CXC-CCIX)

X. Four ordinary folk [M. 11:2F]:

A.   Stories about Balaam: CCX-CCXXXVII

B.   Stories about Doeg: CCXXXVIII-CCXLV

C.   Those not listed who might have been (David): CCXLVI-CCLI

D.   Gehazi: CCLII-CCLVI

We see, therefore, that the entire construction devotes itself to the exposition of the Mishnah. Two units, one on the resurrection of the dead, the other on Messianic crises in Israelite history, complement unit I. Units I, IV-X, systematically work their way through the Mishnah's statements. Units II and III treat the resurrection of the dead, on the one hand, and the coming of the Messiah, on the other. Certainly any effort to expound the theme of the life of the world to come would have to deal with these other two topics, and, what the compositor has done is simply place into the correct context-namely, M. 11:1A-B,--the available materials on these other two components of the principal congeries of ideas at hand. That is, once we take up the world to come, we deal also with the resurrection and the coming the the Messiah. Then, as is clear, the compositor simply proceeded on his way, generally defining the Mishnah's terms, often also greatly expanding on the themes introduced by the Mishnah. So the construction as a whole, seemingly vast and formless, turns out to follow rather simple rules of composition and organization.

11:3A-CC

A. The generation of the flood has no share in the world to come,

B. and they shall not stand in the judgment,

C. since it is written, "My spirit shall not judge with man forever" (Gen. 6:3)

D. neither judgment nor spirit.

E. The generation of the dispersion has no share in the world to come,

F. since it is said, "So the Lord scattered them abroad from there upon the face of the whole earth" (Gen. 11:8).

G. "So the Lord scattered them abroad" -- in this world,

H. "and the Lord scattered them from there" -- in the world to come.

I. The men of Sodom have no portion in the world to come,

J. since it is said, "Now the men of Sodom were wicked and sinners against the Lord exceedingly" (Gen. 13:13)

K. "Wicked" -- in this world,

L. "And sinners" -- in the world to come.

M. But they will stand in judgment.

N. R. Nehemiah says, "Both these and those will not stand in judgment,

O. 'for it is said, 'Therefore the wicked shall not stand in judgment [108A], nor sinners in the congregation of the righteous' (Ps. 1:5)

P. 'Therefore the wicked shall not stand in judgment' -- this refers to the generation of the flood.

Q. 'Nor sinners in the congregation of the righteous' -- this refers to the men of Sodom."

R. They said to him, "They will not stand in the congregation of the righteous, but they will stand in the congregation of the sinners."

S. The spies have no portion in the world to come,

T. as it is said, "Even those men who brought up an evil report of the land died by the plague before the Lord" (Num. 14:37)

U. "Died" -- in this world.

V. "By the plague" -- in the world to come.

W. "The generation of the wilderness has no portion in the world to come and will not stand in judgment,

X. "for it is written, 'In this wilderness they shall be consumed and there they shall die' (Num. 14:35), "The words of R. Aqiba.

Y. R. Eliezer says, "Concerning them it says, 'Gather my saints together to me, those that have made a covenant with me by sacrifice' (Ps. 50:5)."

Z. "The party of Korah is not destined to rise up,

AA. "for it is written, 'And the earth closed upon them' -- in this world.

BB. "'And they perished from among the assembly' -- in the world to come," the words of R. Aqiba.

CC. And R. Eliezer says, "Concerning them it says, 'The Lord kills and resurrects, brings down to Sheol and brings up again' (1 Sam. 2:6)."

I.

A.   Our rabbis have taught on Tannaite authority:

B.   "The generation of the flood has no share in the world to come [M. 10:3A],

C.   "nor will they live in the world to come,

D.   "as it is said, And he destroyed every living thing that was upon the face of the earth (Gen. 7:23) in this world;

E.   "and they perished from the earth in the world to come," the words of R. Aqiba.

F.   R. Judah B. Betera says, "They will live nor be judged, as it is said, And the Lord said, My spirit shall not contend with man forever' (Gen. 6:3)

G.   "It will not contend, nor will my spirit be in them forever."

H.   Another matter: "And the Lord said, My spirit shall not contend: - [Said the Omnipresent,] that their spirit will not return to its sheath.

I.   R. Menahem b. R. Joseph says, [In T.'s version:] "It will not contend -

J.   "Said the Omnipresent, 'I shall not contend with them when I pay the good reward which is coming to the righteous.'

K.   "But the spirit of the evil is harder for them than that of all the others.

L.   "as it is written, Their spirit is a fire consuming them (Is. 33:11)'" [T. San. 13:6A-K].

II.

A.   Our rabbis have taught on Tannaite authority:

B.   The generation of the Flood acted arrogantly before the Omnipresent only on account of the good which he lavished on them, since it is said, "Their houses are safe from fear, neither is the rod of God upon them" (Job 21:9). "Their bull genders and fails not, their cow calves and casts not her calf" (Job 21:10). "They send forth their little ones like a flock, and their children dance" (Job. 21:11). "They spend their days in prosperity and their years in pleasures" (Job 36:11).

C.   That is what caused them to say to God, "Depart from us, for we do not desire knowledge of they ways. What is the Almighty, that we should serve Him, and what profit should we have, if we pray to him (Job 21:14).

D.   They said, "Do we need Him for anything except a few drops of rain? But look, we have rivers and wells which are more than enough for us in the sunny season and in the rainy season, since it is said, And a mist rose from the earth (Gen. 2:6)."

E.   The Omnipresent then said to then, "By the goodness which I lavished on them they take pride before me? By that same good I shall exact punishment from them!"

F.   What does it say? "And I, behold, I bring a flood of water upon the earth" (Gen. 6:17)

G.   R. Yose B. Durmasqit says, "The men of the Flood took pride only on account of [the covetousness of] the eyeball, which is like water, as it is said, 'The sons of God saw that the daughter of men were fair, and they took them wives from all which they chose (Gen. 6:2).

H.   "Also the Omnipresent exacted punishment from them only through water, which is like the eyeball, as it is written, 'All the fountains of the great deep were broken up, and the windows of heaven were opened' (Gen. 7:11)" [T. Sot. 3:6-9]

III.

A. Said R. Yohanan, "As to the generation of the flood, they corrupted their way 'greatly,' and they were judged 'greatly.'

B. "They corrupted their way greatly, as it is said, 'And God saw that the wickedness of man was great in the earth' (Gen. 6:5).

C. "They were judged greatly, as it is said, 'All the fountains of the great deep' (Gen. 7:1 l)."

D. Said R. Yohanan, "Three [of those fountains remained, the gulf of Gaddor, the hot springs of Tiberias, and the great well of Biram.:

IV.

A. "For all flesh had corrupted its way upon the earth" (Gen. 6:12):

B. Said R. Yohanan, "This teaches that [the men of the generation of the flood] made a hybrid match between a domesticated beast and a wild animal, a wild animal and a domesticated beast, and every sort of beast with man and man with every sort of beast."

C. Said R. Abba bar Kahana, "And all of them reverted [to the right way] except for the Tartarian lark [Freedman, p. 740, n. 10]."

V.

A. "And God said to Noah, the end of all flesh is come before me" (Gen. 6:13).

B. Said R. Yohanan, "Come and take note of how great is the power of robbery.

C. "For lo, the generation of the flood violated every sort of law, but the decree of punishment against them was sealed only when they went and committed robbery, for it is said, 'For the earth is filled with violence through them, and behold I will destroy them with the earth' (Gen. 6:13).

D. "And it is written, 'Violence is risen up into a rod of wickedness, none of them shall remain, nor of their multitude, nor any of theirs, neither shall there be wailing for them' (Ez. 7:1 l)."

E. Said R. Eleazar, "The cited verse teaches that [violence] stood up straight like a staff and stood before the Holy One, blessed be he, and said to him, 'Lord of the world, Neither them, nor of their multitudes, nor of any thing belonging to them, nor will there be wailing for them.'"

VI.

A. A Tannaite authority of the house of R. Ishmael [said], "Also the decree of punishment for Noah was issued, but he pleased the Lord,"

B. "as it is said, 'I am sorry that I made them. But Noah found favor in the eyes of the Lord' (Gen. 6:7-8)."

VII.

A. "And the Lord was comforted that he had made man in the earth" (Gen. 6:6).

B. When R. Dimi came, [he said,] "The Holy One, blessed be he, said, 'I did well that I made graves for them in the earth [Freedman, p. 741, n. 6: since the wicked are thereby destroyed].'

C. "How is this indicated? Here it is written, 'And the Lord was comforted' (Gen. 6:6) and elsewhere: 'And he comforted them and spoke kindly to them' (Gen. 50:21)."

D. There are those who say, "[He said,] 'I did not do well that I made graves for them in the earth.

E. "Here it is written, 'And the Lord regretted...' (Gen. 6:6) add elsewhere: 'And the Lord regretted the evil that he had thought to do to his people' (Ex. 32:14)."

VIII.

A. "These are the generations of Noah: Noah was a righteous man, perfect in his generations" (Gen. 6:9):

B. Said R. Yohanan, "By the standards of his generations, but not by the standards of other generations [was he perfect]."

C. R. Simeon b. Laqish said, "By the standards of his generations, and all the more so by the standards of other generations."

D. Said R. Hanina, "As to the view of R. Yohanan, one may propose a comparison. To what may the matter be compared? To the case of a keg of wine, stored in a wine cellar of vinegar.

E. "In its setting, its fragrance is noteworthy, but in any other setting, its fragrance would not be noteworthy."

F. Said R. Oshaia, "As to the view of R. Simeon b. Laqish, one may propose a comparison. To what may the matter be compared? To the case of a bottle of perfumed oil lying in a garbage dump.

G. "If it smells good in such a place, all the more so in a place in which there is spice!"

IX.

A. "And every living substance was destroyed which was upon the face of the ground, both man and beast" (Gen. 7:23):

B. While man sinned, what sin had beasts committed?

C. It was taught on Tannaite authority in the name of R. Joshua b. Qorha, "The matter may be compared to the case of a man who made a marriage banquet for his son. He prepared all sorts of food for the banquet. After some days the son died. The man went and threw out [all the food he had prepared for] the banquet.

D. "He said, 'Did I do anything except for my son? Now that he is died, what need have I for a marriage banquet?'

E. "So too the Holy One, blessed be he, said, 'Did I create domesticated and wild beasts for any purpose other than for man? Now that man has sinned, what need have I for domesticated beasts or wild beasts?'"

X.

A. "All that was on the dry land died" (Gen. 7:22) --

B. But not the fish in the sea.

XI.

A. R. Yose of Caesarea expounded as follows: "What is the sense of the verse, 'He is swift as the waters, their portion is cursed in the earth, [he does not behold the way of the vineyards]' (Job 24:18)?

B. "The verse teaches that Noah, the righteous man, rebuked them, saying to [his generation], 'Carry out an act of repentance, for if not, the Holy One, blessed be he, will bring upon you a flood and your corpses will float on the water like gourds.'

C.   "'So it is written, "He is light upon the waters" (Job 24:18).

D.   "'And not only so, but people will take from your example a curse for all who will pass through the world, as it is said, "Their portion is cursed in the earth" (Job 24:18).'

E.   "They said to him, 'And what is stopping him now?'

F.   "He said to them, '[God] has one dear one to take away from your midst.'

G.   "[They replied], [108B] 'If so, we will not turn aside from the way of the vineyards, [that is, we shall continue in our drunkenness].'"

XII.

A.   Raba expounded as follows: "What is the meaning of the verse, 'He that is ready to slip with his feet is as a stone despised in the thought of him that is at ease' (Job 12:5)?

B.   "This teaches that the righteous Noah rebuked them, saying to them words as hard as stone, but they despised him, saying, 'Old man, what is this ark for?'

C.   "He said to them, 'The Holy One, blessed be he, is bringing a flood on you.'

D.   "They said to him, 'What sort of flood? If it is a flood of fire, we have something called alitha [Freedman, p. 743, n. 7: a fire-extinguishing demon].

E.   "'And if he brings a flood of water, if it comes from the earth, we have iron plates to cover up the earth [and keep the water down].

F.   "'If it comes from heaven, we have aqob (others say, aqosh) [Freedman, p. 743, n. 8: a legendary fungus, which when donned on the head protects against rain].'

G.   "He said to them, 'He will bring it from between your heels [legs, that is, from your penis], as it is said, "He is ready for the steps of your feet" (Job 12:5).'"

H.   It has been taught on Tannaite authority:

I.   The water of the flood was as hard as semen, as it is written, "It is ready for the steps of his feet" (Job 12:5).

XIII.

A.   Said R. Hisda, "By hot fluid they corrupted their way in transgression, and by hot fluid they were judged.

B.   "Here it is written, 'And the water cooled' (Gen. 8:1), and elsewhere: 'Then the king's wrath cooled down' (Est. 7:10)."

XIV.

A.   "And it came to pass after seven days that the waters of the flood were upon the earth" (Gen. 7:10)"

B.   Said Rab, "What is the meaning of these seven days?

C.   "These are the seven days of mourning for Methuselah, the righteous man. This teaches that lamentation for the righteous held back the retribution from coming upon the world.

D.   "Another matter: 'After seven days' teaches that the Holy One, blessed be he, changed the order of the world for them, so that the sun came up in the west and set in the east.

E.   "Another matter: It teaches that the Holy One, blessed be he, first set a long a time for them, and then a short time.

F.   "Another matter: It teaches that he gave them a taste of the world to come, so that they should know how much good he would withhold from them [T. Sot. 10:3C. 4]."

XV.

A.   "Of every clean beast you shall take by sevens, man and wife" (Gen. 7:2).:

B.   Do beasts relate as man and wife?

C.   Said R. Samuel bar Nahmani said R. Jonathan, "It was to be from among those with whom no transgression had been committed."

D.   How did he know?

E.   Said R. Hisda, "He brought them before the ark. Any that the ark received could be known not to have been the object of a transgression, and any that the ark did not receive could be known to be those with whom a transgression had been committed."

F.   R. Abbahu said, "It was from among those who came on their won."

XVI.

A.   "Make an ark of gopher wood for yourself" (Gen. 6:14)"

B.   What is gopher wood?

C.   Said R. Adda, "Members of the house of R. Shila say, 'It is a kind of cedar.'

D.   "Others say, 'It is a hard wood of cedar.'"

XVII.

A.   "A window (SHR) you shall make in the ark" (Gen. 6:16):

B.   Said R. Yohanan, "The Holy One, blessed be he, said to Noah, 'Put up in its precious stones and pearls, so that they will give light for you as at noon [using the root for window]."

XVIII.

A.   "And in a cubit you shall finish the above" (Gen. 6:16)"

B.   In what way will it stand firm [against the rain]

C.   "With lower, second, and third stories you shall make it" (Gen. 6:16)"

D.   It has been taught on Tannaite authority:

E.   The bottom for dung, the middle for beasts, the upper for man.

XIX.

A.   "And he set forth a raven" (Gen. 8:7):

B.   Said R. Simeon b. Laqish, "The raven gave Noah a victorious reply, saying to him, 'Your master [God] hates me, and you hate me.

C.   "'Your master hates me: 'Of the clean, seven, of the unclean, two' [and the raven is unclean]

D.   "'You hate me, for you exempt the species of which you have seven, and send forth a species of which you have only two.

E.   "'If I should be injured by the prince of heat or cold, will the world not end up lacking one species?

F.   "'Or perhaps you need only to make use of my wife?'

G.   "He said to him, 'Wicked creature! Even sexual relations with one normally permitted to me are presently forbidden [since it was not permitted to have sexual relations in the ark. Is it not an argument a fortiori that I should not desire sexual relations with one who normally is forbidden to me [namely, a bird]?'"

H.   And how do we know that sexual relations were forbidden?

I.   As it is written, "And you shall enter the ark, you, your sons, your wife, and the wives of your sons with you" (Gen. 6:18).

J.   And elsewhere: "Go forth from the ark, you, your wife, your sons, and your sons' wives with you" (Gen. 8:16).

K.   And, said R. Yohanan, "On the basis of this statement they said that sexual relations were forbidden in the ark [ad the instruction to go forth once more permitted sexual relations]."

XX.

A.   Our rabbis have taught on Tannaite authority:

B.   Three species had sexual relations in the ark, and all of them were smitten: the dog, raven, and Ham.

C.   The dog [was smitted by being condemned to be] tied up.

D.   The raven was smitted by having to spit [his semen into his mate's mouth].

E.   Ham was smitten in his skin.

XXI.

A.   "Also he sent forth a dove from him to see if the waters had abated" (Gen. 8:8).:

B.   Said R. Jeremiah, "On the basis of this verse [we learn] that the dwellings of the clean fowl was with the righteous man."

XXII.

A.   "And lo, in her mouth was an olive leaf as food" (Gen. 8:11):

B.   Said R. Eleazar, "The dove said before the Holy One, blessed be he, 'May my food be as bitter as an olive leaf but placed in our hand, and let it not be as sweet as honey but placed in the hand of mortals.'

C.   "What gives evidence that the word at hand means 'as food'?

D.   "From the following: 'Feed me [using the same root] with food convenient for me' (Prov. 30:8)."

XXIII.

A.   "After their families they went forth from the ark" (Gen. 8:19).:

B.   Said R. Yohanan, "'After their families' and not they [Freedman: alone]." [Freedman, p. 746, n. 6: While in the ark, copulation was forbiddden. On their exit, it was permitted. That is the significance of "after their families," which denotes that mating was resumed and they ceased to be a group of single entities.]

XXIV.

A.   Said R. Hana bar Bizna, "Said Eliezer [Abraham's servant] to Shem, the eldest [son], 'It is written, "After their families they went forth from the ark" (Gen. 8:19). How was it with you? [How did you take care of all the animals, given their diverse needs, while you were in the ark?]'

B.   "He said to him, 'We had a great deal of trouble in the ark. A beast who usually was to be fed by day we fed by day. One that usually was to be fed by night we fed by night. As to the chameleon, father did not know what it ate.

C.   "'One day he was sitting and cutting up a pomegranate, and a worm fell out of it. [The chameleon] ate it. From that point forth, he would mash bran for it. When it became maggoty, [the chameleon] ate it."

D.   As to the lion, it was fed by a fever, for said Rab, "For no fewer than six days and no more than thirteen, fever sustains."

E.   [Reverting to Shem's statement,] "'As to the phoenix, father found it lying in the hold of the ark. He said to it, "Don't you want food?"

F.   "'It said to him, "I saw that you were occupied and thought not to bother you."

G.   "'He said to it, "May it be God's will that you not die, as it is written, 'Then I said I shall die in the nest, but I shall multiply my days as the phoenix' (Job 29:18).'"'

H.   Said R. Hanah bar Livai, "Said Shem, the eldest [son] to Eliezer, 'When the kings of the east and the west came against you, what did you do?'

I.   "He said to him, 'The Holy One, blessed be he, came to Abraham and set him at his right hand, and [God and Abraham] threw dirt, which turned into swords, and [they threw] chaff, which turned into arrows.

J.   "'So it is written, "A Psalm of David. The Lord said to my master, Sit at my right hand until I make your enemies your footstool" (Ps. 110:1). And it is written, "Who raised up the righteous man from the east, called him to his food, gave the nations before him, and made him rule over kings? He made his sword as the dust and his bowl as driven stubble" (Is. 41:2).'"

XXV.

A.   Nahum of Gam Zo ["This Too"] was accustomed to say, on the occasion of anything that happened, "This too is for the good." One day, the Israelites wanted to end a gift to Caesar.

B.   They said, "With [109A] whom shall we send it? Let us send it with Nahum of Gam Zo, for he is familiar with miracles."

C.   When he got to an Inn, he wanted to lodge there. They said to him, "What do you have with you?"

D.   He said to them, "I'm bringing a gift to Caesar."

E.   They got up in the middle of the night and untied his box, took out everything in it, and filled the box with dirt. When he got there [to the capital], it turned out to be dirt. The [courtiers] said to him, "The Jews are ridiculing us."

F.   They took him out to kill him. He said, "This too is for the good."

G.   Elijah came and appeared to them as one of them. He said to them, "Perhaps this dirt comes from the dirt of Abraham, our father, who threw dirt that turned into swords and chaff that turned into arrows."

H.   They looked, and that is what turned out. There was a province that they had not been able to conquer. They threw some of that dirt against it, and they conquered it. They brought [Nahum] to the treasury and said to him, "Take whatever you want."

I.   He filled his box with gold. When he returned, those who were at the inn came and said to him, "What did you bring to the palace?"

J.   He said to them, "What I took from here I brought there."

K.   They took [dirt] ad brought it there, and [the courtiers] put them to death.

XXVI.

A.   The generation of the dispersion has no share in the world to come [M. 10:3E]:

B.   What did they do wrong?

C.   Said members of the house of R. Shila, "[They said], 'Let us build a tower and go up to the firmament and hit it with axes, so that the water will gush forth."

D.   They ridiculed this in the West, "If so, they should have built it on a mountain!"

E.   Said R. Jeremiah bar Eleazar, "They divided up into three parties. One said, 'Let us go up and dwell there.'

F.   "The second said, 'Let us go up and worship an idol.'

G.   "The third said, 'Let us go up and make war.'

H.   "The party that said, 'Let us go up and dwell there -- the Lord scattered them' (Gen. 11:9).

I.   "The party that said, 'Let us go up and make war' turned into apes, spirits, devils, and night-demons.

J.   "The party that said, 'Let us go up and worship an idol' -- 'for there the Lord did confound the language of all the earth'(Gen. 11:9)."

XXVII.

A.   It has been taught on Tannaite authority:

B.   R. Nathan says, "All of them [went up] intending to worship an idol.

C.   "Here it is written, 'Let us make us a name' (Gen. 11:4), and elsewhere: 'And make no mention of the name of other gods' (Ex. 23:13).

D.   "Just as in the latter passage [name stands for] idolatry, so here too 'name' stands for idolatry."

XXVIII.

A.   Said R.Yohanan, "As to the tower, a third of it burned, a third of it sank into the earth, and a third is yet standing."

B.   Said Rab, "The air of the tower makes people forget."

C.   Said R. Joseph, "Babylonia and Borsif are a bad sign for Torah-study [because people there forget what they learn)Freeman, p. 748, n. 8)]."

D.   What is the sense of Borsif?

E.   Said R. Asi, "An empty pit [bor: pit: sif/shafi: empty]."

XXIX.

A.   The men of Sodom have no portion in the world to come [M. 10:31]:

B.   Our rabbis have taught on Tannaite authority:

C.   The men of Sodom have no portion in the world to come [M. 11:31],

D.   since it is said, "And the men of Sodom were wicked sinners" (Gen. 13:13) in this world

E.   "against the Lord exceedingly" -- in the world to come. [T. San. 13:8A-C].

XXX.

A.   Said R. Judah, "'Wicked' -- with their bodies.

B.   "And 'sinners' -- with their money.

C.   "'Wicked' -- with their bodies, as it is written, 'How then can I do this great wickedness and sin against God?' (Gen. 39:9).

D.   "'Sinners' -- with their money, as it is written, 'And it be a sin unto you' (Deut. 15:9).

E.   "'Before the Lord' -- this is blasphemy.

F.   "'Very much' -- for they intended deliberately to sin."

G.   On Tannaite authority it was taught:

H.   "'Wicked" -- with their money.

I.   "And sinners" -- with their bodies.

J.   "Wicked" -- with their money, as it is written, "And your eye be wicked against your poor brothers" (Deut. 15:9).

K.   "And sinners" -- with their bodies, as it is written, "And I will sin against God" (Gen. 39:9).

L.   "Before the Lord" -- this is blasphemy.

M.   "Very much" -- this refers to murder, as it is written, "Moreover, Manasseh shed innocent blood exceedingly" (2 Kgs. 21:16).

XXXI.

A.   Our rabbis have taught on Tannaite authority:

B.   The men of Sodom acted arrogantly before the Omnipresent only on account of the good which he lavished on them, since it is said, "As for the land, out of it comes bread...Its stones are the place of sapphires, and it has dust of gold. That path, no bird of prey knows...The proud beasts have not trodden it" (Job 28:5-8).

C.   Said the men of Sodom, "Since bread comes forth from our land, and silver and gold come forth from our land, and precious stones and pearls come forth from our land, we do not need people to come to us.

D.   "They come to us only to take things away from us. Let us go and forget how things are usually done among us."

E.   [Following T.'s version:] The Omnipresent said to them, "Because of the goodness which I have lavished upon you, you deliberately forget how things are usually done among you. I shall make you be forgotten from the world."

F.   What does it say? "They open shafts in a valley from where men live. They are forgotten by travelers. They hang afar from men, they swing to and fro (Job 28:4). In the thought of one who is at ease there is contempt for misfortune; it is ready for those whose feet slip. The tents of robbers are at peace, and those who provoke God are secure, who bring their god in their hand" (Job 12:5-6).

G.   And so it says, "As I live, says the Lord God, your sister Sodom and her daughters have not done as you and your daughters have done. Behold, this was the guilt of your sister Sodom: she and her daughters had pride, surfeit of food, and prosperous ease, but did not aid the poor and needy. They were haughty and did abominable things before me. Therefore I removed them when I saw it" (Ez. 16:48-50). [T. Sot. 3:11-2].

XXXII.

A.   Rabba expounded [the following verse]: "What is the sense of this verse: 'How long will you imagine mischief against a man? You shall be slain, all of you, you are all as a bowing wall and as a tottering fence' (Ps. 62:4)?

B.   "This teaches that the [Sodomites] would look enviously at wealthy men, so they would set such a man near a tottering fence and push it over on him and come and take away all his money."

C.   Raba expounded [the following verse]: "What is the meaning of this verse: 'In the dark they dig through houses, which they had marked for themselves in the daytime; they know not the light' (Job 24:16)?

D.   "This teaches that the [Sodomites] would look enviously at wealthy men, so they would deposit with such a man valuable balsam. [The wealthy men] would put it into their treasure rooms. In the night [the others] would come and smell it out like a dog [and so know where there treasure was], as it is written, 'They return at evening, they make a noise like a dog, and go around the city' (Ps. 59:7).

E.   "They would then come and dig there and take away the money.

F.   "[As to the victim"] 'They cause him to go naked without clothing' (Job 24:10), 'that they have no covering in the cold' (Job 24:7). 'They lead away the ass of the fatherless, they take the widow's ox for a pledge' (Job 24:3). 'They remove the landmarks, they violently take away flocks and feed them' (Job 24:2). 'And he shall be brought to the grave and remain in the tomb' (Job 21:32)."

G.   R. Yose interpreted the passage in this way in Sepphoris. That night three hundred houses in Sepphoris were broken into. They came and blamed him. They said to him, "You have shown the way to thieves."

H.   He said to them, "Did I know that thieves would come?"

I.   When R. Yose died, the streets of Sepphoris ran with blood.

XXXIII.

A.   [The Sodomites] said, "Whoever has one ox must guard the herd one day, and whoever has no oxen must guard the herd two days."

B.   There was an orphan, son of a widow, the whom they gave the herd to pasture. He went and killed the [oxen]. He said to them, "He who has one ox may take one hide. He who has no oxen may take two hides."

C.   "Why so" they asked him?

D.   He said to them [109B], "The end of the matter must accord with its beginning. Just as, at the beginning, one who had an ox had to pasture the herd for one day and one who had none had to do it two days, so at the end, one who had an ox takes one hide, and one who has none takes two."

E.   One who crosses a river [by a ferry] pays one _zuz_, and one who does not cross the river by a ferry [but crosses on his own] has to pay two.

F.   If one had a row of bricks [drying in the sun], each one of them would take one, saying to him, "I only took one."

G.   If one had garlic or onions drying [in the sun], each one of them would take one, saying to him, "I only took one."

XXXIV.

A. There were four judges in Sodom, named Liar, Big Liar, Forger, and Perverter of Justice.

B. If someone beat his neighbor's wife and made her abort, they say to him, "Give her to him, and he will make her pregnant for you."

C. If someone cut off the ear of his neighbor's ass, they say to him, "Give it to him, until it grows a new one."

D. If someone injured his neighbor, they say to [the victim], "Pay him the fee for letting blood from you."

E. One who crosses the river in a ferry pays four zuz, one who crosses through the water pays eight.

F. One day a washerman came by there. They said to him, "Pay four zuz."

G. He said to them, "I crossed in the water."

H. They said to him, "If so, pay eight, because you crossed through the water."

I. He would not pay, so they beat him up. He came before a judge, who said to him, "Pay the fee for his having let blood from you, as well as the eight zuz for crossing through the water."

J. Eliezer, Abraham's servant, happened to come there. Someone beat him up. He came before a judge, who said to him, "Pay him a fee for letting blood from you."

K. He took a stone and beat the judge. He said to him, "What's this?"

L. He said to him, "The fee that you now owe me give to this man, and my money will remain where it is."

M. They had beds, on which they would place guests. If someone was too long, they shortened him [by cutting off his legs], and if he was too short, they stretched him [on a rack].

N. Eliezer, Abraham's servant, happened by there. They said to him, "Come, lie down on the bed."

O. He said to the, "I took a vow from the time that my mother died never to sleep on a bed."

P. When a poor man came there, each one of them gave him a denar, on which he wrote his name. But they gave him no bread. When he would die, each one of them came and took back his denar.

Q. They made this stipulation among them: Whoever invited someone to a banquet will have to give over his cloak. There was a banquet, and Eliezer happened to come there, but they did not give him any bread. Since he wanted to eat, Eliezer came and sat down at the end of them all. They said to him, "Who invited you here?"

R. He said to the one who sat nearby, "You were the one who invited me."

S. He said, "Perhaps they will hear that I was the one who invited him and take away the cloak of that man [me]." He took off his cloak and ran away. And so they all did, until all of them were gone, and he ate the entire banquet.

T. A certain girl brought out bread hidden in a pitcher to a poor man. The matter became known. They covered her with honey and put her on the parapet of the wall, and a swarm of bees came and ate her up.

U. For it is written, "And the Lord said, The cry of Sodom and Gomorrah, because it is great" (Gen. 18:20).

V. On this passage, said R. Judah said Rab, "It is on account of the girl [with the consonants for 'girl' and 'great' being the same]."

XXXV.

A. The spies have no portion in the world to come, as it is said, "Even those men who brought up an evil report of the land died by the plague before the Lord" (Num. 14:37). "Died" in this world. "By the plague" in the world to come.

B. "The party of Korah is not destined to rise up, for it is written 'And the earth closed upon them' -- in this world. 'And they perished from among the assembly' in the world to come," the words of R. Aqiba. And R. Eliezer says, "Concerning them it says, 'The Lord kills and resurrects, brings down to Sheol and brings up again' (1 Sam. 2:6).

C. Our rabbis have taught on Tannaite authority:

D. "Korah and his company have no portion in the world to come and will not live in the world to come,

E. "since it is said, 'And the earth closed upon them' (Num. 16:33) -- in this world.

F. "'And they perished from among the assembly' -- in the world to come," the words of R. Aqiba [M. 11:3Z-BB].

G. R. Judah b. Petera says, "Lo, they are like something lost and searched for [T.: They will come to the world to come].

H. "For concerning them it is written, 'I have gone astray like a perishing sheep; seek your servant' (Ps. 119:176)

I. [Following T.:] 'Perishing' is said here, and in the matter of Korah and his company, 'perishing' also is said.

J. "Just as 'perishing' spoken of later on refers to that which is being sought, so 'perishing' spoken of here refers to that which is being sought" [T. San. 13:9C-I].

XXXVI.

A. "Now Korah took..." (Num. 16:1):

B. He took a bad deal for himself.

C. "Korah" -- for he was made a bald-spot ["Korah" and "bald-spot" using the same consonants] in Israel.

D. ""Son of Izhar" -- a son who turned the heat of the entire world against himself, as the heat of noon ["Izhar" and "noon" use the same consonants].

E. "Son of Kohath" -- who set on edge [KHT] the teeth of those who gave birth to him.

F. "Son of Levi" - a son of the company of Gehenna ["Levi" and "company" use the same consonants].

G. Then why not say, "son of Jacob" -- a son who followed to Gehenna [with the letters for "Jacob" and "follow" being shared]?

H. Said R. Samuel b. R. Isaac, ""Jacob sought mercy for himself, [that he should not be listed here], as it is said, 'O my soul, come not into their secret, to their assembly my honor be not united' (Gen. 39:6).

I.   "'O my soul, come not into their secret' -- this refers to the spies.

J.   "'Unto their assembly, my honor be not united' refers to the assembly of Korah."

K.   "Dathan" (Num. 16:1) [colleague of Korah] -- so-called because he transgressed the law [dat] of God.

L.   "Abiram" (Num. 16:1) -- so-called because he strengthened himself [using the consonants of the name] not to carry out an act of repentance.

M.   "On" (Num. 16:1) [whose name means "lamentation"] -- so-called because he sat and lamented [what he had done].

N.   "Peleth [On's father]" (Num. 16:1) -- so-called because wonders [using the same letters as the name] were done for him.

O.   "The son of Reuben" (Num. 16:1) -- who saw and understood [using the consonants of the name] [not to get involved].

XXXVII.

A.   Said Rab, "As to On, son of Peleth, his wife saved him. She said to him, 'What do you get out of this matter? If one master is the greater, you are his disciple, and if the other master is the greater, you are still his disciple!'

B.   "He said to her, 'What should I do? I was in their conspiracy and I took an oath to be with them.'

C.   "She said to him, 'I know that they are all a holy congregation, for it is written, "Seeing all the congregation are holy, every one of them" (Num. 16:3).'

D.   "She said to him, 'Stay here, and I'll save you.' She got him drunk on wine and laid him down in [the tent]. She sat down at the flap [110A] and loosened her hair. Whoever came and saw her turned back. [No one would gaze at her.]

E.   "Meanwhile Korah's wife joined them, saying to them, 'See what Moses is doing! He is king. His brother made him high priest. His brother's sons he has made assistant priests. If heave-offering is brought, he says, "Give it to the priest." If tithe is brought, which you have every right to take [since it is for the Levites], he says, "Give a tenth of it to the priest."

F.   "'Moreover, he has shaved off all your hair [as part of the purification rite, Num. 8:7], and ridicules you as if you were dirt, for he envied your hair.'

G.   "He said to her, 'But he did the same thing to himself?'

H.   "She said to him, 'It was because all the greatness was coming to him, he said also, "Let my soul die with the Philistines" (Jud. 16:30). [Freedman, p. 754, n. 5: This was used proverbially to denote readiness to suffer, so that others might suffer too. Moses, retaining all the greatness himself, did not mind shaving his own hair off, seeing that he had caused all the rest to do so, thus depriving them of their beauty.]

I.   "'And furthermore he has said to you to make [fringes] of blue [on your garments] [Num. 15:38]. But if you think that the blue [fringe] is a religious duty, then produce cloaks of blue and dress your entire academy in them.'

J.   "That is in line with what is written, "Every wise woman builds her house' -- referring to the wife of On, son of Peleth.

K.   "'But the foolish woman tears it down with her own hands' (Prov. 14:1) -- referring to the wife of Korah."

XXXVIII.

A. "And they rose up before Moses, with certain of the children of Israel, two hundred and fifty" (Num. 16:2):

B. They were the distinguished members of the community.

C. "Chosen for the appointed times" (Num. 16:2):

D. For they knew how to intercalate years and designate the beginnings of the new months.

E. "Men or renown" (Num. 16:2):

F. For they were known throughout the world.

XXXIX.

A. "And when Moses heard, he fell on his face" (Num. 16:4):

B. What did he hear?

C. Said R. Samuel bar Nahmani said R. Jonathan, "That people suspected him of having sexual relations with a married woman, as it is said, 'And they expressed jealousy [as to sexual infidelity] of Moses in the camp' (Ps. 106:16)."

D. Said R. Samuel bar Isaac, "This teaches that everyone expressed jealousy of his wife [M. Sot. 1:1] with respect to Moses, as it is said, 'And Moses took the tent and pitched it outside the camp.' (Ex. 33:7) [Freedman, p. 755, n. 5: to avoid all ground of suspicion.]"

XL.

A. "And Moses rose up and went to Dathan and Abiram" (Num. 16:25):

B. Said R. Simeon b. Laqish, "On the basis of this verse we learn that one should not hold on to a quarrel [but should be eager to end it, in the model of Moses, who modestly went out to the other side to seek a resolution]."

C. For Rab said, "Whoever holds on to a quarrel [and does not seek to end it] violates a negative commandment, for it is said, 'And let him not be as Korah and as his company' (Num. 17:5)."

D. R. Ashi said, "He is worthy of being smitten with saraat.

E. "Here it is written, 'As the Lord said to him by the hand of Moses' (Num. 17:5), and elsewhere it is written, 'And the Lord said to him, Put your hand into your bosom [and when he took it out, behold, his hand was leprous as snow' (Ex. 4:6)."

XLI.

A. Said R. Yose, "Whoever contends with the kingdom of the house of David is worthy that a snake bite him.

B. "Here it is written, 'And Adonijah slew sheep and oxen and fat cattle by the stone of Zoheleth" '(1 Kgs. 1:9), and elsewhere it is written, 'With the poison of serpents [using the same consonants as the word Zoheleth] of the dust' (Deut. 32:24)."

C. Said R. Hisda, "Whoever is contentious with his master is as if he were contentious with the presence of God, as it is said, 'When they strove against the Lord' (Num. 26:9). [Freedman, p. 755, n. 14: The reference is to Korah's rebellion; though against Moses only, it is stigmatized as being against God.]"

D.   Said R. Hama b. R. Hanina, "Whoever undertakes to quarrel with his master is as if he had quarrelled with the Presence of God, as it is said, 'This is the water of Strife, because the children of Israel strove with the Lord' (Num. 20:13)."

E.   Said R. Hanina bar Pappa, "Whoever complains against his master is as if he complains against the Presence of God, as it is said, 'Your murmurings are not against us but against the Lord' (Ex. 16:8)."

F.   Said R. Abbahu, "Whoever murmurs against his master is as if he murmurs against the Presence of God, as it is said, 'And the people spoke against God and against Moses' (Num. 21:5)."

XLII.

A.   "Riches kept for the owners to their hurt" (Qoh. 5:12):

B.   Said R. Simeon b. Laqish, "This refers to the riches of Korah."

C.   "And all the substance that was at their feet" (Deut. 11:6)"

D.   Said R. Eleazar, "This refers to the wealth of a man, that puts him on his feet."

E.   And said R. Levi, "A load for three hundred white mules were made up by the keys of Korah's treasury, although all of them were made of leather, both keys and locks [and not metal]."

F.   Said R. Hama b. R. Hanina, "Joseph hid three treasures in Egypt. One of them was revealed to Korah, one of them was revealed to Antoninus, son of Severus, and one of them is hidden away for the righteous in the world to come."

XLIII.

A.   And said R. Yohanan, "Korah was not among those who were swallowed up nor among those who were burned.

B.   "He was not among those who were swallowed up, for it is written, 'And all the men that joined Korah' (Num. 16:32) -- but not Korah.

C.   "He was not among those who were burned, for it is written, 'When the fire devoured two hundred and fifty men' (Num. 16:10) -- but not Korah."

D.   In a Tannaite teaching it was repeated:

E.   Korah was one of those who were burned up, and he was one of those who were swallowed up.

F.   He was one of those who were swallowed up, for it is written, "And swallowed them up together with Korah" (Num. 16:10).

G.   He was one of those who were burned, since it is written, "And there came up a fire from the Lord and consumed the two hundred fifty men" (Num. 16:35) -- including Korah.

XLIV.

A.   Said Raba, "What is the meaning of that which is written, 'The sun and the moon stood still in their zebul, at the light of your arrows they went' (Hab. 3:1)? [Freedman, p. 757, n. 1: There are seven heavens, of which zebul is one. What were they doing in zebul, seeing that they are set in the firmament, a lower heaven?]

B.   "This teaches that the sun and the moon went up to the firmament called Zebul. They said before the Holy One, blessed be he, 'Lord of the world, if you do justice with the son of Amram, we shall go forth, and if not, we shall not go forth.'

C. "He shot arrows at them and said to them, 'On account of the honor owing to me you never objected, but on account of the honor owing to a mortal man, you make a protest!'

D. "Nowadays they go forth only when they are driven out."

XLV.

A. Raba interpreted a verse of Scripture, "What is the meaning of what is written, 'But if the Lord make a new thing and the earth open her mouth' (Num. 16:30)?

B. "Said Moses before the Holy One, blessed be he, 'If Gehenna has been created, well and good, and if not, let the Lord now create it.'

C. "For what purpose? If we say that he was actually to create it then and there, [how can this be so, for] 'There is no new thing under the sun' (Qoh. 1:9)?

D. "Rather, it was to bring its mouth near [to the present place]."

XLVI.

A. "But the children of Korah did not die" (Num. 26:11):

B. A Tannaite authority taught in the name of our Master [Judah the Patriarch]: "A place was set aside for them in Gehenna, and they sat there and recited a song [for God]."

XLVII.

A. Said Rabbah bar bar Hana, "One time I was going along the way, and a Tai [Arab] said to me, 'Come, and I shall show you where the men of Korah were swallowed up.' I went and saw two crevasses, from which smoke came forth. He took a piece of wool, wet it down, and set it on the tip of his spear and passed it over the spot, and it was singed.

B. "I said to him, 'Listen to what you are going to hear.'

C. "And I heard him saying, 'Moses and his Torah are true, and they are liars.'

D. "[110B] He said to me, 'Every thirty days Gehenna turns them over like meat in a pot, and they say this: 'Moses and his Torah are true, and they are liars.'"

XLVIII.

A. The generation of the wilderness has no portion in the world to come [M. 11:3W]:

B. Our rabbis have taught on Tannaite authority:

C. "The generation of the wilderness has no portion in the world to come [M. 10:3W],

D. [T. adds:] "and will not live in the world to come,

E. "for it is said, 'In this wilderness they shall be consumed and there they shall die' (Num. 14:35),

F. "'In this wilderness they shall be consumed' -- in this world,

G. "and there they will die, ' in the world to come.

H. "And it says, 'Of them I swore in my wrath that they should not enter into my rest' (Ps. 95:11)", the words of R. Aqiba.

I. R. Eliezer says, "They will come into the world to come,

J. "for concerning them it is said, 'Gather my saints together to me, those that have made a covenant with me by sacrifice' (Ps. 50:5) [M. 11:3Y] [T. San. 13:10].

K. "What does Scripture mean, 'I swore in my wrath'?

L.   "'In my wrath I swore, but I retract it.'"

M.   R. Joshua b. Qorha says, "These things were spoken only regarding generations to come,

N.   as it is said, 'Gather my saints together to me' -- these are the righteous of every generation [T.: because they did deeds of loving kindness to me];

O.   "'Those that have made a covenant with me' -- this refers to Hananiah, Mishael, and Azariah, who gave themselves up to the fiery furnace on my account.

P.   "'By sacrifice' -- this refers to R. Aqiba and his colleagues, who gave themselves over to the slaughter on account of the teachings of the Torah."

Q.   R. Simeon b. Menassia says, "They will come [into the world to come],

R.   "and concerning them it is said, 'And the redeemed of the world shall return and come to Zion with gladness' (Is. 35:10) [T. San. 13:11].

S.   Said Rabbah bar bar Hannah said R. Yohanan, "R. Aqiba abandoned his love [of Israel, when he said that the generation of the wilderness will not enjoy the world to come].

T.   "For it is written, 'Go and cry in the ears of Jerusalem, saying Thus says the Lord, I remember the loyalty of your youth, the love of your espousals, when you went after me in the wilderness, in an unsown land' (Jer. 2:2). [Freedman, p. 759, n. 1: Thus the merit of this act of faith on the part of the generation of the wilderness stood their decendants in good stead and conferred the privilege on them of a share in the world to come].

U.   "Now if others will come on account of their merit [to the world to come,] how much the more so they themselves!"

The Talmud simply lays forth materials to complement the Mishnah's topics, item by item:

I.   The generation of the flood [M. 11:3A]:
        I - XXV

II.   The generation of the dispersion [M. 11:3E]"
        XXVI - XXVIII

III.   The men of Sodom [M. 111:3I]:
        XXIX - XXXIV

IV.   The spies [M. 11:3S]:
        XXXV

V.   The generation of the wilderness [M. 11:3W]"
        XLVIII

VI.   The party of Korah [M. 11:3Z]"
        XXXV - XLVII

The sole point of note is the change in the order of the Mishnah's topics at the final two items. Otherwise the sequence and topical unfolding are just as expected.

11:3DD-FF

DD. "The ten tribes are not destined to return,

EE. "since it is said, 'And he cast them into another land, as on this day' (Deut. 29:28). Just as the day passes and does not return, so they have gone their way and will not return," the words of R. Aqiba.

FF. R. Eliezer says, "Just as this day is dark and then grows light, so the ten tribes for whom it now is dark -- thus in the future it is destined to grow light for them."

I.

A. Our rabbis have taught on Tannaite authority:

B. "The ten tribes have no portion in the world to come [T.: and will not live in the world to come],

C. "as it is said, 'And the Lord drove them out of their land with anger and heat and great wrath' (Deut. 29:8) -- in this world;

D. "and cast them forth into another land' (Deut. 29:28) -- in the world to come [cf. M. 11:3DD-ff]," the words of R. Aqiba.

E. R. Simeon b. Judah of Kefar Akkum says in the name of R. Simeon, "Scripture said, 'As at this day' --

F. "if their deeds remains as they are this day, they will [not] reach it, and if not, they will (not) reach it."

G. Rabbi says, "[Both these and those] have a portion in the world to come,

H. "as it is said, 'And it shall come to pass in that day that the trumpet shall be blown [and those who are perishing in the land of Assyria and those who are driven away in to the Land of Egypt shall come and worship the Lord in the holy mountain, in Jerusalem]' (Is. 27:13)." [T. San. 13:12].

I. Said Rabbah b. b. Hana said R. Yohanan, "R. Aqiba abandoned his love [for Israel in taking the position that he did.]

J. "For it is written 'Go and proclaim these words toward the north and say, Return, you backsliding Israel, says the Lord, and I will not cause my anger to fall upon you, for I am merciful, says the Lord, and I will not keep my anger forever' (Jer. 3:12)."

K. What is the reference to [Aqiba's] love?

L. As it has been taught on Tannaite authority:

M. "Minors who are children of the wicked of the Land [of Israel] have no portion in the world to come, as it is said, 'Behold, the day is coming, burning like a furnace, and all the proud, and all who do wickedly, shall be as stubble, and the day coming shall burn them up, said the Lord, that it shall leave them neither root nor branch' (Mal. 3:19).

N. "'Root' -- in this world.

O. "'Branch' -- in the world to come," the words of Rabban Gamaliel.

P. R. Aqiba says, "They come into the world to come. For it says, 'The Lord preserves the simple' (Ps. 116:6), and in the coastal towns they call a child 'the

simple one.' And further, 'Hew down the tree and destroy it, nevertheless, leave the
stump of the roots thereof in the earth' (Dan. 4:23)."

Q.   Said Rabban Gamaliel said to [Aqiba], "How shall I interpret, 'He shall leave to them
      neither the root nor the branch'"?

R.   [Joshua] said to Gamaliel, "That the Omnipresent will not leave them [the merit of
      a single] religious duty or the remnant of a religious duty, or for their fathers,
      forever" [T. San. 13:1 A-D].

S.   Another matter:

T.   "Root" -- this refers to the soul.

U.   And "branch" -- this refers to the body.

V.   And the children of the wicked among the heathen will not live [in the world to
      come] nor be judged.

W.   And Rabban Gamaliel?

X.   He derives the same fact from the verse, "And you have made all their memory
      perish" (Is. 26:14).

II.

A.   It has been stated upon Amoraic authority:

B.   As to an infant, at what point does it enter the world to come?

C.   R. Hiyya and R. Simeon b. Rabbi: one said, "From the time that it is born."

D.   The other said, "From the time that it spoke."

E.   The one who has said, "From the time that it is born" -- as it is said, "They shall
      come and declare his righteousness to a people that shall be born, that he has done
      this" (Ps. 22:32).

F.   The one who has said, "From the time that it spoke" -- as it is written, "A seed shall
      serve him it shall be related of the Lord for a generation" (Ps. 22:31).

G.   It has been stated upon Amoraic authority:

H.   Rabina said, "From the time that of conception as it is written, 'A seed shall serve
      him' (Ps. 22:31)."

I.   R. Nahman b. Isaac said, "From the time of circumcision, as it is written, 'I am
      afflicted and ready to die from my youth up, while I suffer your terrors I am
      distracted.' (Ps. 88:16)."

J.   It was taught on Tannaite authority in the name of R. Meir, "From the time that is
      said, 'Amen,' as it is said, 'Open you the gates, that the righteous nation which
      keeps the truth may enter in' (Is. 26:2). Do not read 'which keeps truth' but 'which
      says, "Amen"'' [rearranging the consonants at hand]."

K.   [111A] What is the meaning of "Amen"?

L.   God, faithful king.

III.

A.   "Therefore hell has enlarged herself and opened her mouth without measure" (Is.
      5:15):

B.   Said R. Simeon b. Laqish, "For him who leaves over even one law [unobserved]."

C. Said R. Yohanan, "It is not a pleasing to their Master that you make such a statement to them. Rather: even if one who has not studied a single statute [it will save a person from Gehenna]."

D. "And it shall come to pass that in all the land, says the Lord, two parts therein shall be cut off and die, but the third shall be left therein" (Zech. 13:8):

E. Said R. Simeon b. Laqish, "The third of the descendants of Shem."

F. Said R. Yohanan, "It is not pleasing to their Master that you make such a statement to them [since most of humanity will perish]. Rather: A third even of the descendants of Noah.'"

G. "For I am married to you and I will take you one of a city and two of a family" (Jer. 3:14):

H. Said R. Simeon b. Laqish, "The matter is to be interpreted just as it is written."

I. Said R. Yohanan to him, "It is not pleasing to their Master that you should say this to them. Rather: One in a given city imparts merit to save the entire city, and two of a family impart merit to save the entire family."

J. R. Kahana was in session before Rab and said [in this same context], "The matter is to be interpreted just as it is written."

K. Said Rab to him, "It is not pleasing to their Master that you should say this to them. Rather: One in a given city imparts merit to save the entire city, and two of a family impart merit to save the entire family."

L. Rab saw that he straightened out his hair and then went and took up a seat before Rab. He said to him, "'And it shall not be found in the land of the living' (Job. 28:13)."

M. He said to him, "You curse me."

N. He said to him, "I cite a verse to you: You shall not find Torah in him who worries about his own needs ahead of it."

IV.

A. It has been taught on Tannaite authority:

B. R. Simai says, "It is said, 'I shall take you to me for a people' (Ex. 6:7), and it is said, 'And I will bring you in [to the land]' (Ex. 6:7).

C. "Their exodus from Egypt is compared to their entry into the land. Just as, when they came into the land, they were only two out of the original six hundred thousand [only Caleb and Joshua], so when they lift Egypt, there were only two out of six hundred thousand."

D. Said Raba, "So it will be in the times of the Messiah, as it is said, 'And she shall sing there, as in the days of her youth, and as in the days when she came up out of the land of Egypt' (Hos. 2:17)."

V.

A. It has been taught on Tannaite authority:

B. Said R. Eleazar b. R. Yose, "One time I went to Alexandria, Egypt. I found an old man there, who said to me, 'Come and I shall show you what my forefathers did to your fat forefathers.

C.   "'Some of [your ancestors] did [my ancestors] drown in the sea, some of them they slew with a sword, some of them they crushed in the buildings.'

D.   "And on that account, Moses, our master, was punished, as it is said, 'For since I came to Pharaoh to speak in your name, he has done evil to this people, neither have you delivered your people at all' (Ex. 5:23).

E.   "Said to him the Holy One, blessed be he, 'Woe for those who are gone and no longer to be found! How many times did I appear to Abraham, Isaac, and Jacob, as God Almighty, and they did not complain against what I meted out, nor did they ask me, "What is your name?"

F.   "'I said to Abraham, "Arise, walk through the land in the length of it and in the breadth of it, for I will give it to you" (Gen. 13:17), [yet] he had to go begging for a place in which to bury Sarah, and he found nothing until he acquired a place for four hundred silver shekels, yet he did not complain against what I meted out.

G.   "'I said to Isaac, "Sojourn in this land and I will be with you and will bless you" (Gen. 26:3), and while his servants went begging for water and found none to drink until they had a quarrel, as it is said, "And the herdmen of Gerar did strive with Isaac's herdmen, saying, the water is ours" (Gen. 26:20). Yet he did not complain against what I meted out [to him].

H.   "'I said to Jacob, "The land on which you lie will I give to you and to your seed" (Gen. 28:13). Yet he went begging for a place on which to pitch his tent and found none until he bought it for a hundred pieces of money [Gen. 33:19], yet he did not complain against what I meted out.

I.   "'And none of them said to me, "What is your name?"

J.   "'Yet in the beginning you have said to me, "What is your name?"

K.   "'And now you say to me, "Neither have you delivered your people at all" (Ex. 5:23)!

L.   "'"Now shall you see what I will do to Pharaoh" (Ex. 6:1). You will see the war against Pharaoh, but you will not see the war against Pharaoh, but you will not see the war against the thirty-one kings' [Josh. 12:24]."

VI.

A.   "And Moses made haste and bowed his head toward the earth and worshipped: (Ex. 34:8):

B.   What did Moses see?

C.   R. Hanina b. Gamula said, "He saw [God's attribute of] being long-suffering [Ex. 34:7]."

D.   Rabbis say, "He saw [the attribute of] truth [Ex. 34:7]. "It has been taught on Tannaite authority in accord with him who has said, "He saw God's attribute of being long-suffering."

E.   For it has been taught on Tannaite authority:

F.   When Moses went up on high, he found the Holy One, blessed be he, sitting and writing, "Long-suffering."

G.   He said before him, "Lord of the world, "Long-suffering for the righteous?"

H.   He said to him, "Also for the wicked."

I.   [Moses] said to him, "Let the wicked perish."

J.   He said to him, "Now you will see what you want."

K.   When the Israelites sinned, he said to him, "Did I not say to you, 'Long suffering for the righteous'?"

L.   [111B] He said to him, "Lord of the world, did I not say to you, 'Also for the wicked'?"

M.   That is in line with what is written, "And now I beseech you, let the power of my Lord be great, according as you have spoken, saying" (Num. 14:17). [Freedman, p. 764, n. 7: What called forth Moses' worship of God when Israel sinned through the Golden Calf was his vision of the Almighty as long-suffering.]

VII.

A.   R. Hagga was going up the stairs of the house of Rabbah bar Shila. He heard a child saying, "'Your testimonies are very sure, holiness becomes your house, O Lord, you are for the length of days' (Ps. 93:5).

B.   "And near the same verse: 'A prayer of Moses' (Ps. 90:1)."

C.   He said, "This proves that he saw [the attribute of God's being' long-suffering.]"

VIII.

A.   Said R. Eleazar said R. Hanina, "The Holy One, blessed be he, is destined to be a crown on the head of every righteous person, as it is said, 'In that day shall the Lord of Hosts be for a crown of glory and for a diadem of beauty to the remnant of his people' (Is. 28:5)."

B.   What is the meaning of "a crown of glory and a diadem of beauty"?

C.   It is for those who do his will and look forward to his salvation. [The word for "glory" uses letters that, in Aramaic, also mean "will" or "desire," and the word for "diadem" contains letters that also mean "look forward" or "hope". The whole reads: In that day shall the Lord of hosts be for a crown of desire and for a diadem of hope (Freedman, pp. 764-5, n. 12)].

D.   Might one suppose that it is for everyone?

E.   Scripture states, "For the remnant of his people" (Is. 28:5). For those who make themselves as a remnant [Freedman, p. 75, n. 1: of no value, hence, to the humble].

F.   "And for a spirit of judgment to him who sits in judgment and for strength to them that turn the battle to the gate" (Is. 28:6)"

G.   "For a spirit of judgment" -- this is one who rules over his impulse to do evil.

H.   "To him who sits in judgment" -- this refers to one who gives a true and honest judgment.

I.   "And for strength" -- to him who is stronger than his impulse to do evil.

J.   "To them that turn the battle" -- this refers to one who engages in the give and take of Torah-study.

K.   "To the gate" -- this refers to those who get up early in the morning and go to bed late at night to spend time in synagogues and school houses.

L.   The attribute of justice said before the Holy One, blessed be he, "Lord of the world, how do these differ from those? [Why do those who have these qualities differ from those who do not have them them?]?

M.   He said to it, "'But they also have erred through wine and through strong drink are
      out of the way...they stumble in giving judgment'" (Is. 28:7)."

N.   The word used for "stumble" refers to Gehanna, as it is said, "That this shall be no
      grief to you" (I 1 Sam. 25:31), and the word for "judgment" refers only to judges, as
      it is said, "And he shall pay as the judges determine" (Ex. 21:22).

The Talmud begins by citing Tosefta's complementary material, unit I. I am
somewhat puzzled about the relevance of unit II. Unit III appears equally miscellaneous,
since it speaks now of those who do not inherit the world to come, and this theme
continues at unit IV. Units V-VII deal with the theme of the generation of the Exodus, and
I do not understand why the compositor found them relevant. Unit VIII seems to be
equally difficult to account for. If we stand back, however, we see the group of materials
in a slightly different perspective. They deal with those who do not inherit the world to
come as against those who do, and when unit III and VIII frame a set of entirely
appropriate materials. But that is only a guess on what lay behind the compositor's work.

                                11:4-6

A.   The townsfolk of an apostate town have no portion in the world to come,

B.   as it is said, "Certain base fellows [sons fo Belial] have gone out from the
      midst of thee and have drawn away the inhabitants of their city" (Deut.
      13:14).

C.   And theyare not put to death unless those who misled the [town] come
      from that same town and from that same tribe,

D.   and unless the majority is misled,

E.   and unless men did the misleading.

F.   [If] women or children misled them,

G.   of if a minority of the town was misled,

H.   or if those who misled the town came from outside of it,

I.   lo, they are treated as individuals [and not as a whole town],

J.   and they [thus] require [testimony against them] by two witnesses, and a
      statement of warning, for each and every one of them.

K.   This rule is more strict for individuals than for the community:

L.   for individuals are out to death by stoning.

M.   Therefore their property is saved.

N.   But the community is put to death by the sword,

O.   Therefore their property is lost.

                              M.11:4

A.   "And you shall surely smite the inhabitants of the city with the edge of
      the sword" (Deut. 13:15)

B.   Ass-drivers, camel-drivers, and people passing from place to place -- lo
      these have the power to save it,

C.   as, it is said, "Destroying it utterly and all that is therein and the cattle thereof, with the edge of the sword" (Deut. 13:17)

D.   On this basis they said, The property of righteous folk which happens to be located in it is lost. But that which is outside of it is saved.

E.   And as to that of evil folk, whether it is in the town or outside of it, lo, it is list.

M.11:5

A.   [As it is said,] "And you shall gather all the spoil of it into the midst of the wide place thereof" (Deut. 13:17).

B.   If it has no wide place, they make a wide place for it.

C.   [If] its wide place is outside of it, they bring it inside.

D.   "And you will burn with fire the city and all the spoil thereof, (ever whit, unto the Lord your God)" (Deut. 13:17).

E.   "The spoil thereof" -- but not the spoil which belongs to heaven.

F.   On this basis they have said:

G.   Things which have been consecrated which are in it are to be redeemed; heave-offering left therein is allowed to rot; second tithe and sacred scrolls are hidden away.

H.   "Ever whit unto the Lord your God"

I.   Said R. Simeon, "Said the Holy One, blessed be he: 'If you enter into judgment in the case of an apostate city, I give credit to you as if you had offered a whole burnt-offering before me.'"

J.   "And it shall be a heap forever, it shall not be built agian"

K.   "It should not be made even into vegetable-patches or orchards," the words of R. Yose the Galilean.

L.   R. Aqiba says, "'It shall not be built again' -- as it was it may not be rebuilt, but it may be made into vegetable patches and orchards."

M.   "And there shall cleave nought of the devoted things to your hand [that the Lord may turn from the fierceness of his anger and show you mercy and have compassion upon you and multiply you]" (Deut. 13:18)

N.   for so long as evil people are in the world, fierce anger is in the world.

O.   When the evil people have perished from the world, fierce anger departs from the world.

M.11:6

I.

A.   Our rabbis have taught on Tannaite authority:

B.   "...have gone out..."(Deut. 13:14) -- they and not messengers.

C.   "...fellows..." -- the plural means there must be two.

D.   Another matter: "...fellows..." -- and not women.

E.   "...fellows..." and not children.

F.   "...sons of Belial..." -- sons who have broken the yoke of heaven from their shoulders.

G.   "From your midst" -- and not from the border towns.

H.   "The inhabitants of their city' -- and not the inhabitants of some other city.

I.   "Saying" -- indicating that there must be proper testimony and admonition for each one [who is involved].

II.

A.   It has been stated on Amoraic authority:

B.   R. Yohanan said, "They may divide a single town between two tribes [if the boundary between tribes runs through it]."

C.   R. Simeon b. Laqish said, "They may not divide a single town between two tribes."

D.   R. Yohanan objected to R. Simeon b. Laqish, "...unless those misled the town come from that same town and from that same tribe [M. 11:4C] -- does this not bear the implication that even though the ones who led the town astray come from that town only, if they also come from that tribe as well, the law applies, and if not, it does not apply? Then it bears the implication that a single town may be divided among two tribes."

E.   [He replied,] "No, it may be a case in which part of the town came to [the one who led it astray] through an inheritance, or it was given to him."

F.   He objected, "'Nine cities out of these two tribes' (Josh. 21:16) -- is that not four and a half from one and four and a half from the other, in which case it follows that they do divide a single town among two tribes?"

G.   He replied, "No, it means four from one and five from the other."

H.   If so, it should be made explicit [which one gave which number].

I.   [112A] That is a problem.

III.

A.   The question was raised:

B.   If the inhabitants were led astray on their own, what is the law?

C.   [Do we say that] the All-Merciful has said, "...have seduced the inhabitants" (Deut. 13:14), and not those who were seduced on their own?

D.   Or perhaps, even if the inhabitants were induced on their own, [the law still applies]?

E.   Come and take note: If women or children misled them...[M. 11:4F] -- [the people of the town are exempt from punishment]. Now why should this be the case? Let them be in the status of those who were led astray on their own? [It would follow that if a town is led astray on its own, it would be exempt from penalty.]

F.   [No, the comparison is apt, for] these followed their own will alone, while the others [in the case specified in the Mishnah-rule] were led astray by women and children.

IV.

A.   And unless the majority is misled [M. 11:4D]:

B.   [Since each participant is subject to the usual testimony of two witnesses as well as admonition,] how do we handle the matter [of dealing with the majority of a town]?

C.   Said R. Judah, "The court judges and imprisons, judges and imprisons [again and again, working their way through the population, until a majority has been convicted. Then all are executed.]"

D.   Said Ulla to him, "You turn out to delay the judgment [and execution of those tried earlier, an this is intolerable]."

E.   Rather, said Ulla, "The court judge and executes the death penalty of stoning, judges and executes the death penalty of stoning. [Freedman, p. 769, n. 10: When half of a town have thus been executed and there are still more, the place is declared a condemned city, and the rest are decapitated.]"

F.   It has been stated on Amoraic authority:

G.   R. Yohanan said, "The court judges and executes the death penalty through stoning, judges and executes the death penalty through stoning."

H.   R. Simeon b. Laqish said, "They set up many courts [to judge the community more or less simultaneously and the trials are under the aspect of the condemnation of the town as a whole]."

I.   Is this so? And has not R. Hama, son of R. Yose, said in R. Oshaia's name, "'Then you shall bring forth that man or that woman to your gates' (Deut. 17:5), teaching that a man or a woman do you bring to your gates, but do not bring an entire town to your gates."

J.   Rather, they set up many courts and look into the cases of each of the persons involved [without pronouncing a verdict], then they take the accused out to the high court and complete the trials and put them all to death.

V.

A.   And you shall surely smite the inhabitants of the city with the edge of the sword" (Deut. 13:15):

B.   Our rabbis have taught on Tannaite authority:

C.   Ass-drivers, camel-drivers, and people passing from place to place [M. 11:5B] who spent the night in its midst and became apostates with [the others of the town]

D.   if they spent thirty days in the town, they are put to death by the sword, and their property and the town are prohibited.

E.   But if they did not spend thirty days in the town, they are put to death by stoning, but their property is rescued [T. San. 14:2 A-D]

F.   An objection was raised from the following:

G.   How long must a man be in a town to count as one of the men of the town? Twelve months [M. B.B 1:5].

H.   Said Raba, "There is no contradiction [between the two definitions of residency for,] one serves the purpose of designating a person as one of the men of the town [which takes a year], and the other serves the purpose of designating him as one of the permanent residents of the town [which takes thirty days]."

I.   And has it not been taught on Tannaite authority [in support of that view]:

J.   He who is prohibited by vow from deriving benefit from his town or from the people of his town, and someone came from the outside and lived there for thirty days -- he who took the vow is permitted to derive benefit from him.

K.   But if he was prohibited by vow from deriving benefit from those who dwell in his town, and someone came from the outside and lived there for thirty days, he is prohibited from deriving benefit from him [T. Ned. 2:10A-D].

VI.

A.   <u>Destroying it utterly and all that is therein and the cattle thereof with the edge of the sword</u> (Deut. 13:17) [M. 11:5C]:

B.   Our rabbis have taught on Tannaite authority:

C.   "Destroying it utterly and all that is therein" (Deut. 13:17) --

D.   excluding <u>the property of the righteous which is outside of it</u>, [M. 11:5D].

E.   "And all that is therein" --

F.   encompassing <u>the property of righteous folk which happens to be located in it</u> [M. 11:5D].

G.   "The spoil that is in it" (Deut. 13:17) -- but not the spoil that belongs to heaven.

H.   "All the spoil of it" (Deut. 13:17) -- encompassing the property of wicked folk that is located outside of it.

VII.

A.   Said R. Simeon, "On what account did they rule, <u>The property of the righteous which is in it is lost?</u>

B.   "Because that property caused the righteous to live among evil people.

C.   [T. adds: "And is it not a matter of an argument <u>a fortiori</u>? And if property, which does not see, hear, or speak, because it caused righteous men to live among wicked people, the Scripture has ruled that it must be burned, he who turns his fellow through the way of life to the way of death, all the more so should he be put to death by burning.]" [T. San. 14:4G-K]

VIII.

A.   A master said, "'And all the spoil of it you shall gather' (Deut. 13:17) -- encompassing the property of evil folk that is outside of it."

B.   Said R. Hisda, "[But that applies, in particular, to that which can be] gathered together in it."

C.   Said R. Hisda, "Objects left on deposit with men of an apostate city are permitted [to the original owners]."

D.   To what circumstance does that statement pertain?

E.   If one should say that the property belongs to people of a different city but is now within [the apostate city], then it is self-evident that it is permitted, since it does not fall into the category of "its spoil."

F.   Rather, they would be objects belonging to the inhabitants of the city located in another town.

G.   But if they are capable of being assembled back in the apostate city, then why should they be permitted. And if they are not going to be assembled in he apostate town, he already has made that statement once [and why repeat it in the present form]?

H.   In point of fact the property belongs to inhabitants of another town, and has been deposited in the apostate town. And here with what sort of case do we deal? It is with a case in which the resident of the apostate town accepted responsibility to replace the deposited property if lost. What might you have said? Since he has accepted responsibility for the deposited property if it is lost, it falls into the category of his own property.

I.   So we are informed that that is not the case.

J.   Said R. Hisda, "As to a domesticated beast half of which belongs to a resident of an apostate city and half of which belongs to a resident of another town, it is forbidden. But as to dough half of which belongs to a resident of an apostate city and half of which belongs to a resident of another town, it is permitted.

K.   "What is the difference? The beast is treated as something which has not been divided, while the dough falls into the category of something that already has been divided."

L.   R. Hisda raised the question, "As to a domesticated beast belonging to a resident of an apostate city, what is the law on regarding proper slaughter as an act effective to purify the beast from the uncleanness pertaining to carrion [and so permitting use of the carcass]?

M.   "The All-Merciful has said, '[You shall surely smite...the cattle thereof] with the edge of the sword' (Deut. 13:17), and there is no difference whether the beast is properly slaughtered or merely put to death [and not slaughtered as required for ritual use].

N.   "Or perhaps, once the beast has been properly slaughtered, does the act of slaughter serve [to permit use of the beast]?

O.   "What is the law?"

P.   The question stands over.

IX.

A.   R. Joseph raised the question, "What is the law concerning use of the hair of righteous women [in such a city]?"

B.   Said Raba, "Lo, that of wicked women is forbidden [if it is shaved off before they are executed].

C.   "Scripture states, 'You shall gather...and you shall burn...' (Deut. 13:17), thus referring to something that lacks only being collected together and burned. Then the present matter is excluded, for it also lacks cutting off, as well as gathering and burning."

D.   Rather, said Raba, "We deal with a wig made from the hair of a gentile woman."

E.   If it is a wig made from the hair of a gentile woman, then what is the condition of the wig? If it is attached to her body, it is in the status of her body [and of course is not burned].

F.   No, it is a question in a case in which the wig is hung on a peg.

G.   Does it fall into the category of the property of the righteous that are located
      in the town, in which case it is destroyed?

H.   Or perhaps, since it is put on and taken off, it falls into the category of the
      woman's clothing [and is preserved].

I.   The question stands.

X.

A.   "And you shall gather all the spoil of it into the midst of the wide place
      thereof" (Deut. 13:17):

B.   Our rabbis have taught on Tannaite authority:

C.   "If it does not have a wide place, it is not declared to be an apostate city," the
      words of R. Ishmael.

D.   R. Aqiba says, "If it has no wide place, they make a wide place for it" [M.
      11:6B].

E.   What is at issue here?

F.   One authority takes the view that "its wide place" has the sole meaning of a
      wide place already present.

G.   The other authority maintains that "wide place" also bears the meaning of a
      wide place existing only at present.

XI.

A.   [112B] Things which have been consecrated which are in it are to be
      redeeemed; [heave-offering left therein is allowed to rot; second tithe and
      sacred scrolls are hidden away] [M. 11:6G]:

B.   Our rabbis have taught on Tannaite authority:

C.   If there were Holy Things in it, things that have been consecrated for use on
      the altar are left to die; things which are consecrated for the upkeep of the
      Temple building are to be redeemed; heave-offering left therein is allowed to
      rot; second tithe and sacred scrolls are hidden away.

D.   R. Simeon says, "'Its cattle' -- excluding firstlings and tithe of cattle.

E.   "'And its spoil'-- excluding money which has been consecrated, and money
      which has taken on the status of second tithe" [T. San. 14:5A-D]

XII.

A.   A master has said, "If there were Holy Things in it, things that have been
      consecrated for use on the altar are left to die:"

B.   Now why should they be left to die? Rather, let them pasture until they are
      permanently disfigured, at which point let them be sold, and let the proceeds
      fall for the purchase of a freewill offering [as would be done under ordinary
      circumstances with such donations].

C.   R. Yohanan said, "'The sacrifice of the wicked is an abomination' (Prov.
      21:27)."

D.   R. Simeon b. Laqish said, "It is property belonging to its original owner, for
      here we deal with Holy Things which the donor is liable to replace if lost."

E.   At hand, then, is the viewpoint of R. Simeon, for he hwasaa said, "It remains
      the property of the owners."

F.   But since the next clause [M. 11:6I] represents the view of R. Simeon, it must follow that the present clause does not stand for his opinion at all.

G.   [Rather, we try a different tack:] the passage speaks of Lesser Holy Things and is framed in accord with the position of R. Yose the Galilean, who has ruled, "Lesser Holy Things fall into the category of property owned by the original donor."

H.   Then what would be the rule for Most Holy Things? They should be redeemed [since they belong to the Temple and not to the original donor, that is, the resident of the apostate city].

I.   If that is the case, then the framer of the passage should have given the rule concerning things consecrated for the upkeep of the Temple building not separately, but as part of the rule covering Most Holy Things, framing matters in this way:

J.   "Under what circumstances? In the case of Lesser Holy Things. But as to Most Holy Things, they are to be redeemed." [That would have covered both matters.]

K.   [The reason he could not frame matters in that way is that is hand also is a sacrifice such as] a beast designated as a sin-offering, the owner of which now is put to death. [Such a beast is killed, but not as a sacrifice.] Accordingly, the framer of the passage could not state matters as a general rule [since the rule would contradict the case of the sin-offering].

L.   Now we can understand why R. Yohanan did not rule as did R. Simeon b. Laqish, for it is written, "The sacrifice of the wicked is an abomination" (Prov. 21:27).

M.   But why did R. Simeon b. Laqish not reply in the way in which R. Yohanan did [since Yohanan gave a good reply]?

N.   He may say to you, "Where we invoke the rule, 'The sacrifice of the wicked is an abomination,' it is where the beast is present and at hand, but in the present case, since the status of the beast has changed, [for it is redeemed], the rule likewise may differ [and the cited verse will not apply]."

XIII.

A.   R. Simeon says, "'Its cattle' -- excluding firstlings and tithe of cattle" [T. San. 14:5C].

B.   With what sort of case do we deal?

C.   If we say that we deal with those that are unblemished, then this falls into the category of the spoil belonging to heaven.

D.   Rather we deal with those that are blemished.

E.   In that case, the beasts fall into the category of "the spoil of it" [the city itself, and are to be destroyed].

F.   Said Rabina, "In point of fact we deal with blemished beasts. What falls into the category of "the cattle thereof" [to be destroyed] are beasts that are eaten as 'its cattle,' excluding the ones at hand, which are not eaten in the category of 'its cattle,' but rather in the category of firstlings and tithes [under a different rule entirely, not as ordinary animals], and so the fall into the category of 'the spoil of heaven.'"

G.   That then differs from the view of Samuel for Samuel has said, "Everything may be sacrificed and everything may be redeemed."

H.   What is the sense of his statement?

I.   This is what he means to say: Whatever may be offered if it is unblemished or redeemed if it is blemished falls into the category of "the spoil of it" [that is to say, all animals designated for offerings of a lesser sanctity, except for firstlings and tithes].

J.   "But whatever may be offered if unblemished, while not subject to redemption if blemished, for example, the firstling and tithe of cattle, would be excluded by the phrase, "And the cattle thereof." [This would stand at variance with Rabina's position.]

XIV.

A.   Heave-offering left therein is allowed to rot [M. 11:6G]:

B.   Said R. Hisda, "That rule applies only to heave offering in the possession of ordinary Israelites, but as to heave-offering in the possession of a priest, to whom the produce actually belongs, it must be burned."

C.   To this proposition R. Joseph objected, "Second title and sacred scrolls are hidden away [M. 11:6G]. Now lo, second tithe in the possession of ordinary Israelites is in the same classification as heave-offering in the possession of a priest. And yet, the Mishnah-passage states, It is to be hidden away."

D.   Rather, if a statement on Amoraic authority has been made, this is how it has been made:

E.   Said R. Hisda, "The stated rule [at M. 11:6G] applies only to heave-offering in the possession of priests. But as to heave-offering in the possession of ordinary Israelites, let it be handed over to a priest located in some other town [than the apostate city]."

XV.

A.   It has been taught on Tannaite authority:

B.   "Dough prepared from produce in the status of second tithe [e.g., grain set aside as second tithe that has been milled into flour and made into dough], is exempt from the requirement of the separation of dough-offering," the words of R. Meir.

C.   And sages declare it liable.

D.   Said R. Hisda, "The dispute concerns second tithe that is located in Jerusalem. For R. Meir takes the view that produce in the status of second tithe is the property of the Most High [and hence it will not be subject to the requirement of the separation of an additional holy offering, namely, dough-offering.]

E. "Sages, by contrast, maintain that it is in the ownership of the ordinary person [and hence, even in Jerusalem, remains liable to the separation of dough-offering. Since, in Jerusalem, the farmer can eat the produce, it is regarded as his own property, and not property belonging to the Most High].

F. "But in the provinces, all parties concur that it is exempt to the separation of dough-offering [because the farmer may not make use of the produce as he likes but is subject to the obligation to bring it to Jerusalem. Hence it is subject to God's claim.]"

G. To this proposition R. Joseph object, "Second tithe and sacred scrolls are hidden away [M. 11:6G]. Now with what case do we deal? If we say that it is produce in Jerusalem, can Jerusalem ever fall into the category of an apostate city? And has it not been taught on Tannaite authority: 'There are ten rules stated with respect to Jerusalem, and this is one of them: it may not be declared an apostate city'?

H. "If, furthermore, we deal with another town, the second tithe produce of which they brought up to Jerusalem, then the walls of Jerusalem have enveloped the produce [and imparted to it the status of such produce as it is defined in Jerusalem. It cannot be redeemed for money and removed.] Thus do we not deal with a case of produce in the status of second tithe located in the provinces, and it has been taught in the Mishnah that it is hidden away! [So it is treated as secular property, not as holy property, when it is in Jerusalem, contrary to Hisda's thesis.]"

I. [In behalf of Hisda, this is the reply:] No, in point of fact it is produce in the status of second tithe that derives from some other town, which people brought to Jerusalem. There it became unclean. [Freedman, p. 776, n. 6: In this case it may not be eaten; consequently, it must be hidden away.]

J. But then should one not redeem the produce [that has become unclean]? For said R. Eleazar, "How do we know that even in Jerusalem people are to redeem produce in the status of second tithe that has become unclean? Scripture says, "When you are not able to bear it, then you shall turn it into money" (Deut. 14:25).

K. "The word for bear has the meaning of 'eat,' as it is said, 'And he took and sent them gifts to them from before him' (Gen. 43:34. [So Freedman, p. 776, n. 10: Thus he translates, If you are not able to eat it -- since it is defiled -- then you shall turn it into money, that is, redeem it]."

L. [No, one need not redeem this produce, for] here with what do we deal? It is with produce that has been purchased [113A] [with the money received in the redemption of the original produce in the status of second tithe. Now the newly purchased produce has become unclean. Freedman, p. 776, n.11: At this stage it is assumed that only the original second tithe can be redeemed if made unclean, but not produce later purchased with the redemption money].

M. But why not redeem [that produce, too], for it has been taught in the Mishnah:
    If produce that has been pruchased with money received for the second tithe
    has become unclean, it is to be redeemed [M. M.S. 3:10].

N. The passage accords with the view of R. Judah, who has said that it should be
    buried.

O. If that is the case, then why do you maintain that at issue is produce in the
    status of second tithe deriving in particular from an apostate city? Even a
    city in general [would be subject to the same rule. So we have gained nothing.]

P. Rather, we deal with produce in the status of second tithe which is clean, and
    which has come within the fallen walls of Jerusalem.

Q. This accords with the statement of Raba, for Raba has said, "The rule that one
    must eat produce in the status of second tithe within Jerusalem's walls derives
    from the Torah.

R. "The rule that the walls of Jerusalem envelope the produce [and impart to it
    the status of second tithe, so that once the produce has entered the walls of
    the city, it cannot then be redeemed for money and be removed from the city]
    derives only from the authority of rabbis, "Now when rabbis made that decree,
    it applied to a time in which the walls were there [to form a barrier], the rule
    does not apply. "[Freedman, p. 777, n. 2. Hence in this case since it actually
    belongs to the condemned city, and Jerusalem cannot assimilate it to itself,
    because its walls had fallen, it must be destroyed, but being sacred, it is
    hidden instead of burned.]"

XVI.

A. Sacred scrolls are hidden away [M. 11:6G]:

B. The cited passage of the Mishnah does not accord with the view of R. Eliezer.

C. For it has been taught on Tannaite authority:

D. Eliezer says, "Any city in which is to be found even a single muzuzah is not
    declared to be an apostate city, as it is said, 'And you shall burn the city with
    fire, and all the spoil thereof, every whit' (Deut. 13:17).

E. "Now if it contains even a single mezuzah, this would be impossible, as it is
    written, 'You shall not do so to the Lord your God' (Deut. 12:4)."

XVII.

A. R. Simeon says, "the Holy One, blessed be he, said..." [M. 11:6I]:

B. [With reference to the dispute of Yose the Galilean and Aqiba at M. 11:6K-L],
    may one propose that they dispute about the matter at issue in what R. Abin
    said R. Ilaa said?

C. For said R. Abin said R. Ilaa, "In any passage in which you find a generaliza-
    tion concerning an affirmative action, followed by a qualification expressing a
    negative commandment, people are not to construct on that basis an argument
    resting on the notion of a general proposition followed by a concrete
    exemplification only the substance of the concrete exemplification.
    [Freedman, p. 777-8, n. 8: The rule in such a case is: the general proposition

includes only what is enumerated in the particular specification. But when one is thrown into the form of a positive command and the other stated as a negative injunction this does not apply. Now, in the passage under discussion, "And it shall be an heap forever" is a general proposition, implying that it may not be turned even into parks or orchards; whilst "it shall not be built again" is a particular specification, denoting a prohibition against the erection of houses, etc., which require building, but not against parks, etc. Now had they both been expressed in the for of a positive or negative command, the rule of exegesis would be as stated, the particularized expression defining the general proposition. Thus "It shall be an head for ever," and that only in respect of rebuilding, but not i respect of parks, etc. Since, however, they are not both expressed in the same form, this method of exegesis is not followed, but the two clauses are regarded as distinct, a different exegetical rule being followed; viz., 'That which as included in the general proposition and was then separately stated is intended to illumine the former' (for "it shall not be built again," which refers to houses, etc., was really included in the general proposition). Thus: "And it shall be an heap for ever" implies a prohibition of parks and orchards. Now, how is this implication understood? Because Scripture continues, "it shall not be built again," from which we deduce, just as a building is anything erected in a human settlement, so "it shall be an heap for ever" prohibits everything that finds a place in civilization, and therefore includes gardens, etc.]

D. It would follow [in accord with this theory of what is at issue] that one authority [namely, Yose] concurs with R. Abin, and the other [Aqiba] does not? [Accordingly, Aqiba prohibits building alone, while Yose prohibits all sorts of land-use].

E. No, all parties concur with the principle of R Abin, and what is at issue here? One authority [Yose] takes the view that the word "again' bears the meaning, 'entirely, hence, never again," while the other [Aqiba] understands the word to the "again -- as it had been" [allowing space for some other usage than the original one].

XVIII.

A. It may not be rebuilt, but it may be made into vegetabel patches and orchards [M. 11:6L]:

B. Our rabbis have taught on Tannaite authority:

C. If the town contained trees that had already been cut down [prior to the trial], they are forbidden. If at the time of the verdict they were yet attached to the ground, they are permitted. But as to the trees of another city, whether they are cut down or attached to the ground, they are forbidden [T. San. 14:5E-G].

D. What is this "other city'?

E. Said R. Hisda, "It is Jericho, as it is written, 'And the city shall be herem to the Lord' (Josh. 6:17)."

XIX.

A. "And Joshua adjured them at that time, saying, Cursed be the man before the Lord who rises up and builds this city, Jericho. He shall lay the foundation thereof in his firstborn, and in his youngest son shall he set up the gates of it." (Josh. 6:17).

B. It has been taught on Tannaite authority:

C. One may not rebuild it and call it by the name of some other town, and one may not build some other town and call it Jericho." [T. San. 14:6L].

XX.

A. It is written, "In his days did Heil the Bethelite build Jericho; he laid the foundations thereof in Abiram his firstborn and set up the gates thereof in his youngest son Segub, according to the word of the Lord which he spoke by Joshua the son of Nun" (1 Kgs. 16:4).

B. It has been taught on Tannaite authority:

C. "In Abiram his first born" (1 Kgs. 16:34):

D. That wicked man! To begin with [with Abiram] he had no example from which to learn, but in the case of segub, he had an example from which to learn [T. San. 14:9A-C].

E. What did Abiram and Segub do [that they, who were not wicked, did not learn the reason for the death]?

F. This is the sense of the passage: "From the case of Abiram, his first born, that wicked man should have learned [what would happen to] Segub, his youngest son."

G. Since it is said, "In Abiram, his first born" (1 Kgs. 16:34), do I not know that Segub was his youngest son? Why then does Scripture state, "Segub his youngest son"?

H. This teaches that he continued burying his sons, from Abiram down to Segub.

I. Ahab had been his groomsman. He and Elijah came to greet him at the house of mourning. [Ahab] went into session and stated, "Perhaps when Joshua made that curse, this was the sense of the curse:

J. "'One may not rebuild it and call it by the name of some other town, and one may not build some other town and call it Jericho [T. San. 14:6L]'?"

K. Elijah said to him, "Indeed so."

L. He said to him, "Now if the curse of Moses has not been carried out --

M. "for it is written, 'And you turn aside and serve other gods and worship them' (Deut. 11:16), followed by, 'And he shut up the heaven that there be no rain' (Deut. 11:17), while if someone sets up an idol at the end of every furrow, the rain will not allow him to go and bow down to them --

N. "will the curse of Joshua, his disciple, be carried out? [Surely not!]"

O. Forthwith: "And Elijah, the Tishbite, who was one f the inhabitants of Gilead, said to Ahab, As the Lord God of Israel lives, before whom I stand, there shall not be dew or rain these years, but according to my word" (1 Kgs. 17:1).

P.   He sought mercy, and the key of rain was given to him. He got up an went his way.

XXI.

A.   "And the word of the Lord came to him, saying, Go away and turn eastward and hide yourself by the brook Cherith, that is before Jordan...And the ravens brought him bread and flesh in the morning" (1 Kgs. 17:2, 6).

B.   Where did they get [validly slaughtered meat]?

C.   Said R. Judah said Rab, "They got it from the butchery of Ahab."

D.   "And it came to pass, after a while, that the brook dried up, because there had been no rain in the land" (1 Kgs. 17:7):

E.   When [God] saw that there was suffering in the world, it is written, "And the work of the Lord came to him saying, Arise, go to Zarephath" (1 Kgs. 17:8-9).

F.   And it is written, "And it came to pass after these things that the son of the woman, mistress of the house, fell sick" (1 Kgs. 17:17).

G.   [Elijah] prayed for mercy that the keys of the resurrection of the dead might be given to him.

H.   They said to him, "Three keys are not handed over to a messenger: those of birth, rain, and the resurrection of the dead.

I.   "For will people say, 'Two already are in the hand of the disciple [he already had the one for rain] and one in the hand of the master?'

J.   "Bring the one and take the other."

K.   For it is written, "Go, appear to Ahab, and I will send rain upon the earth" (1 Kgs. 18:1).

XXII.

A.   A Galilean gave an exposition before R. Hisda, "To what may Elijah be compared? To the case of a man who locked his gate and lost the key. [Elijah locked up the rain and could not unlock it]"

B.   R. Yose gave an exposition in Sepphoris, "Father Elijah [113B] was an impatient man."

C.   [Elijah] had been used earlier to come to visit [Yose], but he refrained from visiting him for three days and did not come. When he did come, he said to him, "Why did master not come?"

D.   He said to him, "You called me impatient!"

E.   He said to him, "But before us the master has shown himself to be impatient!"

XXIII.

A.   "And there shall cleave nought of the devoted thing to your hand' (Deut. 13:18), for so long as evil people are in the world, fierce anger -- is in the world [M. 11:6M-N]:

B.   Who are these wicked?

C.   Said R. Joseph, "Thieves [who steal property from the apostate city]."

XXIV.

A.   Our rabbis have taught on Tannaite authority:

B.   When the wicked come into the world, fierce anger comes into the world, for it is written, "When the wicked comes, then comes also contempt, and with ignominy, reproach" (Prov. 18:3).

C.   When the wicked departs from the world, goodness comes into the world and retribution leaves the world, as it is written, "And when the wicked perish, there is exultation" (Prov. 11:10).

D.   When righteous people leave the world, evil comes into the world, as it is said, "The righteous man perishes, and no one lays it to heart, and merciful men are taken away, none considering that the righteous is taken away from the evil to come" (Is. 57:1).

E.   When the righteous come into the world, goodness comes into the world, as it is written, "This one will comfort us in our work and in the toil of our hands" (Gen. 5:29) [T. Sot. 10:1-3]

Unit I provides a scriptural basis for the passage at hand. Unit II is inserted because it cites the Mishnah-paragraph. Unit III raises a secondary question. Units IV, V, VI then cite and gloss further passages of the Mishnah-paragraph. Unit VII inserts Tosefta's complement, which introduces a considerable amplification of the Mishnah's rule, units VIII-IX. Units X, XI-XIII, XIV (to which XV is attached prior to insertion here), XVI, XVII, XVIII all begin with a citation of the Mishnah, passage by passage, followed by amplification of one kind or another. Unit XIX-XXII complete the matter by reference to Jericho, as the best example of the city that is completely wiped out, and unit XXIII concludes with a citation and Toseftan gloss of the Mishnah. So the entire composition is organized and worked out in relationship to the Mishnah.